THE IRAN-IRAQ WAR
AND WESTERN SECURITY 1984-87:

Strategic Implications and Policy Options

THE RUSI MILITARY POWER SERIES

Since 1831 the RUSI has provided a forum for the analysis and discussion of defence and international security issues. Its studies are policy orientated, with a practical and operational focus. They are aimed at those with a legitimate interest in the military sciences and international security, particularly decision-makers and opinion leaders.

The RUSI Military Power Book series is a selection of concise books providing expert views for both the professional and general reader.

THE IRAN-IRAQ WAR AND WESTERN SECURITY 1984-87:

Strategic Implications and Policy Options

Anthony H. Cordesman

JANE'S

To Bridget, Justin, Alexander, and Rachel for closely related reasons.

Contents

List of Figures

Acknowledgements

The author would like to thank the Hoover Institution for a grant that funded part of the initial research for this book, and James Noyes and Gary Sick for their help and advice. Similar thanks go to the Royal United Services Institute for its support during some phases of the research, and to a number of U.S. and British officials for their support. More generally, the author would like the thank the many reporters whose work he has drawn on and whose reporting is referenced in the footnotes.

List of Abbreviations

AAM	air-to-air missile
ACDA	Arms Control and Disarmament Agency (US)
ADIZ	air defense interception zone
AEW	airborne early warning
AFV	armored fighting vehicle
APC	armored personnel carrier
ARM	anti-radiation missile
ASM	air-to-surface missile
ATGM	anti-tank guided missile
AWACS	airborne warning and air control system
AWX	all weather interceptor
BM	battle management
BPD	barrels per day
C^2	command and control
C^3	command, control, and communications
C^3I	command, control, communications and intelligence
C^3I/BM	command, control, communications and intelligence/battle management
CGE	central government expenditure
CIA	Central Intelligence Agency (US)
DIA	Defense Intelligence Agency (US)
DOD	Department of Defense (US)
DOE	Department of Energy (US)
ECM	electronic countermeasures
ECCM	electronic counter-counter measures
EIA	Energy Information Agency (US)

ESM or ESSM	electronic support measures
EW	electronic warfare
EXIM Bank	Export Import Bank
FMS	foreign military sales
FRG	Federal Republic of Germany
GCC	Gulf Cooperation Council
GDP	gross domestic product
GNP	gross national product
GPO	Government Printing Office (US)
IDS	interceptor day strike
IFF	Identification of Friend or Foe
IFV	Infantry Fighting Vehicle
IISS	International Institute for Strategic Studies
IMF	International Monetary Fund
INOC	Iranian National Oil Company (also see NIOC)
JCSS	Jaffe Center for Strategic Studies
KDP	Kurdish Democratic Party
KDPI	Kurdish Democratic Party of Iran
MAF	Marine Ampibious Force
MBD	thousands of barrels per day
MMBD	millions of barrels per day
MICV	mechanized infantry combat vehicle
MOU	memorandum of understanding
MPA	maritime patrol aircraft
MRL	multiple rocket launcher
MRLS	Multiple Rocket Launcher System
NA	not applicable
NIOC	National Iranian Oil Company
NSC	National Security Council (US)
NSSD	National Security Study Directive
NSDD	National Security Decision Directive
OAPEC	Organisation of Arab Petroleum Exporting Countries
OPEC	Organisation of Petroleum Exporting Countries

PDRY	People's Democratic Republic of Yemen
PHOTINT	photo intelligence
PRC	People's Republic of China
PUK	Patriotic Union of Kurdistan
RPG	rocket propelled grenade
SAM	surface-to-air missile
SHORAD	short range air defense system
SIGINT	signals intelligence
SIPRI	Stockholm International Peace Research Institute
SNIE	Special National Intelligence Estimate
SSM	surface-to-surface missile
UAE	United Arab Emirates
UK	United Kingdom
ULCC	ultra large cargo carrier
UN	United Nations
USCENTCOM	United States Central Command
USGS	United States Geological Survey
VLCC	very large cargo carrier
YAR	Yemeni Arab Republic

Chronology

1968   Ba'ath coup in Iraq brings Hassan Al-Bakr and eventually Sadam Hussein to power.

1973-1975   Iraqi troops prove unable to suppress Kurdish rebels, which have backing of Shah and covert support from CIA.

1975   Algiers Treaty settles most of the boundary and political issues between Iran and Iraq. Shah stops support of Kurdish rebels in Iraq. Iraq stops support of groups hostile to Shah.

1978   Shah of Iran begins to lose control of Iran.

  September   Iraq expells Khomeini in effort to appease Shah.

1979

  January   Shah falls, Khomeini comes to power.

  April   Iraq attempts to appease new regime with public statements praising Khomeini.

  July   Sadam Hussein becomes President of Iraq.

  August   Iraq gives up attempts to placate new regime in Tehran.

1980

  January   Bani-Sadr elected President of Iran.

April	Khomeini calls upon Iraqi armed forces to depose Sadam Hussein.
	Pro-Iranian elements attempt to assassinate Tariq Aziz.
August	Sadam Hussein visits Saudi Arabia. Discusses idea of war with Iran.
September	Border clashes between Iraq and Iran.
17	Iraq abrogates the 1975 Algiers Treaty.
20	Iran begins mobilization.
22	Iraq invades Iran, attempting to seize southwestern oil area or "Arabistan". It launches massive air raids against Iran's air bases, but with little military effect. Its armored forces show limited skill in the attack, and Iraqi forces do not take major cities or strategic objectives.
22	Iraqi aircraft bomb Kharg Island and Iran's refineries. The oil war starts.
30	U.S. sends AWACS aircraft to Saudi Arabia.
October	Fighting rages for control of Khorramshar and the Abadan refinery.
	Iranian naval forces take Iraq's oil terminals in the Gulf and cut off most of Iraq's oil export capability.
7	Air war escalates to attack oil and economic facilities and cities on both sides.
13	Khorramshar is taken by Iraqi forces.
14	Iranian aircraft raid Baghdad.
27	Iraq announces a joint military command with Jordan.
November	Iraqi forces lose offensive momentum as Iran fully mobilizes and redeploys forces.

| December | Iraqi forces fail to secure Iran's refinery at Abadan or take the major cities in the border area. Fighting dies down for winter. |

1981

January 5	Bani-Sadr launches unsuccessful counteroffensive near Susangerd.
February 4	Gulf Cooperation Council established
May	Heavy fighting begins in Khuzistan in late May. Iraq does not make progress.
June	
7	Israeli fighters hit Osriak.
10-22	Bani-Sadr ousted as commander of armed forces and dismissed as President.
July	Mujahideen bombing attacks start in Iran.
August	Iran launches new air strikes against Iraq's oil facilities.
30	Mujahideen bomb kills Iran's new President, Mohammed Ali Rajavi.
September	Pasadran forces relieve Iraqi seige of Abadan in Thamin ul-Aimma offensive, and push towards Khorramshar.
October	First Iranian air raid on Kuwait. Kuwait recalls its ambassador.
	Mohammed Ali Khomeini elected President of Iran.
November	Iran launches the Tariq ul-Quds offensive near Bostan in an accelerating effort to recover its territory. It pushes Iraqi forces back towards the border in the area opposite Al Amarah.

December	Iranian troops make limited gains in the mountains just above and in a long line south of Qasr-e-Shirin.
	Bahrain uncovers and suppresses an Iranian sponsored coup attempt.

1982

January	Iraq's pipeline through Turkey is sabotaged.
March	Iraq launches Fath ul-Mubin offensive and scores major gains in recovering its territory, moving from positions west of Dezful to the border area northeast of Al Amarah. Sadam Hussein calls for ceasefire.
April	Iran prepares for a major effort to reconquer its lost terrority and scores major gains, pushing towards the border in the area extending from Al Amarah to Khorramshar. Iraqi forces show little interest in attempting to hold positions in Iran.
May 3-11	Major Iranian offensive begins in Khuzistan and reaches Iraqi border.
24	Iran recaptures Khorramshar in Bait ul-Mugaddas offensive.
June	Iran continues to advance, taking numerous Iraqi prisoners and capturing substantial amounts of equipment.
20-30	Iraq announces it will withdraw all forces from Iran. Iran immediately states it will continue the war.
	Iraq withdraws its troops from Iranian soil in the central front opposite Baghdad, regardless of the Iranian announcement.

July	Iranian forces invade Iran for the first time in an effort to take Basra called Operation Ramadan. They score limited gains along the "square" in the border area northeast of Basra. Both sides step up the air war on each other's cities.
August	Iraqi fighters strike heavily at Kharg Island for the second time in the war.
September 7	Iraqi aircraft strike again at Kharg Island.
15	Ex-Foreign Minister Ghotbzadeh executed for supposed plot against Khomeini.
30	Iranian army launches Muslin Ibn Aqil offensive near Mandali.
October	Muslin Ibn Aqil offensive scores significant gains in the border area south of Qasr-e-Shirin and just northeast of Baghdad. More Mujahideen bombing incidents in Tehran. Further peace efforts fail.
November	Iran scores limited gains in Operation Muharram in the border area west of Dezful.
December	Pause in fighting at onset of winter.

1983

February	Iran launches its first "Behold the Dawn" (Val Fajr) offensive, in a major attack on Iran near Basra. It scores only limited gains.
March-April	Iran launches Val Fajr-1 offensive in the area near Khuzistan, but makes little progress.
May	Iran makes Tudeh Party illegal. Expells 18 Soviet diplomats.
July	Iran's Val Fajr-2 offensive is launched west of Piranshahr, but stalls after token gains and considerable casualties.

August	Iran launches Val-Fajr-3 offensive in the area west of Meheran, in early August, but it again achieves only limited initial gains and results in high casualties.
October	France delivers five Super Etendard fighters equipped with Exocet to Iraq.
19	Iran launches Val Fajr-4 near Pajwin and scores limited gains.

1984

February	Iraq launches Scud attacks against Dezful. Iran uses artillery and air against Basra.
14	Iran launches Val Fajr-5 offensive near Meheran. It has little success.
18	Ceasefire agreement on attacks on civilian targets.
22	Iran launches major Val Fajr-6 offensive near Dehloran in effort to capture Basra.
26	Iraq starts major air attacks on Iranian oil export facilities in Kharg Island and tankers.
	Iraq makes extensive use of chemical weapons.
29	Iranian human wave assaults by poorly trained Basij and Pasdaran forces result in massive Iranian casualties, but Iran does take part of Majnoon Islands.
March	Iraq accelerates tanker war in the Gulf.
	Iraq drives Iranian forces back north of Basra, recaptures part of Majnoon Islands.
27	First Iraqi use of Super Etendards. Iraqi Exocet missile hits Greek tanker.

April-May	"Tanker War" accelerates, then ends in temporary ceasefire as Iraq again seeks peace.
May 13	Iran begins strikes on ships and tankers in Southern Gulf waters. Ceasefire ends.
June 5	Saudi Arabia shoots down two Iranian F-4s attacking tankers in Saudi waters. Iran halts most air attacks in southern Gulf waters.
12	Another temporary ceasefire in attacking civilian targets and tankers. It collapses after its becomes clear Iran is not interested in peace.
June-September	Iran reoganizes Pasdaran and Basij for more systematic land warfare. Iraq fails to adopt flexible patrol and counterattack tactics.
	Continuing Iraqi strikes on Kharg and tankers force Iran to create a "tanker shuttle" moving oil from Kharg to transloading facilities near the island of Sirri in the lower Gulf.
September-December	Little military action other than tanker war.

1985

January-March	Iraq continues tanker war, hitting 30 ships. It starts a new round of air strikes on Iranian cities. Iran responds with first Scud strikes.
	Iraq commences to dominate the air war as Iranian pilots and equipment lose ability to compete in air-to-air combat, and most Iranian radars and Hawk sites suffer from manpower or spare parts problems.

March	Iran launches Fatima Zahra offensive north of Qurna in an effort to cut off Basra. The offensive fails, but both sides suffer high casualties and Iranian performance is much better than in 1983 and 1984.
May	Beginning of U.S. covert arms negotiations with Iran.
August	Iran scores limited gains in central and northern sectors in moderately sized attacks.
14 and 25	Iraq begins major air strikes on Kharg using improved ordnance and larger numbers of fighters.
September	Israel delivers 508 TOW missiles to Iran as part of covert U.S. arms deal.
11	Iran attacks at Majnoon. Result is stalemate.
	Iranian attack near Neimak scores limited gains in the north.
	Iraq again launches major raids on Kharg. Iran begins serious planning to find alternative oil export routes, but runs into time and resource problems.
October– December	
	Iraqi air units keep up the pressure on Iran. Iraq raises the total number of air strikes against Kharg to 60.
	Both sides sporadically exchange artillery, missile, and air strikes against civilian targets.

1986

January	Iranian forces build-up for a massive offensive in the south. They may benefit from intelligence passed to Iran by Colonel Oliver North, and covert U.S. arms shipments.
	Iraq prepares for an attack north of Basra, but largely ignores the southern front along Faw.
16-17	The U.S. ends its use of Israeli and private go-betweens and starts direct shipment of arms to Iran.
February 9	Iran launches a two pronged Al Dawa (Dawn 8) offensive. It bogs down to the north, but catches Iraq by surprise at Faw and scores massive gains as Iraqi troops flee, leaving much of their equipment.
15	Iraqi troops rally and gradually contain the Iranian advance.
17	U.S. TOW missiles and Hawk parts arrive in Tehran.
24-25	Iran launches Al Dawa 9 attack in the northeast of Kirkuk and scores limited gains.
March	Land fighting dies down into stalemate, but Iran retains Faw, and now is far more able to threaten Basra and Kuwait.
April	Iraqi counterattacks in Faw fail. Iraq increasingly relies on air attacks on Iranian ground forces.
	Added Kurdish rebel activity and attacks in northern Iraq.
	Limited purges of Iraqi command.
May	Iraq launches major raid on refineries in Tehran. Forces Iran to start importing refined product.

10-17	Iraq attacks weakly held Iranian positions near Meheran and takes the nearly abandoned city, but does not consolidate its position or take the high ground.
28	McFarlane makes abortive visit to Tehran.
	Iran blocks Jordanian effort to get Syria to reopen its pipeline to Iraq, by offering cheap oil and ignoring Syrian failure to pay for past deliveries.
June	Tanker war continues. Most of the fighting is in the air.
July 1-10	Iran builds up forces in the hills around Meheran and launches Kerbala 1 attack to retake. Poorly prepared Iraqi forces are driven out of Meheran with serious casualties.
	Tehran calls for 100,000 more Basij volunteers.
	Iraq starts massive series of air raids against Iranian towns and economic targets.
14	Colonel Ali Sayyad Shirazi replaced as Iran's ground force commander. Growing reports of rivalry between the regular forces and Pasdaran.
August 10	Iraq bombs the Iranian refinery at Tabriz.
12	Iraq hits tankers near Sirri Island in its first long range air strikes in the Gulf.
18	Iran announces it will resume gas exports to USSR.
	Iraq steps up the air war. By late August, it has flown 120 sorties against Kharg alone in the preceding 12 months. Number of attacks on Gulf shipping since March, 1984 is raised to 144.

	Iran fires first Scud at Iraq in thirteen months.
	GCC fails to agree on extending AWACS patrols to cover the entire Gulf.
September	Iran makes limited gains in small attacks near the Haj Omran basin in Kurdistan. Iranian naval brigades temporarily seize the Al Bakr oil platform in the Gulf and destroy an Iraqi radar.
	Iran steps up its naval intercepts in the Gulf and temporarily detains the Soviet vessel Pytor Yemstov.
16	Iraqi aircraft raid Iranian loading points at Lavan, and launch successful raids on Kharg.
	Iran's airpower is so weak it can do little more than fire the occasional Scud at Baghdad.
29	Iraqi raids on Kharg on September 29 and October 6, temporarily cut much of Iran's oil exports.
October	Iraq continues its air strikes against Iran's oil export facilities and economic targets in Iran. There have been 97 strikes on tankers since the start of the year, and 259 since the start of the war.
	Iran has already hit three times as many ships as in all of 1985.
	There is little fighting on the ground.
	A major power struggle seems to develop between Montazeri and those around Khomeini. Many of Montazeri's staff and supporters are arrested.

November 4	An article in *As Shirra*, evidently planted by Montazeri's supporters, exposes the covert U.S. arms sales to Iran, creating a massive scandal in the U.S.
25	Iraq launches its longest air raid yet, and hits Iranian targets near Larak – showing Iran has little hope of creating a secure oil export facility.
	Iran is down from 400 fighters under the Shah to as little as 40 operational fighters.
	Iran continues sporadic Scud strikes against Baghdad, and hits facilities at the Abu Boosk offshore oil field of the UAE.
December	The air war continues as Iraq hits tankers, oil facilities, and other economic targets in Iran.
	Iran sporadically bombards Basra.
10	Montazeri's aide Hashemi is reported to have confessed to treason.
	Iran reports 100,000 more Basij have left for the front.
23-24	Iran launches Kerbala 4 attack against well prepared Iraqi forces near Basra, takes heavy casulaties and is forced to halt the attack. The attack is poorly prepared and may have been rushed for internal political reasons.
	A meeting of foreign supporters in Tehran reveals the Iranian leadership is as committed to the war as ever.

1987

January 6
In sharp contrast to Kerbala 4, Iran launches a well prepared offensive against Basra and then north of Baghdad. The first attack is called Kerbala 5 and seriously threatens Basra and Iran troops drive Iraqi forces back from the border and to their main line of defenses around Basra.

The USSR attack Iran for continuing the war and its anti-Soviet attitude.

13
As the fighting still ranges around the Fish Lake near Basra, Iran launches Kerbala 6 to the north, near Qasr-e-Shirin. The northern offensive is conducted largely by regular Iranian forces and lacks the fervor of the attacks in the south. It scores only limited gains, mostly recaptured Iranian territory.

16
A bloody stalemate develops around Basra, as both sides take heavy casualties. Iran loses nearly three times as many men as Iraq, but both armies suffer.

Iraq launches waves of air raids against Iranian cities.

16-30
Iran makes several more assaults on Basra, but does not make significant further advances, and is repulsed in several positions. Basra is effectively under seige by Iranian artillery.

20
Three fires are set in oil installations in Kuwait. Iran issues a new series of threats against the southern Gulf states aiding Iraq.

Iran buys more tankers for its "tanker shuttle" in the Gulf. The tanker and oil wars continue. Iranian ships start firing Sea Killer missiles at ships bound for Kuwait.

February	Total number of ships hit since start of war rises to 284.
	Iran launches small new assaults around Basra.
	Iraqi air units continue to strike Iranian cities.
20-25	A "ceasefire" in strikes against population centers fails after five days.
22-23	A new Iranian assault on Basra only scores token gains.
25	US prematurely announces it will provide military escorts for shipping to Kuwait only to be rebuffed later by Kuwait, who fears Iraqi and Soviet anti-US reaction.
26	Iran announces that Kerbala 5 has come to an end, but fighting continues around Basra.
March	Iraq attacks three ships in the Gulf in the "Tanker War"; Iran attacks three.
1	Iran defeats limited Iraqi counterattack in the area around Basra.
4	Kerbala 7 begins in the Germand Heights in the Haj Omran area in the North. Iran scores limited gains and slightly improves its position in the mountain area.
15	Saddan Hussein calls high-level meeting with senior commanders and confidants in Baghdad.
	Turkey again warns Iran against attacks on the Iraqi Turkish oil pipeline.
19	Iranian new year. Iranian leadership pledges continued offensives and victory by the next Norruz.

April	Iraq attacks two ships in the Gulf in the "Tanker War"; Iran attacks three.
	Iran claims Kurdish rebels have killed 1,500 Iraqis in recent attacks in Northern Iraq.
3-11	Kerbala 8 offensive leads to minor Iranian advances on the front near Basra west of the Jassim River and Fish Lake.
9	Kerbala 9 offensive takes place near Qasr-e-Shirin, about 100 miles north of Baghdad. Iran makes slight improvements in its strategic position in the mountainous border area.
15	Iran warns USSR against chartering tankers to Kuwait.
20	Argentina agrees to help Iran finish its Bushehr nuclear power plant.
22	Iran sentences an American, John Pattis, to 10 years in jail on charges he spied for the CIA.
24	US intelligence sources confirm that Iran now has a Silkworm ship-to-ship missile site on the Faw Peninsula opposite Kuwait, as well as two sites at the mouth of the Gulf.
25	Iran launches Kerbala 10 offensive and claims to have liberated 11 Iraqi Kurdish villages in recent fighting in the north.
27	Secret summit meeting takes place between Saddan Hussein of Iraq and Hafaz Assad of Syria in which both sides seem to agree to halt support of the opposition to the opposing regime.

29	Iran claims Kerbala 10 offensive in the north has taken 115-square miles of territory in Silaimaniyeh Province in Iraq near Sardasht, Baneh, and Marivan and Iranian troops are 16 miles inside Iraq.
	Commander of the Iranian Navy, Commodore Mohammed Hoseyn Malekzadegan, warns that Iran could close Straits of Hormuz.
May 2	Iranian marines board 14 tankers in Gulf as Iran continues its pressure on shipping to Kuwait in aid of Iraq.
5	US-Iranian Tribunal orders US to return $541 million in frozen assets to Iran.
6	Iranian attack ships start operations from Al-Farisyah Island, midway between northern Saudi Arabia and the mainland, and attack Japanese supertanker believed to be moved to Kuwait.

Major battle areas in the Iran-Iraq War from 1984-1987
Maps by Derrick Ballington

Introduction

The Iran-Iraq War can be viewed at many different levels: as a human tragedy, as a threat to the security of Southwest Asia, as a threat to the world's main supply of imported oil, and as the source of new lessons regarding the nature of modern war. All of these insights are important to understanding the strategic implications of the war and the meaning of the recent fighting. Without this understanding, the West can neither understand the risks inherent in the conflict, or what can be done to end it.

The Enduring Strategic Importance of the Conflict

One fact is all too clear. The Iran-Iraq War is of critical importance to Western security. More than half of all the world's proven oil reserves are located in Iran, Iraq, and the smaller Southern Gulf states. All of these states are affected by the war, and an Iranian victory could threaten the stability of the West's access to oil for decades to come.

Even a peace settlement that did not involve a major defeat for either side could threaten the West. It could leave Iran or Iraq so dependent on the USSR for arms or political support that it could weaken the delicate balance in the Gulf between the U.S. and USSR. Even if the war does nothing to strengthen the Soviet position, it could leave the region so unsettled that every nation would be forced to continue the present regional arms race indefinitely.

The war may also polarize much of Islam between Sunni and Shi'ite, and help divide the Arab world between secular states and those that adopt some form of Islamic revolution. While Khomeini is scarcely a popular example of Islamic government in most of the Arab world, he has still demonstrated that Islamic revolutions and governments are possible. He also is a powerful sectarian example to the Shi'ites in Bahrain, Lebanon, Saudi Arabia, Syria, and the Yemens.

In fact, it is hard to decide which would be worse, placing the USSR in a dominant position in either Iraq or Iran, or an Iranian victory over Iraq

I

that unleashed religious and cultural divisions that could divide the entire Middle East. Either outcome could rapidly move the West from a brief few years of "oil glut" to decades of oil crisis. Either outcome could require a level of military intervention that would strain the West's limited power projection capabilities to the breaking point.

While little hard data has emerged on the war over the last two years from either Iran or Iraq, neither the West nor its friends in the Middle East can feel safe until the war ends. In spite of three years of near stalemate, the war can radically change the balance of power in Southwest Asia and the Northern Gulf at any time. While Iraq has many strengths, no amount of arms or money can give it the ability to sustain the war indefinitely. At the same time, the war is imposing strains on Iran which may ultimately undermine its present regime and make it vulnerable to Marxist influence or Soviet penetration.

A War of Lies

Unfortunately, the forces that are shaping the course of the Iran-Iraq war are exceptionally difficult to understand. All wars create their own fog of myths and misstatements. In this case, however, two closed societies deny the world press the kind of access needed for accurate reporting. There are no reliable unclassified sources of information on the course of the fighting.

For both Iran and Iraq, the war is a "war of lies". Each side seeks to distort the perceptions of its own populace and the outside world for propaganda reasons. Each leadership lives at least partly in a world of self-inflicted illusions. As a result, neither side knows or tells the truth and the press must often guess. It is all too common to see directly contradictory press reports about the same battle appear on the same day.

While some Western intelligence information has been made public, it often has proved to be no more accurate than press sources. The most advanced intelligence technologies cannot accurately interpret a war where so much of the fighting takes place at night or in poor weather, where both sides are constantly mobilized for new fighting, where so much of the fighting is done by dispersed infantry forces, and where it centers around fixed defenses that do not change from day to day. No one can accurately interpret the communications of forces which routinely communicate in a mixture of deliberate lies and self-delusion. No one can analyze orders of battle where the readiness and effectiveness of individual units is unknown, and there is no clear standardization of unit type.

The political and economic situation are equally uncertain. A great deal of speculative writing has appeared about the internal views and power struggles of Iran's religious leaders and new revolutionary elite. The same is true of reports on Sadam Hussein and Iraq's Ba'ath Party. Few of these reports, however, have stood the test of time, and several coup attempts and executions have been reported that simply did not occur.

A great many statistics are being generated on the economies of both Iran and Iraq, but intelligence experts in the U.S., U.K., Germany, and France all privately agree that the data involved are generally very uncertain, and that many reports are almost useless. The same is true of area experts in the UN, World Bank, IMF, and Departments of State and Commerce. In most cases, the most that can be done with such statistics is to compare a wide range of sources and try to pick the number that does the most convincing job of explaining the most recent facts. This, however, defeats the whole purpose of statistics and economic analysis.

The Unpredictability of War and Revolution

There is also a natural tendency to ignore the sheer scale of the uncertainty surrounding the war and the Iranian revolution. Both news reporting and academic analysis struggles for precision and predictability. In many cases this creates the illusion of understanding when the most that is available is guesswork. The uncertainty is also greatest when it comes to the two most critical issues affecting the war.

First, it simply is not possible to predict the course of the Iranian revolution. Even if one could understand the details of the forces now affecting the Iranian revolution – and no source of data exists to make this possible – the history of true popular revolutions raises serious doubts about the relevance of studies based on the revolutions, initial leadership. Most revolutions take twenty to thirty years to run their course, and the history of the French, Soviet, and Chinese revolutions is littered with the bones of brilliant studies that failed to understand and predict the true course of what would happen.

Second, the outcome of the Iran-Iraq War cannot be predicted, only guessed at. The war is in its seventh year precisely because the military forces and strategic capabilities of both sides have remained in so close a balance. In fact the strategic situation in the Iran-Iraq war has been oddly similar to that in World War I. Both sides have different mixes of forces, but neither has a decisive edge.

There is relatively static trench warfare on the ground. This has led to long bloody battles of attrition against strong points and even gas warfare. At the same time, it has led to constant efforts to find some other flank theater in which one side can break out of the stalemate that has been created in the key central front. Even the war against tankers and oil facilities roughly parallels World War I's naval battles against each side's economy, sources of arms, and lines of communication.

The end result has been a war whose outcome may be determined far more by whether Iran or Iraq can maintain political and economic cohesion under the strain of prolonged combat than by military tactics and strategy. It is a war that is far easier to lose by making a critical series of mistakes, than to win by effective planning and strategy.

Sources, Data, and Uncertainties

Given this background, it should be clear that this book involves a great deal of guesswork. It not only must be written at a time when the facts are remarkably difficult to establish, it concentrates on the fighting during 1984-1987. This is a period in which neither Iraq or Iran has generally permitted press access to the fighting, and it is a period in which the relative stalemate along the border has made it difficult to verify either side's claims by observing the outcome of the fighting. There are no real "experts" on the war, only "students", and even the most informed students often disagree.

Both Iraq and Iran have operated in a climate of growing economic, political, and social strain. Little of their central statistical reporting, or that of outside sources, has come to grips with the true costs of the war, or has separated the fiction of paper plans from the grim reality of societies operating in a climate of "total war". International statistics are unconvincing at the best of times, but they have often become hopeless in trying to understand what is really happening to Iran and Iraq.

As a result, this book draws heavily on the day to day reporting in the press, and relies largely on wide-ranging comparisons of different media sources. The U.S. press is the source which is most often referenced, but this is largely to permit other researchers to trace the chronological basis for the analysis. Extensive use has also been made of sources like the Foreign Broadcast Information Service, Iranian and Iraqi news releases, television and radio transcripts, academic studies and articles, material gained at various conferences on the war, and interviews and discussions in the region, Europe, and the United States.

References to specific newspapers do not generally indicate the true source of a report. U.S. newspapers have very few foreign correspondents. Much of the actual input to U.S. newspaper reporting consists of French and British wire service data, background briefings by Western governments, and stringers in the Middle East. Many of these sources have consistent biases which are disguised by the failure to cite them in U.S. newspapers, and the tendency to mix different sources.

Nevertheless, it is the news media which provide most of the pieces that can be used to put together the puzzle of the Iran-Iraq War. Reporters have to deal in real time and work with many conflicting sources. If they make errors, many are corrected by their colleagues or in subsequent reporting. Further, the better reporters have far better informal access to intelligence sources than academics and are able to get estimates which are current at the time an event occurs. Most official or academic reporting occurs long after an event or long before it.

The reader should be fully aware of these problems because it is not possible to issue endless qualifications throughout this book, or to provide comparative reporting in many cases where there is really little agreement on the data.

The reader should also be aware that names and transliterations are generally provided in the form taken from the original source. Only a limited effort has been made to standardize such terms. Having travelled extensively in Iran and Iraq, the author would caution that both Iran and Iraq often use place names carelessly or issue communiques which simply do not seem to match the terrain. Similarly, Iran and Iraq report unit designations carelessly, as well as force numbers and casualties. These are highly political societies, and this is one case where truth was not the first casualty of war. It was dead long before the war began.

There is also considerable uncertainty in the Western estimates of military forces and casualties used throughout this book, and to estimates of military damage and short term oil production, oil exports, and oil revenues. Most intelligence officers place little confidence in their estimates of the operational strength of Iranian and Iraqi forces or casualty reports. Many reports on war damage overestimate the damage done, and many reports have been issued telling of virtual cutoffs of Iranian oil exports which have proved to be untrue over the weeks which have followed.

Even the spelling of the sites of many battles is not standardized. For example, U.S. Army and U.S. Air Force maps often use different spellings for smaller towns, and no agreed name exists for many of the mountains and hamlets along the border area. No agreement exists on how the names of many individuals shown be transliterated into English, and it is not uncommon to get letters from Iran and Iraq in which individuals change the English spelling of their own last names.

The Problem of Policy

Military history is always uncertain, even when it is limited to well-documented battles and written long after the fact. Trying to write a strategic analysis in the midst of a war, imposes far greater uncertainties. It has many of the characteristics of a detective story where the author is only slightly more aware of many of the facts than the reader. Fortunately, many of the broad issues and strategic themes shaping the war are not dependent on accurate knowledge of the details.

The reader should treat the analysis accordingly. If historians are ever given access to Iran and Iraq, and their records of the war, they may rewrite much of the West's current knowledge of the war. At the same time, there can be no real question regarding the risks the war creates for the

West and the region, or regarding the major strategic objectives of the U.S. and its allies. It is also clear from a policy viewpoint that the main issue is not how to cope with detailed uncertainties, but rather how to structure broad policy objectives.

The final chapter of this book discusses these policy objectives. At the risk of spoiling any suspense, it reaches the following major conclusions:

- The war is far too dangerous to Western interests to be treated as a means of paralyzing Iranian and Iraqi regional ambitions. The West must make every effort to end the war as soon as possible.

- The best outcome of the war is to preserve the present national structure of Iran and Iraq, without one side dominating the other. Both nations can act as major buffers between the Gulf and the USSR, but only if they remain strong independent states.

- Iraq is now threatened by the risk of a successful Iranian invasion. Western policy must be shaped to limit the risk of any Iranian victory and a successful invasion. At the same time, the U.S. will not benefit from directly supporting Iraq with weapons shipments or other major assistance. U.S. support must be indirect, and linked to efforts to open lines of communication to Iran and to strengthen the southern Gulf states. In practice, this means using every political means to limit arms shipments to Iran, providing indirect economic aid to ensure that Iraq can continue to finance the war, providing quiet intelligence support, and providing political support for every serious peace initiative.

  In contrast, the role that European nations like France are playing in providing arms to Iraq is vital. These arms sales are providing Iraq with the technology it needs to both defend and force Iran to a peace settlement. They also are helping to ensure that Iraq will not become dependent on the USSR. Any break in the flow of French arms to Iraq could be very dangerous to Western security.

- Iran is only beginning its current revolution. The West cannot hope to create a stable and friendly relationship with Iran for many years to come. The Reagan Administration's disastrous flirtation with covert arms shipments to Iran has demonstrated that Western efforts to maintain and expand communications with Iran must be limited to political and economic contacts, and that these should be structured to act as incentives towards peace, not as bribes to Iran's government.

  At the same time, the West cannot afford to ignore the various opposition movements in Iran. It is possible that Iran's current ruling elite may remain in power for the next decade, but it is not likely. This means the West must try to maintain low level ties with every major faction, and to build a relationship based on economic self-interest, not common political and social goals.

- No Western effort to buy the support of either Iraq or Iran will secure the safety of Americans in the Middle East, protect Israel, or ease the problems of terrorism and hostage taking. It is stable, well-balanced policy initiatives based on strength and consistency of purpose that will do most to win the enduring support of an Iranian and Iraqi regime.

- The West cannot hope to make Iran or Iraq military allies. Neither state is likely to act as any kind of proxy for Western security interests in the Gulf. The most the West can hope for is that Iranian and Iraqi economic ties to the West can be rebuilt and strengthened to the point where these ties dominate political attitudes and actions. The West also will not benefit from major arms sales to either state. This is an area where our European allies can accomplish far more by ensuring that neither state has to depend on the USSR for arms after the war, and that a superpower rivalry does not develop as part of an Iranian-Iraqi arms race.

- No outcome of the war offers a secure hope of long term stability in the Gulf unless the Gulf Cooperation Council (GCC) states can be built up into a significant and unified political and military deterrent. The U.S., in particular, needs to revitalize its efforts to strengthen the GCC states, and its military ties to Saudi Arabia – the only southern Gulf state large and strong enough to underpin a regional military effort.

- The West, however, cannot rely on regional forces to protect its oil exports. This presents a special problem at a time that European nations are steadily reducing their already limited out of area capabilities. The U.S. must continue to strengthen USCENTCOM (U.S. Central Command) and its power projection capabilities in the region. It must have the military option of ensuring the flow of oil through the Gulf, and be able to provide "over-the-horizon" reinforcements to any Southern Gulf state threatened by one of its larger northern neighbors.

  In shaping its forces, the U.S. must not only consider the risks inherent in an Iranian victory, but the threat of Iranian and Iraqi efforts to limit southern Gulf oil production after the war, the threat from Soviet backed radical states in the Red Sea, and the long term threat of a Soviet victory over Afghanistan's freedom fighters. The U.S. is the only Western nation that can play this role.

In the longer term, the West must return to a far more realistic policy towards its dependence on imported energy. The present "oil glut" will not last beyond the early 1990s, and could end sooner. At that point, one central strategic reality will remain: well over 50% of all the world's proven oil reserves will be in the Gulf. The West must act to secure this flow of oil, but it must also revitalize its efforts to create safe sources of nuclear power and energy from coal, to develop advanced means of oil recovery, to create a commercial synfuels industry, and to exploit alternative sources of energy like solar and geothermal power.

In fact, the "oil glut" has done more than reduce the flow of Western money to the Organization of Petroleum Exporting Countries (OPEC). It has virtually killed every major Western effort at reducing the West's long term dependence on oil imports. No Western security policy can be successful which does not recognize this fact. Unless the West acts to put its own house in order, no regional policy can ever provide it with the degree of security it needs.

Chapter One

The Strategic Implications of the Iran-Iraq War

From a Western viewpoint, the most critical strategic implications of the war are: (a) its impact on the future government and policy of Iran and Iraq, (b) its impact on their role as buffers between the Soviet Union and the West, and (c) its impact on the future availability of oil exports. All of these strategic implications involve serious threats to Western interests.

The War's Impact on the Future of Iran and Iraq

While the West naturally thinks of the war in terms of oil and the security of the Gulf, the conflict is a human tragedy with its own strategic implications. The Iran-Iraq War has become one of the most bloody and enduring conflicts of the modern era. While any estimates of the losses on either side are highly speculative, the total number of dead may now be 1,000,000, and the total wounded exceed 1,700,000. Iran seems to have lost at least 300,000 killed and 600,000-750,000 wounded, and Iraq 120,000 dead and 300,000 wounded.[1] These estimates are highly conservative, however, and U.S. experts have estimated that the total killed on both sides is over 1,000,000. In addition, at least 8,000 Iranians and 15,000 Iraqis are prisoners of war.[2]

The war now costs each nation as much as $1 billion a month in direct expenses and indirect costs to its economy. It has cost Iraq at least $120 billion since the war began. Iran's total costs are far harder to estimate, but probably total well over $70 billion in direct costs and over $140 billion in indirect economic costs and wartime damage.

These costs place an obvious strain on both societies. The pressure of trying to match Iran's military manpower has meant that a generation has had to be mobilized for war that would have been crucial to Iraq's development. Iraq's losses in manpower, the disruption of its educational system, the expenditure of capital, the growth of international debt, the failure to develop civil plant and infrastructure have seriously hurt Iraq's economy. Even if the war ends on favorable terms, it will slow down Iraq's economic development for at least a decade.

The war will also have serious regional effects. Iran's artillery and missile attacks on Basra and neighboring areas have cost Iraq a great deal of its oil shipping, refinery, and steel and iron capacity in the southeast. In the northeast, the war has created a new wave of Kurdish nationalism, and led to a rebirth of separatism that may plague Iraq for years to come.

Iran's wartime losses compound the effects of the collapse of most of its major development projects after the Shah's fall, of continuing revolutionary turmoil in the economy, of even more serious disruption of its educational system, and of population growth. Every major sector of the economy has suffered from contraction and decline, and while Iran often issues accurate statistics on its domestic economy to the Majlis, it omits reporting on key data like monthly oil exports and foreign exchange reserves, and Iran's economic development plans are now little more than an exercise in statistical illusion.[3]

The combination of war and revolution may lead to serious cuts in Iranian living standards which extend over the next quarter century. Agriculture, manufacturing, and education have all experienced serious contraction and decline. There has been at least some permanent loss of oil reserves due to damage to oil facilities or mishandling of oil production, and the trade sector has suffered in virtually every dimension. The war has created over one million refugees and iron/steel, refinery, and petrochemical facilities have all suffered severely. The massive Bandar Khomeini petrochemical plant is only one of many critical facilities that have been damaged or lost.

The war has exposed the darkest side of religion. Like similar periods of stress in the Christian West, and in the history of ancient Israel, conflict and social change in Iran have combined with religious faith to create a new Shi'ite ideology that often glorifies xenophobia and religious prejudice and which transforms opposition into the forces of "Satan".

It is inaccurate to call this "Islamic fundamentalism". Khomeini has given birth to a radical form of Iranian Shi'ism which so far has only found sympathetic resonance in an equally troubled Lebanon. There is no doubt, however, that it has threatened many Islamic states with the emergence of religious challenges to secular rule, and encouraged other challenges to modernization and social evolution throughout the Middle East.

While no one can be certain how these political, economic, and social impacts of the war will combine with the deep ethnic divisions in Iraq and Iran, and the overall process of internal change, there is no question that the war has increased the internal strains in both nations. Even if the war finally ends in a stalemate, it may alter the politics of each nation in ways which threaten both its neighbors and the West.

In the case of Iraq, the war may lead to the rebirth of divisions between Shi'ite and Sunni and new coups or coup attempts. It seems unlikely that Sadam Hussein and the present Ba'ath elite will lose power during the war unless Iraq suffers further major defeats. The regime is too entrenched and there are few illusions that Iran would welcome any secular regime as an acceptable substitute for Iraq's current government. The aftermath of the war, however, may well lead to major pressures for change from both the Iraqi population and Iraq's military.

Even if the war or its outcome do not lead to a change in Iraq's governing elite, the war is certain to have other effects. A new Kurdish civil war has already broken out in the North, and the political and strategic pressures of the war have already led Iraq to quietly reopen the issue of the control of Bubiyan and Waribah, the two Kuwaiti islands near Iraq's small Gulf coast. In the case of Iran, the eventual backlash to the human and financial costs of the war may lead to the strengthening of either Marxist elements or an even more xenophobic regime.

Expert opinion differs sharply over the stability of Iran's present religious elite. Most U.S. experts feel, however, that the religious leadership has largely consolidated its power, and that any short term shifts are likely to take the form of power struggles over the succession to power after Khomeini's death. It is unclear under these conditions whether a "pragmatist" or "true believer" succession would be more dangerous. Both are likely to be heavily ideological, anti-Western, and aggressive in at least political terms. Both might also be willing to deal with the Soviet Union on a basis that could seriously undermine Western interests.

There is little mid-term prospect of a shift towards any form of middle class or secular régime. The most successful of the present exile groups are at least broadly Marxist in character, and the strongest rivals to Iran's present religious regime are more likely to be its emerging new military elites than any exile group.

For all the present and potential rivalries between Iran's present religious and political leaders, the group that actually seizes power is more likely to be led by some unknown that any of the figures the West can now recognize by name. Such leaders may also have only limited personal and ideological tenure. True popular revolutions rarely have any quick or predictable outcome. The French and Soviet revolutions are classic examples of the fact that a revolution can take more than half a century to move towards relative political stability.

Equally importantly, virtually any outcome of the war may help create an enduring split or rise in tension between Iraq and Iran, Persian and Arab, and Sunni and Shi'ite throughout the Gulf area or Middle East.

Coupled to the other problems in the region, these forces may well lead to new arms races, tensions, and conflicts.

Most outcomes of the war are also likely to lead to at least some political and economic conflict over access to the world's oil markets – particularly if the end of the war occurs before the end of the present oil glut. Both Iran and Iraq will have a strong incentive to maximize production while keeping prices high. This means new struggles for oil quotas, many of which may occur with southern Gulf states like Saudi Arabia and Kuwait. Even Iraq's efforts to repay its war debts and oil exchanges lead to high Iraqi export levels that could renew past tensions between it and its conservative neighbors.

The Role of Iraq and Iran as Buffers Between the USSR and the West

The war would be dangerous if it only affected the future politics and development of Iran and Iraq, but the war has much broader strategic dimensions. One of these is the extent to which Iran and Iraq are independent enough to limit the expansion of Soviet influence. Iran and Iraq are key buffer states between East and West. As long as both are strong and independent, the U.S. and USSR have little incentive for military involvement in the Gulf, and the USSR has few prospects of gaining control over a critical portion of the world's oil reserves.

If, however, the war ends with either a major Iranian or Iraqi defeat – or in sheer financial and political exhaustion for both sides – it will gravely weaken at least one nation's ability to act as a strategic buffer. Even if defeat or stress does not radicalize the internal politics of Iraq or Iran, either nation may be forced to desperately seek arms and new sources of military supply. This might well force Iraq or Iran to align itself with the USSR. Even if this does not occur, the broader tensions and problems the war has created may have the same effect. Long after the war is over, the war's legacy of internal divisions and stress may lead to the emergence of new Marxist or pro-Soviet factions that could give the USSR new influence in the Gulf.[4]

The Impact on Oil Exports

The Iran-Iraq War is also of major strategic importance because it affects the West's access to oil. The war not only threatens the day-to-day flow of oil, it threatens the long term stability of the West's access to the Gulf's oil reserves. Today's low oil prices, and surplus oil export capacity, disguise the importance of this threat. After the early 1990s, however, the world demand for oil exports will increase steadily, and oil prices will rise. Given the lack of alternative sources of oil and energy, this means the Gulf will steadily increase in importance.

In spite of a decade of intense Western effort to find alternative energy supplies and oil outside the Middle East, the U.S. Geological Survey (USGS) shows virtually no increase in either proven oil reserves or the estimated undiscovered oil reserves outside the Gulf area. Further, the ratio of reserves to consumption has increased in the Gulf, and decreased virtually everywhere else. The USGS has concluded that, "Demonstrated reserves of crude oil have declined over the past 10 years ... discoveries have lagged over the same period ... Rates of discovery have continued to decline over the past 20 years even though exploratory activity has increased..."[5]

Long term U.S. dependence on Gulf oil reserves is as strategically important as the dependence of Western Europe and Japan. Regardless of where today's oil imports come from, all importing nations compete for the same total pool of global resources. To put this in perspective, the USGS cut its estimate of U.S. offshore oil reserves by 55% in 1985, the USSR is experiencing major problems in exploiting even its proven reserves, expected major discoveries in the PRC (People's Republic of China) have not occurred, and increases in Mexican consumption are now expected to consume its increase in production.

The West is in trouble not only in spite of the so-called oil glut, but *because* of it. The massive drop in oil prices in early 1986, made most Western synfuel efforts and attempts at creating other alternative energy supplies hopelessly uneconomic. Most are now halted indefinitely. It has sharply reduced European efforts to find oil and gas, and has led to a more than 60% cut in U.S. drilling efforts and drops in U.S. oil production. Many marginal oil wells are to be closed while the others overproduce. As a result, oil production in the U.S. dropped in 1986 for the first time since 1980. At the same time demand rose 2.5%. This situation is likely to occur again in 1987.[6]

This is just the tip of the iceberg. In spite of the fact that major oil exploration activities began in 30 new countries between 1979 and 1984, the total increase in all world reserves during that period was less than 1% and most occurred in the Gulf area. Further, several key OPEC countries outside the Gulf are now rapidly consuming their reserves: these include Algeria, Ecuador, Gabon, Indonesia, and Nigeria. None are likely to be oil exporters by the mid-1990s.[7]

Figure 1 shows that Iran and Iraq are already credited with nearly 20% of the world's oil reserves. While the true size of these reserves cannot be reassessed until the end of the war, it now seems likely that Iraq will emerge as having much larger reserves than are now estimated. Many oil experts feel that Iraq's proven reserves will equal those of Kuwait after three to five years of peacetime exploration. In contrast, Iran may experience slowly declining proven reserves, although it will remain a major oil producer.

Figure 1   World Oil Reserves

Region and Country	Estimated Proven Reserves	
	Billions of Barrels	Percent of World Reserves
GULF	369.18	56.7
Bahrain	.17	.02
Neutral Zone	(5.4)	.8
Iran	48.5	6.9
Iraq	44.5 (65.0)[a]	6.4
Kuwait[b]	92.7	13.3
Oman	3.5	.5
Qatar	3.35	.5
UAE	32.49	4.6
Abu Dhabi	(30.5)	—
Dubai	(1.44)	—
Ras al Kaimah	(0.1)	-
Sharjah	(.45)	-
Saudi Arabia[b]	171.7	24.6
OTHER MIDDLE EAST	2.2	.3
Israel	.75	.1
Syria	1.45	.2
TOTAL MIDDLE EAST	398.38	57.0
AFRICA[c]	55.54	7.9
Algeria	9.0	1.3
Angola	1.8	.3
Egypt	3.2	.5
Libya	21.1	3.0
Nigeria	16.65	2.4
WESTERN HEMISPHERE[c]	117.69	16.8
U.S.	27.3	3.9
Mexico	48.6	7.0
Canada	7.075	1.0
Venezuela	25.845	3.7
WESTERN EUROPE[c]	24.425	3.5
Britain	13.59	1.9
Norway	8.3	1.2
ASIA PACIFIC[c]	18.5299	2.7
Australia	1.5	.2
Brunei	1.4	.2
India	3.0	.42
Indonesia	8.65	1.2
Malaysia	3.5	.5

Figure 1   World Oil Reserves

Region and Country	Estimated Proven Reserves	
	Billions of Barrels	Percent of World Reserves
TOTAL NON-COMMUNIST	614.567	88.0
Communist	84.1	12.0
USSR	63.0	9.0
China	19.1	2.7
Other	2.0	.2
TOTAL WORLD	698.667	100

a. The current official estimate is 44.1 billion, which has not been revised because of the Iran-Iraq War but most U.S. officials now estimate Iraqi proven reserves at 65 billion or more.

b. Neither Kuwait or Saudi Arabia provide up to date estimates of proven reserves. The reserves for each country include half of the Neutral Zone. Source: Adapted from *Oil and Gas Journal*, December 1984 and December 1985.

c. Breakdown by individual countries includes only major exporting or reserve holding countries

It is Iraq and Iran's ability to threaten the rest of the Gulf, however, which makes the Iran-Iraq War so dangerous. Saudi Arabia alone has proven oil reserves of over 170 billion barrels. This is nearly 25% of the world's proven oil reserves and 28% of the free world's reserves. Yet, even these percentages are artificially low. Saudi Arabia has had little incentive to prove additional reserves over the last five years. Saudi Arabia can almost certainly continue to prove more reserves than it consumes for at least the next half-decade and may well be able to do so for the next decade.

The five smaller southern Gulf states also have major strategic importance. Kuwait, Qatar, Bahrain, the UAE, and Oman are now linked together with Saudi Arabia in the Gulf Cooperation Council (GCC). These five small states have a total of 130 billion barrels worth of proven reserves. This is a total of 19% of the world's proven oil reserves and 21% of the free world's oil reserves. In fact, these five small Gulf states have 10% more proven oil reserves than the entire Western Hemisphere, including Canada, Mexico, Venezuela, and the United States.[8]

Equally importantly, the six GCC states have a total maximum sustainable oil production capacity of 15.8 million barrels a day and, if Iran and Iraq are included, total Gulf production capacity is about 20-25 million barrels per day. This is equivalent to roughly 50% of all OPEC production capacity. Saudi Arabia alone can produce up to 10.2 million barrels per day, or more than 40% of all the oil production capacity of all the Gulf states.[9]

While it is unlikely that any near-term outcome of the Iran-Iraq war will lead to a major interruption of oil flow from the Gulf, the escalation of the war could still disrupt world markets and lead to sudden rises in price. An Iranian victory could also have much more serious effects. Iran has already put heavy pressure on OPEC and the GCC states to restrict production and raise oil prices. A triumphant Iran could lead to constant Iranian pressure on the GCC states to accommodate Iran by keeping their production low and prices high.

The West has to recognize its long term strategic dependence on the Gulf. It is not only Western efforts in coal, synfuels, alternative energy, and nuclear power which are lagging. Most of the Western effort in these areas has been far less successful than anyone predicted even in the early 1980s.

As a result, the combined strategic importance of Gulf reserves and production capability will grow steadily as time goes by. Even the most conservative estimates of oil demand, indicate that oil will provide at least 30% of the energy for OECD (Organization for Economic Cooperation and Development) countries through the end of the 1990s. While the total oil import needs of the West and the Free World will fluctuate with political and economic conditions, today's "oil glut" is almost certain to disappear by the early 1990s as the result of world economic recovery and economic growth.

Notes

[1] *New York Times*, February 7, 1987; *Washington Post*, February 9, 1987; *Washington Times*, March 14 and 31, 1986 and Insight section, pp. 28-30. This estimate adjusts for losses in the Val Fajr offensives of early 1987, but any such estimates are highly uncertain. One September, 1985, estimate of those killed went as high as 300,000 Iraqis and 420,000-580,000 Iranians: Drew Middleton, "5 Years of Iran-Iraq War", *New York Times*, September 23, 1985. Iraqi estimates of Iraqi dead during the same time period ran as low as 78,000: Joyce Starr, "For Iraqis Good Times May End", *International Herald Tribune*, August 28, 1985. U.S. intelligence experts informally estimated in early October, 1985, that Iran has suffered 550,000 casualties with 250,000 killed, and Iraq had suffered 250,000 casualties with 100,000 killed.

[2] Source: Statement of George B. Crist, U.S. Marine Corps, Commander in Chief, U.S. Central Command Before the Senate Armed Services Committee on the Status of the U.S. Central Command, January 27, 1986. p. 17.

[3] The best detailed reporting is available in the various publications of the Economist Intelligence Unit, particularly the quarterly country reports. The Department of Commerce and State Department country reports are dated and often very limited in coverage. The Economist data are, however, extremely uncertain, as are the press sources used elsewhere in this report.

[4]Any Soviet invasion of Iran seems an unlikely contingency, even in support of some major Marxist faction in Iran. The terrain is difficult, the USSR does not have combat ready forces in good position, and the lessons of the Afghan conflict have been too striking. Nevertheless, the USSR has conducted one major command post exercise of an invasion of Iran. This exercise was held in August 1980, and helped trigger the formation of the U.S. Rapid Deployment Force. The USSR has since held much larger field exercises which could have the same purpose, including the "Kavaz 85" exercise in 1985, which involved some 25,000 troops. This exercise took place when Soviet troops were already in Afghanistan. The USSR did not call up all the support units and air power necessary for a full scale invasion in either case, and would probably need 30 days to mobilize a full invasion force regardless of such exercises. *New York Times*, December 15, 1985, p. A-14. A full description of Soviet plans for such an invasion dating back to World War II is presented in Marshall Lee Miller, "The Soviet General Staff's Secret Plans for Invading Iran," *Armed Forces Journal*, January 1987, pp. 28-32.

[5]Excerpted from an unclassified USGS working paper dated June, 1983.

[6]*New York Times*, December 11, 1986, p. D-1.

[7]See *World Petroleum Outlook*, 1984, Committee on Energy and Natural Resources, U.S. Senate, Ninety-Eighth Congress, January 30, 1984; Office of Technology Assessment, *U.S. Vulnerability to an Oil Import Curtailment*, Report OTA-E-243, September, 1984; Department of Energy, *International Energy Outlook, 1985, With Projections to 1995*, DOE-EIA-0484(85) March 19, 1986, pp. 1-24; and Department of Energy, *International Energy Annual*, 1984, DOE/EIA-0219(84), pp. 11-45.

[8]See *World Petroleum Outlook*, 1984, Committee on Energy and Natural Resources, U.S. Senate, Ninety-Eighth Congress, January 30, 1984; Office of Technology Assessment, *U.S. Vulnerability to an Oil Import Curtailment*, Report OTA-E-243, September, 1984; Department of Energy, *International Energy Outlook, 1985, With Projections to 1995*, DOE-EIA-0484(85) March 19, 1986, pp. 1-24; and Department of Energy, *International Energy Annual*, 1984, DOE/EIA-0219(84), pp. 11-45.

[9]Ibid.

Chapter Two

The Forces Now Shaping the Course of the Iran-Iraq War

As the fighting in 1986 has demonstrated, the apparent stalemate in the Iran-Iraq War is misleading. Although neither side has made decisive strategic gains in the land fighting since 1984, several important shifts have occurred during the last two years.

- Iran has slowly been able to dominate the bloody war of attrition on the ground. It has succeeded to the point where it can achieve a steady series of small gains from Iraq, and can inflict steady casualties, and strain Iraqi morale and political cohesion.
- In contrast, Iraq has been able to keep Iran from winning decisive victories because it has dominated the race for new arms imports. Iraq has received more economic aid and has been able to afford a higher level of mobilization. It is only its superior access to arms, however, which has so far allowed it to limit the scope of Iran's strategic gains.
- As the threat on the ground has grown, Iraq has responded by steadily escalating its attempts to deny Iran the ability to export oil. Iraq has had considerable success, but it has not yet been able to reduce Iran's oil exports to the point where this has threatened Iran's ability to continue the war.
- Both sides have come under growing stress. While no reliable economic statistics are available, it is clear that Iran has had to cut back on its civil budget, curtail arms imports, and introduce draconian import controls and some rationing. Iraq no longer is able to afford both "guns and butter." Its people are having to make more and more economic sacrifices, as well as pay the human cost of a war that has wounded or killed nearly one out of ten Iraqi males.

At present, these forces have created a delicate military balance. Chance and/or a single major military mistake could tip the war decisively in favor of one side of the other. At the same time, both Iraq and Iran have reason to escalate the conflict, and to threaten or include other states.

Iraq must seek to cripple Iran economically by striking at its oil exports, and must continue political pressure on its neighbors in the Southern Gulf to ensure they provide economic and political support. It increasingly will need the option of allowing its long range fighters to use air bases in the Southern Gulf States.

Similarly, Iraq has reason to continue to use, and even expand its use of, gas warfare. Its chemical complex near Samarra, north of Baghdad, is now capable of producing both Tabun and Sarin nerve gases. Iraq has already used mustard gas, cyanotic agents, and Tabun with limited success, and Sarin is nearly 10 times more lethal than Tabun. While Iran is acquiring its own capability to manufacture nerve gas, and has had limited aid from Syria in developing such capability, it still lags well behind Iraq.[1]

Iran's incentives to escalate are somewhat different. It currently lacks the air and naval power to halt Gulf shipping in the face of even limited U.S. opposition. It cannot mine or otherwise close the Straits of Hormuz, and it lacks sufficient operational fighters to conduct major air strikes. It does, however, have every reason to try to force the Southern Gulf states to halt their aid to Iraq. Iran's seizure of Faw in 1986 has given it far more capability to intimidate Kuwait, and its limited victories in the land fighting seem to have persuaded the Arab states to be more accommodating in OPEC.

Iran also retains enough remaining naval strength to inspect and harass Gulf shipping. Further, some key Gulf states like Bahrain are vulnerable to subversion and political pressure. Iran may still, therefore, find it desirable to broaden the war through limited strikes or acts of escalation, and its capabilities may rise significantly as it takes delivery on more PRC aircraft and anti-ship missiles.

In terms of the overall course of the fighting, Iran is less vulnerable for both ideological and strategic reasons. Iran still has considerable revolutionary fervor to help it sustain the conflict. Iraq is running out of the resources to provide the kind of economic security and stability that have helped persuade its people to keep up the conflict. Iran can afford to concentrate its resources on its offensives. Iraq has little ability to counterattack, and there is no decisive strategic objective in Iran anywhere as near to the border as Basra, the Kirkuk oil fields, or Baghdad are in Iraq.

Iranian Superiority on the Ground

The key to much of what has happened since 1984, is the emergence of Iranian superiority on the ground. Iran has been able to steadily improve its performance in the "war of attrition" that has characterized the fighting along the Iranian-Iraqi border. Although it continues to make serious mistakes, Iran has steadily improved its ability to use its superiority in manpower and has developed superior tactical skills in infiltration and assault techniques, close infantry fighting, exploiting mountain and marsh terrain, and night combat. It has demonstrated that it can dominate many battles and encounters as long as these are fought for limited objectives and near the initial front.

In spite of continuing large scale purchases of new weapons and technology, Iraq has experienced steadily growing difficulties in countering Iran's major offensives and smaller attacks whenever these achieve tactical surprise and do not run head on into well-prepared Iraqi defenses.

Iraq has had massive superiority over Iran in air power, firepower, and armor since 1982, but it has faced two crippling limitations in land combat:

- First, Iraq has very little strategic depth and must try to defend its entire border against even limited losses while Iran has immense strategic depth and does not offer Iraq any major objective worth the cost of a counterattack.

- Second, Iraq has been unable to take the casualties which are inevitable in any aggressive pattern of land warfare and counter attacks. While Iran has had far more casualties than Iraq, it can afford to do so. Iran is a nation of over 46 million and Iraq is a nation of 16 million. There are well over 12 million Iranians in the labor force, and only about 3.9 million Iraqis, although Iraq has had up to one million expatriate workers. About 462,000 Iranians come of military age each year versus a little over 177,000 in Iraq. There are about 6.6 million Iranian males fit for military service versus only 2.1 million Iraqis.[2]

There are also critical political and cultural differences in each side's ability to take casualties. Iran's population has limited expectations regarding material wealth and it is now governed by the leader of a mass revolution who possesses Messianic charisma. Its branch of the Shi'ite faith has a strongly institutionalized glorification of martyrdom which is far less apparent in Iraq's Sunnis and Shi'ites.

Iran is 93% Shi'ite and 63% ethnic Persian. Its only other large minority is Turkic, with 18% of the population. Iran's Kurds make up only 3% of the population and its Arab minority makes up only about 2%.[3] This gives Iran a high degree of unity, and Iran is fighting as a nation that was invaded in the midst of a popular and highly xenophobic revolution. While its wartime losses have inevitably lead to some protest from the people, it has far greater political and cultural ability to take losses than Iraq.

In contrast, Iraq is a secular state governed by a small elite with relatively limited popular support. In spite of the often vociferous politics of

Iraq's Ba'athist leaders, most Iraqis have little interest in Ba'athist ideology. They see Iraq's government as more a Takriti elite than a national leadership.[4] The regime is personified in President Sadam Hussein, who came to power through a series of violent coup d'etats. While Sadam Hussein and the Ba'ath are not unpopular, most of their popularity has stemmed from the nation's dramatic increase in oil wealth after 1973 and from the resulting improvement in popular living standards and security.

This is an uncertain base upon which to sustain either high casualties, or major sacrifices in the living standards of the general populace. Aside from a brief burst of popularity during Iraq's initial easy advances into Iran, the war has never had broad popular support. It became all too apparent to both Iraq's military forces and the Iraqi public after the first months of the war that there was no Arab population in Iran's southwest that wanted or welcomed Iraqi liberation. Many Iraqis came to recognize that the war stemmed more from rivalries between Sadam Hussein and Khomeini than any other cause.

Most Iraqis have seen the defense of Iraq as a patriotic duty since Iran's first major counter-invasions in 1983. Nevertheless, this feeling has never transformed itself into popular fervor or into support for the Ba'athist regime. If anything, it has tended to transfer loyalties from political leaders to the individual commanders, technocrats, and officials whose personal performance or courage has commanded popular respect. There are no signs that this is creating an organized opposition, but it is creating an Iraqi society with far less tolerance for political posturing, profiteering, or Ba'athist ideology.

Iraq's people and armed forces are very conscious of the personal costs of the war. Iraq did a surprisingly good job of maintaining the flow of both "guns and butter" until 1984, but it has since had to slowly cut back on welfare payments, development, housing, educational deferments, payments to survivors and wounded, and a host of other areas. This has not sharply undermined popular living standards so far, but the detailed data issued by the Iraqi Central Statistics Organization do show a significant decline in gross domestic product, per capita income, employment, rate of construction, improvement in transportation services, growth of education, imports of civilian goods, and agricultural production of major crops since the war began, and this situation is certain to grow much worse in 1987, with oil prices at less than half their 1985 level.[5]

Iraq is also more ethnically divided than Iran. Although it is 75% Arab, its Kurds make up 15-20% of the population and have a far stronger tradition of separatism than the Kurds in Iran. Turkomans and Assyrians make up another 5-10% of the population. Iraq has sharp religious divisions. It is 55% Shi'ite, 40% Sunni, and 10% Christian and "other". While Iraq's Shi'ites have generally supported the defense of

Iraq, they resent the fact that the Ba'ath leadership is largely Sunni and has been careless of Shi'ite beliefs and traditions. There is still some risk that any major defeat could lead Iraq to divide along religious lines.[6]

This mix of politics, domestic considerations, and ethnic divisions creates a potentially dangerous military climate for Iraq. These dangers are reinforced by a fundamental strategic asymmetry in the military positions of Iraq and Iran. Iraq has little strategic depth between its border and major cities and oil facilities, and its political structure does not allow it to sustain high surges of casualties. Iran now has no major cities or facilities vulnerable to limited Iraqi thrusts into Iran and the Iranian regime can afford to sustain high casualties.

Iraq failed to achieve any decisive results with its initial invasion, but destroyed most of the key targets within easy reach. Even then, it had no objective near the border that could credibly force Iran to a peace settlement, much less any form of major concession. As a result, Iraq has since faced a situation where it has become steadily more difficult to counterattack or use its ground forces to try to force an end to the fighting.

Any counterattack means higher initial Iraqi casualties in an Iraq where each additional casualty undermines political unity. Any defeat or set back – e.g. the Iraqi failure to hold Meheran in 1986 – may seriously undermine morale. Even if Iraq does seize and hold some limited objective in Iran, any "successful" Iraqi counteroffensive might well increase Iranian popular support for the conflict.

Iraq is having steadily greater problems in accepting the casualties that are the inevitable price of war. It has had to place increasing limits on the number of public funerals and has tried to conceal the number of military dead. Bodies are now often delivered to families with little warning, and Iraqi publicity concentrates almost solely on Iranian losses.

These tactics, however, have only limited success. During the fighting in early 1986 – when as many as 10,000 Iraqis were killed – funerals occurred constantly at key burial centers like Al Najaf. Even though bodies were refrigerated and only slowly released to the next of kin – to conceal the rate of losses during heavy battles – virtually every Iraqi family was all too well aware of the war's cost.[7]

Iraq thus faces potentially disastrous political risks if it tries to inflict enough Iranian losses to force an end to the war. Iraq has constantly faced the problem that even if three or four Iranians die for every Iraqi, Iran can stand the manpower loss and Iraq cannot. Every Iraqi casualty contributes to undermining popular support for the war, and increases the cumulative risk of an eventual overthrow of its regime.

This helps explain why the Iraqi army and air force have been so reluctant to carry out even small counterattacks and to push them home, and why Iraq has to fight so defensively in low level encounters along the border. The net effect, however, has almost been paralytic. Iraq cannot react aggressively in the marshes or match Iran's willingness to infiltrate through the mountains in the north. It cannot conduct aggressive infantry attacks or counterattacks. Iraq has become heavily dependent on static defenses and mass firepower, and tended to freeze its military development at a level where its army and air force are making far slower progress in assault and infantry tactics, and basic maneuver and counterattack capabilities, than they should.

There is also no way in which Iraq can use fixed defenses, airpower, and long range land firepower to shield its entire border. The Iranians can always exploit weather, night, marshes and water, and mountains or rough terrain to infiltrate and close on Iraqi ground troops or surprise any area that is weak. Iraq has learned that modern military technology is far more effective in killing modern weapons than in dealing with sudden massive infiltrations by well dispersed infantry.

Iraqi Superiority in Arms and Technology

Iraq does, however, have an area of superiority which allows it to largely counterbalance Iran's superiority in manpower, willingness to take casualties, and tactical skills. Iraq has drawn great benefits from its superior ability to import arms. While any estimates of the flow of such arms are extremely uncertain, Figure 2 is valid to the extent it shows a broad illustration of this Iraqi superiority in obtaining new weapons in both numbers and weapons type.

Figure 2 is also correct to the extent it shows that Iran has been unable to get any major replacement of its U.S. supplied weapons and Iraq has been able to obtain more and better weapons in virtually every category. Iran has suffered particularly badly from the fact it has not gotten any deliveries of modern high performance combat aircraft and new major surface-to-air missile (SAM) systems – although it has obtained important deliveries of aircraft parts and Hawk missiles and parts.[8]

Equally importantly, Iraq has been able to import a much larger total flow of weapons and military goods of all types. This Iraqi superiority is reflected in Figure 3, which shows the cash value of all the arms each side received between 1979 and 1983 by source. While the data involved are again uncertain, and only cover the period up to 1983, they are based on far more reliable CIA estimates than the SIPRI (Stockholm International Peace Research Institute) data in Figure 2.

It is striking to note that Iraq received a total of $17.6 billion worth of arms between 1979 and 1983 versus only $5.4 billion for Iran, at least $2 billion of which came before the Shah's fall.

Iraq also enjoyed much greater freedom in being able to buy from a vendor of its own choice, and in finding reliable sources of supply. During

Figure 2. Estimated Deliveries of Major Weapons to Iraq and Iran: 1981-1986[a]

Part One – Shipments to Iran

Sources and Weapons	1981	1982	1983	1984	1985	1986
CHINA						
F-6/F-7	—	20?	20?	20?	3?	6?
T-59	–	100	100	100	100?	100?
CSA-1 SAM	—	—	—	—	50?	50?
Type 54 122 mm howitzers	—	—	—	—	—	—
Type 60 122 mm guns	—	—	—	—	—	—
Type 63 107 mm MRLS	—	—	—	—	—	—
122 mm MRLs						
NORTH KOREA						
SA-2	—	—	—	—	60?	—
T-62	—	75	75	—	—	—
Artillery	—	—	—	400[b]	—	—
AA Guns	—	—	—	1200[b]	—	—
SYRIA						
T-55	—	120	—	—	—	—
T-62	—	100	—	—	—	—
SA-7 launchers	—	—	—	150[b]	—	—
SA-7 Missiles	—	—	—	400[b]	—	—
LIBYA						
Scud B	—	—	—	40?	40?	—
T-54	60?	—	—	—	—	—
T-55	65?	—	—	—	—	—
T-62	65	—	—	—	—	—
Katyusha rockets	—	—	—	—	—	—
SA-7s	—	—	—	—	—	—
ISRAEL	?	?	?	?	?	?
Tow ATGM	—	—	—	—	500	—
USA						
TOW ATGM	—	—	—	—	—	2,008
Hawk Assemblies	—	—	—	—	—	235
UK						
Hengam Class LS	—	—	—	2	—	—
FRANCE						
Kaman FAC	3	—	—	—	—	—
ARGENTINA						
TAM MT	—	—	25	—	—	—
SOUTH AFRICA	?	?	?	?	?	?
VIETNAM						
F-5s	—	—	—	—	—	—

Other suppliers include: Brazil, Chile, Czechoslovakia, Ethiopia, India, Italy, Japan, Netherlands, Pakistan, Poland, Portugal, South Korea, Spain, Sweden, Switzerland, Taiwan.

Part Two – Shipments to Iraq

Sources and Weapons	1981	1982	1983	1984	1985	1986
SOVIET BLOC						
MiG-23BU	—	20	20	20	30	—
MiG-25	10	—	—	15	15	—
MiG-27	—	10	10	—	—	—
Su-20	—	—	—	—	—	30?
T-55	—	50	50	100	100	—
T-62	—	—	—	150	150	—
T-72	100	50	50	300	300	—
SA-6	60	60	60	60	60	—
SA-8	—	72	72	72	72	—
SA-9	—	40	40	40	40	—
FRANCE						
Mirage F-1C/E	—	12	27	15	14	24
Super Etendard (loan)	—	—	5	—	—	—
Roland-2	—	150	150	150	150	—
EGYPT						
F-6	—	—	10	—	—	—
F-7	—	—	40	—	—	—
T-55	50	100	200	—	—	—
CHINA						
T-59	—	130	120	—	—	—
POLAND						
T-55	300	—	—	—	—	—
USA						
M-48/M-60 (Captured)	—	60?	60?	—	—	—
ITALY						
Lupo Class frigate	—	—	—	—	1	1
Wadi Class frigate	—	—	—	4	2	—

Other suppliers include: Brazil, Kuwait, GDR, FRG, U.K., and Spain

a. Adapted from work by Mark Cleveland and various editions of the Stockholm International Peace Research Institute yearbook, *World Armaments and Disarmament*, Oxford, Oxford University Press, 1980-1986, and Anthony H. Cordesman, "Arms Sales to Iran: Rumor and Reality," *Middle East Executive Reports*, February 1986, pp. 8-19. Estimates are extremely uncertain. Sales with exceptional uncertainty have question marks.

b. Total as of this date for 1981-1984.

1979-1983, Iraq received $7.2 billion from the USSR, $3.8 billion from France, $280 million from the U.K., $140 million from the FRG, $410 million from Italy, $1.5 billion from the PRC, $850 million from Poland, $400 million from Romania, $40 million from Czechoslovakia, and $3 billion from a wide variety of other countries. Iraq has had much freer access than Iran to the world's most advanced arms suppliers. It has been able to get more advanced technology, a much higher degree of standardization, and far freer flows of spare parts.

In contrast, Iran received $975 million worth of arms from the USSR, $1.2 billion from the U.S., $20 million from France, $140 million from the U.K., $5 million from the FRG, and $150 million from Italy during 1979-1983, but this was virtually all delivered before the war started. Its only other major sources of arms were $230 million from the PRC, $40 million from Poland, $5 million from Romania, and $2.6 billion worth from a wide range of other countries.

It is also important to note that Iran began the war after a revolution that cost it many of its U.S.-trained officers and technicians, and that the Shah fell long before his ambitious military plans resulted in effective forces. Although Iran had spent close to $17 billion on U.S. arms before the Shah's fall, it had not achieved a fully balanced force structure when the revolution occurred.

Many critical systems, including its computerized logistic and supply system, radar system, and surface based missile system were still in the process of development when the Shah fell. Many spare parts and munitions deliveries had not occurred, and some $12.2 billion of additional orders were in the pipeline.

The U.S. signed a Memorandum of Understanding (MOU) with Iran on February 1, 1979 – the day before Khomeini returned to Iran – that gave it the authority to cancel these contracts and use the proceeds to pay off Iran's FMS debts. The U.S. used this authority to cancel many orders and arms shipments ceased after the hostage crisis. Further, Khomeini began to formally cancel some $9 billion worth of these orders even before the hostage crisis. U.S. military deliveries dropped in value from about $2.6 billion in 1979 to about $14 million in 1980.[9]

After the hostage crisis, Iran faced a virtual embargo on the delivery of U.S. arms and spare parts.[10] Some key weapons already in the Iranian forces, including the fire control systems on the F-14As and some of the Hawk missile and radar units, were sabotaged by anti-Khomeini officers before the revolution took power.

Accordingly, Iran suffered severely when it could not obtain U.S. arms, and was forced to improvise new sources of supply once the war began. It got much lower quality weapons than it had previously obtained from the U.S. but could not use its U.S. weapons effectively because of the existing shortfalls in its inventories and stocks and its extreme difficulty in getting an adequate supply and mix of U.S. parts and munitions – particularly for its more advanced U.S. weapons.[11]

This situation has not changed radically since 1983. Iraq continues to get advanced weapons from France and substantial deliveries from the USSR – although often cloaked as deliveries from the East European states. About 55% of Iraq's arms have come from the USSR and other Soviet bloc countries, 20-25% from France, and the remaining 20-25% from other countries. Iraq has also had substantial financial aid from the Arab world, and has been able to turn to nations like Egypt for rapid arms transfers in an emergency. For example, Egypt rushed deliveries of ammunition and other military goods to Iraq in 1986 when it suffered a defeat at Faw.

While U.S. government sources caution that any estimates are very uncertain, they indicate that Iraq was able to buy more than $8.2 billion worth of arms from the USSR alone between the time the war began and the end of 1985 (although many of these arms were shipped from Eastern Europe). This total is now close to $10 billion. Iraq has also bought at least $5.6 billion worth of arms from France, and at least another $5 billion worth of arms from other sources. U.S. estimates of Iraq's total arms and military imports from all sources since the start of the war go as high as $24 billion, and Iraq has consistently been able to spend over $5 billion annually on arms and other war material.

Iran, in contrast, has been limited to about $2.325 billion worth of arms in 1983, $2.9 billion worth of arms in 1984, $2.158 billion worth of arms in 1985, and $860 million in the first half of 1986.[12] It is also important to note that in spite of covert U.S. and arms sales to Iran, the U.S. effort to halt all arms transfers to Iran has had considerable success. Iran has had more and more trouble in obtaining the Western arms, parts, and ammunition it needs the most, and has had to pay more and more layers of middlemen to obtain even limited quantities.

More is involved than the dollar value of such arms flows. Iraq's ability to openly buy arms in large amounts – and to buy integrated packages with a suitable follow-on flow of ammunition and spare parts – has given Iraq far more value per dollar than Iran has been able to obtain since early 1980. Iran has had to buy most of the ammunition, spares, and replacements for its Western supplied arms on the black market. It often has had to make helter-skelter arms deals and buy only part of its needs. Where Iraq was able to achieve a mix of counter-trade and cash arms deals worth $3 to $5 billion during the first four months of 1986, Iran has had to deal almost solely in cash.[13]

This helps explain why Iran has responded to the virtual cutoff of open Western arms sales since the American Embassy hostage crisis by organizing a massive effort to obtain arms from the West and by buying arms from nations like the PRC and North Korea. Buying from the PRC and North Korea has eased the strain Iran has faced in trying to assemble the parts, ammunition, and equipment it needs for its Western arms from black and grey markets.

Iran has contacted virtually every possible source of arms in the West, legal and illegal. It has organized a large Logistic Support Centre in the Iranian National Oil Company building in London, near Britain's Department of Trade and Industry. This office coordinates Iran's arms purchase efforts in Europe and aids in its illegal and covert purchase efforts in the U.S., Israel, the Arab world, and Latin America. This office has succeeded in obtaining important supplies like new engines for some British-made Chieftain tanks. It also, however, has been trapped in numerous frauds, including a false effort to sell some 8,000 TOW missiles.[14]

Iran also has used countless middle men ranging from Iranian expatriates to Israeli intelligence officials and ex-U.S. military officers. Some of the middlemen have been useful, but many have been outright frauds. Others have been able to supply a few systems, but then have been caught – like Saeid Asefi Inanlou, who was able to obtain some stolen F-14 parts but whose operation was uncovered by U.S. customs officials. Some have shipped obsolete or used parts of little value, and in one case Iran got a shipment of dog food instead of the F-5 parts it had ordered.[15] All have been expensive, often delivering less than a dollar worth of arms for every three dollars Iran has spent.

Further, most of these illegal sources have only been able to sell part of the equipment Iran needs to keep a weapons system functional. This often has left Iran with most of the spares it needs for some critical weapon, but without the final deliveries of spares needed to make a weapon fully operational. Dependence on illegal sources has also meant that Iran can assemble only part of the balanced mix of supplies, spares, and weapons it needs to support a major offensive.

Iran's situation has also grown steadily worse since 1984. Buying on the black and grey arms markets has increasingly meant long delays and deliveries of defective or second rate goods. It also increasingly means buying at exorbitantly high prices. In spite of its years of experience, Iran has increasingly been caught up in major frauds, including some involving significant corruption by Iranian officials.

In April 19, 1986, Iran was caught in a two billion dollar U.S. customs "sting" operations that led to 17 indictments, and from mid-1983 to late 1986, it was involved in a complex sales program called the Demavand Project where U.S. and Israeli intelligence officials attempted to obtain captured Iraqi weapons like the T-72 tank in return for tolerating a largely spurious private offer of 39 F-4 fighters, 50 M-48 tanks, and at least 25 attack helicopters. Iran was never able to tell whether it was dealing with serious offers, frauds, or sales being partly controlled by Western intelligence.[16]

It is not surprising, therefore, that Iran has turned to those few nations that will openly sell it weapons on a government-to-government basis. North Korea and the PRC have emerged as Iran's main sources of arms. These countries alone provided about 43% of all Iranian military imports in 1985 and nearly 70% in 1986.[17]

Iran spent at least $1 billion on North Korean military imports between the start of the war and late 1986. This included such weapons as 150 T-62 tanks, 400 artillery pieces, 1,000 mortars, 600 antiaircraft guns, and 12,000 machine guns and rifles. While Iran has recently shifted most of its arms purchases to the PRC, it still spent some $495 million on North Korean arms in 1985 – the last year for which reasonably accurate data are available.

Iran has bought $2.4 billion worth of arms from the PRC, since the war began, and seems to have signed at least one $1.6 billion dollar arms agreement. Many of these orders have been placed since 1984. Iran bought only about $200 million worth of arms from the PRC between 1979 and 1983, but ordered $430 million worth of arms in 1985 and at least $600 million worth in 1986.

Some reports indicate that Iran may have gotten delivery on the first of some 50 J-7 (F-7 or MiG-21 variant) fighters, as well as Chinese made SA-2 surface-to-air missiles, and Chinese SS-N-2 naval surface-to-surface missiles.[18] While the extent of Chinese deliveries of J-6 and F-7 fighters is very controversial, and none have yet been seen in combat, it is fairly clear that the PRC has sold SA-2 surface-to-air missiles, coastal defense anti-ship missiles, at least 200 T-59 tanks, Type 60 122 mm guns, Type 54 122 mm howitzers, Type 59, 130 mm guns, Type 63 107 mm MRLs, Katyusha artillery rockets, SA-7 man-portable surface-to-air missiles, antitank missiles, armored personnel carriers, antiaircraft guns, and large amounts of ammunition.[19]

At the same time, such purchases had serious disadvantages for Iran since none of this Chinese and North Korean equipment is interoperable with U.S. equipment. Iran also has had to retrain its forces to use such equipment and create a new chain of maintenance facilities and new stocks of spare parts. Most PRC and North Korean equipment is inferior to that available from the USSR, and even more inferior to that available from the West. Buying North Korean and PRC arms thus means Iran gets far less military effectiveness per dollar spent than Iraq.

Further, these purchases have also had their problems. Reports of the $1.6 billion Iranian-PRC arms deal may be exaggerated. Iran has had financing problems in meeting the PRC's terms, and the PRC has attempted to conceal its arms sales because of its desired to maintain close relations with the Arab states. North Korea has delivered at least some substandard equipment, and seems to have reduced deliveries after the break between Iran and the USSR over the suppression of the Tudeh Party.

Iran's other arms purchases have been much more chaotic, and it is often hard to separate rumors from reality. Nevertheless, Iran has received three Combattante II class missile boats and large amounts of 155 mm and other artillery ammunition from French factories. While the French government has claimed such ammunition sales were made illegally by a French corporation – Luchaire – U.S. experts privately doubt such claims.

Britain too has tended to disclaim or down play the size of its sales to Iran. It is clear, however, that Iran has bought numerous Chieftain tank parts from Britain, including obvious military spares as well as engines. It also has recently bought Plessey air defense radars, replenishment tankers, logistic support ships, and other equipment from the U.K.[20]

More significantly, Iran has received large amounts of ammunition and light weapons from Portuguese and Spanish arms factories, and Portugal has often acted as a transit point for illegal arms smuggled from the U.S.[21] Portugal shipped Iran at least $150 million worth of arms between early 1984 and early 1987, many from the port of Setubai. Although Portugal recalled one shipment of arms in the Spring of 1987, after it threatened to become a minor scandal, it was still continuing major shipments in early 1987.[22] Iran's total arms imports from Spain were worth $35 million in 1985, and $80 million in the first half of 1986. Iraqi sources feel that Spain and Portugal were the main sources of Iran's supplies of Western ammunition in its late 1986 and early 1987 offensives.

The ambiguities in U.S. policy towards Iran and Iraq have also done much to help Iran. As the result of U.S. efforts to free American hostages and win influence with so-called Iranian "moderates", Iran obtained at least five separate covert shipments of U.S. arms, worth some $30-87 million, between August, 1985 and November, 1986.[23] These shipments included at least 2,008 TOW missiles, extensive deliveries of Hawk parts and 235 missiles, and five ships of spare parts.[24]

The full details of these shipments are still under investigation, but preliminary studies by the U.S. Senate indicate they began in August, 1985, when Israel sent 508 TOW anti-tank missiles to Iran with the understanding that the U.S. would replace Israeli stocks. Iran paid about $6.2 million for the missiles.[25] This shipment was rapidly followed in September 14, 1985 by another delivery of 408 TOWs.

The largest Iranian outlay occurred in November, 1985, when Iran paid some $41-64.7 million for 80-120 Hawk missiles, but Iran only obtained 18 obsolete missiles, and an Iranian middleman – Manucher Gorbinfar – and Israeli middlemen seem to have defrauded Iran of much of the money. In February, 1986, the Iranians paid $5 million for 1,000 more TOW missiles as part of another arms-for-hostages deal that was eventually supposed to lead to the sale of 4,000 TOW missiles. These were eventually delivered in two lots of 500 each on February 18 and 27 1986.

[26] On May 28, 1986, Iran paid some $8 million for Hawk missile parts. One pallet of these parts was delivered in May and the bulk on August 3, 1986. The final weapons shipment included 500 more TOW missiles worth $4.7 million and more Hawk parts and missiles. These were shipped in October 29, 1986.

Further, Iran has had substantial covert arms deliveries from Israel ever since 1980. In 1981, when Israel was still afraid of an Iraqi victory, it shipped up to $135 million worth of critical items. Israeli agents may have signed a contract with Iran in July, 1981, that included such critical items as 40 155 mm field guns, 68 Hawk missiles, and M-48 tanks, although rumors that Israel sold 50 Lance missiles and 3,730 Copperhead laser guided 155 mm artillery shells seem to be totally false. Reports of these sales later led to claims that Secretary of State Alexander Haig at least informally approved the sale, although Haig denied that such advanced technology weapons were shipped and that he gave any "green light" to such sales.[28]

Other deliveries have since been made by a wide range of Israeli agents, and have included badly needed F-4 and F-5 parts, Hawk surface-to-air missiles and parts, some of the arms and ammunition that Israel captured from the PLO in 1982, at least 500 TOW missiles, some 360 tons of spare parts for U.S. tanks, and large amounts of ammunition.

Some U.S. experts estimate that these ammunition sales included at least 100,000 155 mm shells, 150,000 203 mm howitzer shells, 50,000 105 mm shells, and 100,000 rounds of 106 mm recoilless rifle shells between 1982 and late 1985. Israeli agents also seem to have recently brokered the sale of some reconditioned U.S. tanks – which did not arrive in combat capable condition.[29]

While the exact scale of such sales is still uncertain, the recent volume of sales has been substantial. Work by Gary Sick indicates that some 5,000 tons of arms worth $500-1,000 million and involving 9-12 shipments went from Israel to Iran by sea between May and November, 1986.[30] Other reports by officials of the Danish sailors' union indicate that as many as 40 Danish cargo ships have carried illegal arms to Iran.[31] Danish sailors may also have been involved in carrying covert shipments by a Northern European 'consortium' that was to illegally ship arms to Iran.

Israel has continued such arms sales for several reasons. First, to paralyze any threat from Iraq. Second, to secure the position of Iranian Jews, third in hopes of influencing Iran to ease its hostility to Israel while strengthening a broader threat to the Arab world; fourth, to earn hard currency; fifth, to reduce the growing Shi'ite threat to Israel in Southern Lebanon, and finally, for intelligence reasons. For example, Israel sought to trade arms for captured Soviet tanks. At one point in 1985, it came close to obtaining a T-72 as part of a $50 million arms deal involving the sale of mortars, 155 mm howitzers, bombs, and ammunition. This only fell through because Iran sought to add 500 TOW missiles to the deal.[32] Israel has also continued to sell to Iran since the US-Iranian arms scandal and a key Israeli agent – Amiram Nir – met with Iranian arms sales agents in mid-March 1987.

Iran has bought arms from at least 41 countries and these include many Western ones. It has acquired grenades, light arms, and evidently F-4 and F-5 parts and engines from Greek dealers although the origin of these weapons is unknown. It has bought a significant amount of engineering equipment with military value from the FRG – including ribbon bridges.

Iran has purchased 200 trucks and large numbers of 13 meter fast patrol boats from Sweden. It also illegally bought arms from the Bofors division of Nobel, including at least 200 to 400 RBS-70 laser-guided antiaircraft missiles, and 200 tons of military explosives, it is alleged.[33] It bought six Swiss PC-7 military training aircraft in August 1984 for $4 million, which may have been part of a total order for 30. These so-called civilian trainer aircraft are shipped with detailed conversion plans to make them into military light attack aircraft.

Iran has also dodged around Swiss export control laws by buying at least 20 Contraves Skyguard radar guided antiaircraft systems in Italy. Italy has since sold Iran parts for Iran's U.S.-made military helicopters in spite of U.S. objections. Further, Iran has had at least some Hawk parts and U.S.-type military electronics and spares from Italy.

There are reports that Iran has bought armored cars, hand grenades, and Avibras ASTROS rocket launchers from Brazil – although total Brazilian arms sales to Iran are only estimated at $4 million in 1985. It bought some $40 million worth of arms from Argentina in 1985, and past deliveries seem to include 100 TAM fighting vehicles. Other deliveries include machine guns and light arms. While Argentina considered selling Iran a nuclear power plant and two British Type-42 destroyers, these deals do not seem to have gone through. Iran also seems to have bought Ethiopia's aging U.S.-made F-5 fighters, although these had little value even as parts.

Iran's arms purchases from Asia include numerous arms transfers through Singapore – some of which may have originated in the PRC. It has bought a small amount of F-4 and F-5 parts, and mortar grenades and uniforms, from South Korea. South Korean arms sales have risen from $1 million in 1985 to $17 million in the first half of 1986.

Iran has reportedly acquired up to $400 million worth of arms from Vietnam, largely captured U.S.-made equipment. The government of Vietnam seems to have signed a deal with Iran in July, 1985, to sell 80 M-48 tanks, 200 M-113 APCs, 12 F-5 fighters, 12 Cobra Gunships, Sidewinder missiles, and large amounted of captured U.S. parts and ammunition it acquired as the result of its defeat of South Vietnam. Some of this equipment was new – the F-5 fighters were still in crates – but deliveries were slow and the Vietnamese sales could not provide the range and types of parts and equipment to repair and sustain most of Iran's U.S.-equipped forces.[34] Other reports indicate, however, that deliveries were substantially smaller and that much of this has been worthless except as spare parts.

Iran has bought Kawasaki C-1 transports and small boats from Japan. It has bought 10,0000 tents, several thousand jeeps, and trucks from India, and has some arms on the black market in Pakistan – some of which may originally have been intended for the Mujahideen. It has received U.S. aircraft parts and maintenance assistance from Taiwan.

Iran has also obtained assistance from other radical states in the Middle East: Scud B surface-to-surface missiles, Katyusha rockets, SA-7s, antiaircraft guns, antitank missiles, artillery shells, and some tanks and APCs (armored personnel carriers) from Syria and Libya. While precise figures are difficult to come by, Iran ordered at least $100 million worth of arms from Libya in 1985, and got $15 million worth of Scuds from Syria in 1986. Iran has also has at least some military deliveries transit through the UAE.

The USSR does not seem to have made direct deliveries of arms to Iran since Iran clamped down on the Tudeh Party and expelled many of its Soviet diplomats. Iran has, however, purchased light arms, ammunition, and chemical warfare gear from Czechoslovakia; and antiaircraft guns, rocket propelled grenades, and ammunition from Poland. There are also indications that the flow of Soviet style arms for Eastern European states has slowly increased since mid-1986, along with the thaw in Iranian-Soviet relations.[35]

This is far too wide a group of arms suppliers to provide Iran with an effective mix of arms, and has still left Iran without the parts and munitions it needs to operate most of its U.S.-made equipment. Iran has been forced to try to buy on the black market and to obtain stolen U.S. parts and military equipment.

Whatever the failures of U.S. policy inherent in the covert U.S. arms sales to Iran, it is also important to note that the U.S. effort to halt shipments to Iran called "Operation Staunch" had considerable success during 1985 and 1986. Nations like South Korea had to recall some of their arms shipments to Iran, and Iran was forced to buy more and more indirectly. Where it once used only two agents to disguise the purchaser, it must now use up to four agents, and each of these agents raises the cost of Iran's purchases substantially.

During 1986, Iran was increasingly being forced to concentrate on items with both civil and military uses to disguise the nature of its purchases, and to buy items like raw phosphorous, pontoons, small craft, bridging equipment, and diving equipment. Where it bought $2 billion

Figure 3. Iraqi and Iranian Arms Imports By Importing Country: 1979-83
(Current $ millions)

Importer		Seller Nation			
	Total	USSR	US	FR	U.K.
IRAN-IRAQ					
Iran	5,365	40	2,400	1,200	575
Iraq	17,620	7,200	—	3,800	280
Sub-Tot.	22,985	7,240	2,400	5,000	855
OTHER GULF					
Saudi					
Arabia	12,125	—	5,100	2,500	1,900
Kuwait	450	30	180	—	50
Bahrain	120	—	10	40	—
Qatar	765	—	10	440	310
UAE	620	—	20	350	90
Oman	565	—	80	20	430
GCC	14,645	30	5,400	3,350	2,780
Sub-Tot.	37,630	7,270	7,800	8,350	3,635
RED SEA					
Sudan	640	—	110	10	10
Ethiopia	1,900	1,800	—	—	—
Somalia	580	—	30	5	5
YAR	2,355	1,200	200	30	—
PDRY	1,510	1,500	—	—	—
Sub-Total	6,985	4,500	340	45	15
LEVANT					
Israel	3,805	—	3,800	—	—
Syria	10,530	9,200	—	200	180
Jordan	3,430	230	970	1,000	1,100
Lebanon	395	—	250	90	10
Sub-Tot.	18,160	9,430	5,020	1,290	1,290
OTHER					
Turkey	1,865	—	750	10	5
India	4,695	3,400	40	80	875
Pakistan	1,830	20	550	550	10
Afghan.	1,830	1,800	—	—	—
Sub-Tot.	10,220	5,220	1,340	640	890

Source: ACDA, *World Military Expenditures and Arms Transfers, 1985*, Washington, GPO, 1985.

Figure 3. Iraqi and Iranian Arms Imports By Importing Country: 1979-83
(Current $ millions)
Seller Nation

FRG	IT	CZ	PRC	Ro	Po	Others
210	320	—	300	—	50	550
140	410	40	1,500	400	850	3,000
350	730	40	1,800	400	900	3,550
525	200	—	—	—	—	1,900
70	110	—	—	—	—	10
40	10	—	—	—	—	20
—	—	—	—	—	—	5
110	30	—	—	—	—	20
—	10	—	5	—	—	5
745	350	—	5	—	—	1,960
1,095	1,895	1,235	1,805	400	900	5,510
270	10	—	70	—	60	100
—	20	10	—	—	—	70
—	410	—	50	—	10	70
10	5	—	—	250	10	650
—	—	—	—	—	—	10
280	445	10	120	250	80	900
—	—	—	—	—	—	5
40	—	470	90	20	30	300
5	—	—	10	—	—	110
—	10	—	—	—	5	30
45	10	470	100	20	35	445
850	150	—	—	—	—	100
5	50	120	—	5	—	120
190	40	—	390	—	—	80
—	—	20	—	—	—	10
1,045	240	140	390	5	—	310

worth of major weapons and ammunition in 1985, it only seems to have bought $800 million worth in 1986.

Iran also has had to concentrate more and more of its resources on buying spare parts, and on trying to use its own military industries. The Iranian arms industry now produces over $200 million worth of arms a year, including small arms and machine guns, radios, tank ammunition, BM-21 multiple rocket launchers, 106 mm recoilless guns, RPG-7 rocket propelled grenades, and 60 mm, 81 mm, and 120 mm mortars.

Ironically, while Iran once had a substantial ability to rebuild armor and aircraft, these were facilities managed by U.S. and European firms and staffed largely by skilled foreign technicians. These repair facilities virtually collapsed after the revolution.[36] As a result, Iran has many of the industrial facilities to support relatively static, infantry-dominated warfare, but few internal manufacturing and major overhaul and repair resources to support its U.S. equipment or any other high technology force.

The Role of Western Intelligence

In theory, Iraq has also benefited from informal intelligence support from its Arab neighbors and from several Western intelligence services, including those of France and the United States. In practice, however, this situation is even more tangled and uncertain than that surrounding Western arms shipments.

Iraq has had informal intelligence support from France since the beginning of the war, although this support has varied in quality and has been counterbalanced by selective Israeli intelligence support and leaks to Iran. The principal difference between the two states has been Iraq's access to the advanced national technical means – including photo and signals intelligence – available to the U.S. and to some of the data obtained by U.S. maritime reconnaissance systems and the USAF E-3A AWACS aircraft on station in Saudi Arabia.[37]

The provision of U.S. intelligence support to Iraq began in 1983, when Iraq first faced the threat of an Iranian invasion and possible defeat. The U.S. then steadily expanded its cooperation with Iraq as U.S. and Iraqi relations improved, and as the Iranian threat to Iraq became more serious. The U.S. expanded its intelligence in mid-1985, and then again in August, 1985, providing increasingly more detailed data on warning and the military situation.[38]

While the details remain classified, the data the U.S. provided seems to have been valuable in estimating Iranian force strength, tracking Iranian military movements and arms shifts, providing warning of Iranian attacks, and targeting Iraqi air strikes in the Gulf and Iran against Iranian military concentrations, civilian targets, oil facilities, and possibly tankers.

By late 1985, however, the U.S. shifted to a different posture. As part of the same effort that led it to try to trade covert arms shipments to Iran for the release of U.S. hostages and better relations with the "moderates" in the Khomeini government, the U.S. began to provide tailored intelligence to both sides. This created a situation where the U.S. simultaneously:

- Provided overt support to Iraq in its defense and efforts to end the war, and limited economic aid in the form of credits.
- Sold arms to Iran and tolerated increased Israeli transfers of U.S. equipment and technology.
- Gave unreliable intelligence on the war to Iran and may have altered the intelligence on the war provided to Iraq.
- Gave exaggerated intelligence on the Soviet build-up near Iran to Iran, and accurate data on Soviet efforts.
- Provided covert support to various emigrant groups attempting to overthrow the Khomeini regime.

The full details of what happened are not yet available, but it seems clear from press reporting, and the *Report on Preliminary Inquiry* of the U.S. Senate Committee on Intelligence, that senior officials in the National Security Council and the CIA ignored the advice of the State Department, Department of Defense, and career intelligence experts in the CIA and began a complex campaign to convince Iran that it faced a significant new Soviet threat as part of the broader U.S. attempt to improve relations with Iran.[39]

The main thrust of the U.S. effort seems to have begun considerably later than the covert U.S. arms sales to Iran, and as the result of the effort surrounding the preparation of President Reagan's January 17, 1986 determination formally authorizing a covert program to influence Iran. U.S. intelligence officials then met several times with Iranian officials during 1986 in cities like Frankfurt. During the meetings the U.S. provided details of Soviet contacts with the Iranian Communist Party and certain elements of the Mujahideen, and data on Soviet exercises and force improvements in the areas near Iran.

The US also inadvertently helped Iran by failing to control the sale of equipment allowing Iran to directly read the output of the LANDSAT satellite. This equipment was delivered in 1986. While the signal from the satellite is public, the equipment to read the output is directly under US export control and can be used for mapping and other military purposes.

It is unclear how much of the data provided to Iran represented actual disinformation, if any, as distinguished from selective information designed to give that impression. It is important to note, however, that later press reports showed that the CIA circulated estimates, including a Special National Intelligence Estimate (SNIE) in both 1983 and 1985 that reduced previous U.S. estimates of the risk of a Soviet invasion or intervention.[40]

What is even more controversial is how much data the U.S. provided Iran which was of value in its war effort. It is clear that Colonel Oliver North provided such data on at least one critical occasion, and during the period just before Iran's successful attack on Faw. There were also reports in late February, 1987, that a CIA study had been issued which indicated that North may have provided data of critical value to Iran in estimating the weaknesses in the Iraqi position.

Another key uncertainty surrounds the provision of U.S. intelligence data to Iraq just before the Iranian attack on Faw.[41] The U.S. does seem to have provided data that led Iraq to believe the main thrust was coming to the north of Basra, and which led it to keeps its reserves near Basra when it otherwise might have committed them to halt the Iranian attack on Faw. This may, however, have been a legitimate error by U.S. intelligence – which failed to inform Iraq that its satellites could not cover the area in the south because of cloud cover – and not disinformation.[42]

The issue is particularly important because virtually all sources agree that neither Iraq or Iran have organized an effective intelligence effort of their own since the war has begun. They have failed to make more than the most basic use of SIGINT and Electronic Support Measures for either the interception and jamming of communications or targeting.

Although Iraq has reasonably sophisticated. reconnaissance aircraft, including five MiG-25s and several Mirage F-1s with photo and electronic warfare capabilities, it has never effectively organized its photo intelligence effort, and has failed to even procure adequate stocks of tactical sensor equipment like night vision devices.

Similarly, Iran cannot use most of the sensors on its P-3F Orion maritime patrol aircraft and RF-4E. Neither side has been able to remove the political bias from its human intelligence effort to the point where it can accurately assess the data it gathers on enemy forces.

Iraqi and Iranian Spending on Military Forces and Arms Imports

The military economics of the Iran-Iraq War are as uncertain as most of the other data on the conflict. Nevertheless, it seems likely that the broad trends in the CIA data reported in Figure 4 are correct. These data again show that Iraq has been able to buy massive amounts of new arms since the war began, while Iran's purchases have been comparatively limited.

They also, however, show that Iraq has been able to shift from a 3:1 inferiority in total defense spending relative to Iran in 1974 – the period just before the Algiers accord that was intended to create a lasting peace between Iraq and the Shah's Iran – to a nearly 2:1 superiority in 1983.

Figure 4. The Iranian and Iraqi Military Effort: 1979-1983

Year	Military Manpower (1,000s)		Military Expenditure $M		Arms Imports $M		Military Spending as % of GDP		Military Spending as % of CGE		Arms Imports as % of Total	
	Iraq	Iran	Iraq	Iran	Iraq	Iran	Iraq	Iran	Iraq	Iran	Iraq	Iran
1973	105	285	1486	3112	625	525	25.5	8.3	57.7	30.2	69.9	15.4
1974	110	310	2453	6732	625	1000	21.6	11.8	45.1	29.0	26.3	18.4
1975	155	385	2390	9417	675	1200	16.9	14.3	29.0	31.9	28.8	11.6
1976	190	420	2882	11549	1000	2000	17.2	13.5	37.5	32.0	28.8	15.5
1977	140	350	3621	9928	1500	2500	18.7	11.3	42.1	25.1	38.4	17.0
1978	140	350	4006	12066	1600	2200	17.0	15.8	24.7	35.5	37.9	16.2
1979	212	415	5129	6045	2300	1600	14.9	6.2	24.9	19.1	31.8	16.4
1980	350	305	8629	6737	1900	400	21.7	7.3	NA	19.7	13.5	3.2
1981	400	440	11823	7403	3700	1000	48.2	7.8	NA	20.7	17.6	8.0
1982	450	470	12541	8499	4300	1500	49.7	8.2	NA	21.7	19.7	8.2
1983	500	470	11900	5520	5100	750	47.2	5.0	NA	14.9	42.3	4.1

This defense spending has come at the cost of a considerable strain to Iraq's economy: its military spending has risen from 25% of GDP to nearly 50% and its arms imports are nearly 45% of all imports.

The full extent of Iraq's superiority in military spending is difficult to determine. The CIA estimates in Figure 4 probably understate the scale of the Iranian effort since the war began, and more recent working estimates show that Iran is spending far more of its resources on the war. Nevertheless, Figure 4 is probably broadly correct in indicating that Iran has had considerable difficulty in mobilizing its economy and government spending behind the war.

The more recent data on each country's military economy are discussed in the context of their impact on the fighting during 1984-1987, but it is also clear that both nations have gradually been strained to their limits. This strain has been compounded by the "oil war" they have conducted to reduce each other's revenue from oil exports, and by the crash in world oil prices in early 1985. While both Iran and Iraq have the financial resources to continue fighting, it is clear that both face a growing strain on their economy, and that both have steadily had to give up "butter" for "guns".

The Shift in Total Forces

Iraq's superior military resources are also clearly reflected in the major shifts in the Iranian-Iraqi military balance shown in Figure 5. The revolution cost Iran much of the Shah's massive arms build-up before the war began. Wartime attrition and the inability to import critical spare parts (advanced combat fighters have over 20,000 critical parts per aircraft) have since reduced Iran to a shell of its former military capability.

As Figure 5 shows, Iran has lost a major portion of its aircraft, helicopters, and armor. In fact, Iran's real losses are probably far greater than Figure 5 indicates, since there is no real way to estimate the amount of equipment that is inoperable from limited combat damage or the loss of spare parts. In contrast, Iraq has had a constant flow of replacements, critical spares, and munitions through its logistic pipeline while Iran's buys have been erratic, had major gaps, and have been fed into a chaotic logistic system.

As the following chapters show, this superior access to arms has allowed Iraq to dominate the skies, conduct its oil war against Kharg and Iranian tanker traffic with comparative impunity, and launch air and missile raids against Iranian cities and rear areas without fear of retaliation. It also has tended to make the land war one in which the Iranians can constantly score minor gains they cannot fully exploit because of their lack of armor. Iran has lost much of its ability to fight in the open or to maneuver outside the areas it can hold with masses of well dug-in infantry, and has limited ability to rapidly extend and support offensives much beyond the initial area of attack.

The Struggle in Manpower

These differences in the Iranian and Iraqi approach to war, and arms import capability, help explain why the struggle in manpower has become so important. If one adjusts for current population growth rates, and uses CIA estimates, one gets the manpower estimates shown in Figure 5.

There are considerable uncertainties in these estimates, but it is important to note that if the CIA estimates are correct, the demographics relating to militarily fit males are more favorable than is commonly estimated. Iran's population has a different age structure, is more rural, and has different medical services. Accordingly, it has only about twice as many militarily fit males, although it has more than three times the work force. Iraq is also better able to substitute imports and foreign labor for its own military manpower and work force, and this also helps it overcome Iran's advantage in total population.

More is involved, however, than demographics and economics. As Figures 3 and 4 have shown, Iran has a surprisingly limited advantage over Iraq in terms of trained combat manpower. The practical problem for Iran is that it lacks the mix of combined arms, the logistic and supply systems, and probably the wealth to use its manpower numbers effectively. Iran is forced to rely on training and equipping most of its manpower for light infantry roles, and on temporary call-ups of masses of volunteers for particular offensives.

Figure 5. Iranian and Iraqi Military Manpower in Early 1987

Category	Iran	Iraq	Iran Times Iraq
Total Population	49.4	16.5	3.0
Work Force			
Native	14.9	4.2	3.5
Foreign	—	0.85	—
Total	14.9	5.1	2.9
Military Manpower			
Males Ages 15-49	11.4	3.8	3.0
Militarily Fit	6.8	2.2	2.1
Annual Total Reaching			
Military Age (Age 21)	2.7	0.49	0.18

Source: Adapted from the Central Intelligence Agency, *The World Factbook, 1986*, Washington, CIA, GPO, 1986, pp. 117-120.

Iran has also had severe difficulties in using such volunteers to do more than score short term gains near the front. A successful offensive requires mobility and firepower, and Iran needs far more armor, artillery, air defenses, and logistic support than it now possesses to exploit its potential lead in manpower with full effectiveness.

Further, Iran has lost many of the trained personnel in the regular armed forces that served under the Shah, and its regular forces often do not fully commit themselves to its offensives. Some have been lost due to age and combat and others to defection. Further, many of the rest have not been fully committed to the war. The bulk of Iran's regular forces are kept in position opposite Baghdad, and have not been heavily committed in most of Iran's offensives since 1984.

At the same time, Iran has taken very high casualties among its trained Revolutionary Guards forces, while other Pasdaran cadres tend to have become institutionalized in urban and rural security roles or in Iran's new emerging power elite. Poor medical care has also sometimes increased the death to wound ratio, while erratic political campaigns have rotated volunteer manpower in and out of service that needed more training and experience to become properly effective. This has limited Iran's ability to absorb popular reserves and use them effectively. The effectiveness of military forces is never simply a matter of manpower quantity, manpower quality is at least as important.

This mix of manpower, equipment, and economic problems may also help explain why Iran so far has been unable to launch more than one or two major offensive thrusts at a time, in spite of the fact that Iran's best strategy for exploiting its superiority in manpower is to attack simultaneously on several fronts. Such a simultaneous attack strategy

Figure 6. The Trends in Iranian and Iraqi Military Forces: 1980-1987

Force Category	1980/81		1986/87	
	Iran	Iraq	Iran	Iraq
TOTAL ACTIVE MILITARY MANPOWER SUITABLE FOR COMBAT	240,000	242,250	750,000-1,050,000	750,000-850,000
LAND FORCES				
Regular Army Manpower				
Active	150,000	200,000	305,000	800,000
Reserve	400,000 +	256,000	NA	(230,000)
Revolutionary Guards/	—	—	350,000	—
Basij/People's Army	—	—	150,000	400,000
Hezbollahi (Home Guard)	—	—	2,500,000	—
Arab Volunteers	—	—	—	6,000?
Division Equivalents				
Armored (Divisions/Brigades)	6 + 4	12 + 3	?	5
Mechanized	3	4	3-4? (a)	3
Infantry and Mountain	0	4	8-11 (a)	10 + 9 (b)
Special Forces/airborne	—	—	1/1	3/2
Pasdaran/People's Militia	—	—	9?/?	—/15
Major Combat Equipment				
Main Battle Tanks	1,740	2,750	900-1,250	4,600-6,000
Other Armored Fighting Vehicles	1,075	2,500	1,190-2,000	3,550-4,000
Major Artillery	1,000 +	1,040	600-1,300	4,000-5,500
AIR FORCES				
Air Force Manpower	70,000	38,000	35,000	40,000
Combat Aircraft	445	332	63-105 (c)	500 (d)
Combat Helicopters	500	41	45-75	120-170
Total Helicopters	750	260	150-370	360-410
Surface to Air Missile Batteries (e)	—	—	12	75
NAVY				
Navy Manpower	26,000	4,250	14,500	5,000
Destroyers	3 (f)	0	3(f)	0
Frigates	4 (g)	1 (h)	4(g)	2 (h)
Corvettes	4	0	2	6 (i)
Missile Patrol Craft	9 (j)	12(k)	3-8(j)	8(k)
Major Other Patrol Craft	—	—	4-8	7-13
Mine warfare vessels	—	5	5-7	5
Hovercraft	14	0	10-12	0
Landingcraft and Ships	—	17	8	7
Maritime Patrol Aircraft	6 P-3F	0	2 P-3F	0

(a) Estimates differ sharply. One detailed estimate of the regular army shows 7 mechanized divisions with 3 brigades each and a total of 9 armored and 18 mechanized battalions. Also 2 special forces divisions, 1 airborne brigade, plus eight Revolutionary Guard divisions and large numbers of other brigades and battalions.

(b) Includes 5 infantry divisions and 4 mountain divisions. There are 2 independent special forces divisions, 9 reserve brigades, and 15 People's Volunteer Infantry Brigades.

(c) Includes 20-50 F-4D/E, 17-50 F-5E/F, 10-14 F-14A, and 3 RF-4E. Large numbers of additional combat aircraft are in storage due to lack of parts. Some Argentine A-4s and PRC or North Korean F-6 and F-7 may be in delivery. The number of attack helicopters still operational is unknown.

(d) Includes up to 7-12 Tu-22, 8-10 Tu-16; 4 FGA squadrons with 20 Mirage F-1EQ5 (with Exocet), 23 Mirage F-1EQ200, 4 FGA squadrons with 40-60 MiG-23BM/MiG-27, 3 with 75-95 Su-7 and Su-17/20, and 1 training unit with 12-15 Hunter FB-59/FR-10. There is 1 recce squadron with 5 MiG-25; and 5 interceptor squadrons with 25 MiG-25, 40 MiG-19, 150-200 MiG-21, and 30 Mirage F-1EQ. Figures for Mirage strength vary sharply according to assumptions about delivery rates and combat attrition. Typical estimates of combat helicopters are 40-50 Mi-24, 50-70 SA-342 Gazelle (some with HOT), 30 SA-316B with AS-12 and 44 MBB BO-105 with SS-11.

(e) The number of operational SAM units on each side is unknown. Many of Iran's 12 Hawk batteries are not operational. Iran also has extensive holds of SA-7s and some RBS-70. Iraq has shown very limited ability to use its Soviet made SAMs and some sites do not seem to be fully operational. Counts of Iraq's missile strength are controversial but Iraq seems to have roughly 20 SA-2 (120 launchers), 25 SA-3 (150 launchers), and 25 SA-6 batteries. It also has SA-7 and SA-9 units and some 60 Roland fire units.

(f) 3 equipped with Standard Arm SSMs. One Battle-class and two Sumner-class in reserve.

(g) Equipped with Sea Killer SSM

(h) 1 Lupo class with 8 Otomat-2 missiles and 1x8 Albatros/Aspide, plus 1 helicopter. 1 Yugoslav training frigate. 3 Lupo-class Italian made frigates on order

(i) 6 Wadi-class Italian made 650 ton corvettes. Each has 1X4 Albatros/Aspide. 2 have 2 Otomat-2 and 1 helicopter each; 4 have 6 Otomat 2 SSMs.

(j) Equipped with Harpoon surface to surface missiles.

(k) Equipped with Styx missiles.

Adapted from various editions of the IISS: *The Military Balance*, JCSS, *The Middle East Military Balance*, and work by Drew Middleton for the *New York Times*

would deny Iraq the ability to reinforce its defenses against any given thrust by drawing on manpower in other parts of the front and to match a single major Iranian thrust with an equivalent mix of Iraqi manpower and technology.

At the same time, Iraq has also had problems. It has managed to mobilize a large part of its male population, and it has provided far better training, equipment, support, living conditions, and medical services for its troops. Iraq has, however, had to deal with the problem of securing its Kurdish regions, which has forced it to commit significant military manpower to a diversionary effort. It also continues to substitute ideology for effective training and leadership. Many opportunities to improve training and professionalism have also been ignored, allowing troops to stay in static defensive positions without proper improvement in their fighting quality.

The Civil Economics of the Iran-Iraq War

The civil economics of the war are very difficult to quantify, and most of the data available are so uncertain and so lacking in comparability, that analysis is often more misleading than useful. It is clear, however, that both sides have faced growing problems.

Iraq began the war with massive foreign exchange reserves, but lost its Gulf oil terminals during the first weeks of the war, and then its pipelines through Syria. Its balance of trade shifted from a $14.7 billion surplus in 1980 to a $10.9 billion deficit in 1982, and it has taken Iraq five years to build back up to an oil export capability approaching two million barrels per day (2 MMBD).[43] Only $25-35 billion in foreign aid and loans, a 75% cutback in domestic development expenditure, continuing debt rescheduling, massive countertrade deals which have traded current arms deliveries for future oil exports, and Saudi and Kuwaiti willingness to market oil for Iraq on a future exchange basis, have allowed Iraq to continue the war.

Iran was able to rely on its oil exports and civil economy with more success than Iraq until 1984-1985, but was unable to obtain any major source of foreign credits during that period. It has since had major problems in maintaining its oil exports and suffered from the same dramatic cut in oil prices as Iraq.

Iran now is experiencing rationing and a rate of inflation which is over 50%. It has virtually halted development, has massive unemployment, and serious underemployment in agriculture. Agricultural production has actually declined since the beginning of the war, although substantial increases in output have been needed to keep up with Iran's more than 3% annual population increase, and reduce its dependence on over $2 billion annually in food imports.

While any statistics on Iran's reserves and balance of trade since 1982 are sheer guesswork, it is clear than Iran is experiencing serious problems. Iran also has only been able to average about 2.2 MMBD oil exports during the war, and since 1984, most Iranian exports have been sold at substantial discounts. Iran almost certainly has only been able to finance the war because so many of its volunteers are virtually unpaid and because of mass popular contributions.

Unfortunately, the economic data available on Iran and Iraq are even more uncertain when one attempts to provide an accurate picture of each side's current problems and capabilities. The recent budget and economic data available on Iraq are erratic and do not provide a good picture of

Iraq's true credit position or of Iraq's position in terms of the total cash flow available to finance the war.

The economic and budget statistics available on Iran and Iraq since 1984 are so untrustworthy that quantitative analysis of such data is virtually meaningless. Nevertheless, it is clear that the civil economies of both Iraq and Iran are now strained to their practical limits.

Iraq has also faced serious manpower and labor force problems. In spite of cuts in development and industry, Iraq is still badly short of labor. Iraq still has a million or more foreign workers to finance. It has become steadily more dependent on Egyptian and Sudanese workers, on imports of food and industrial products.

While the full details are unclear, Iraq has had to lower its conscription age and expanded its recruiting base. It has cut back steadily on leave and deferments since early 1985. Iraq has faced growing economic strains in financing arms imports since early 1983, and this strain often led to cancellations and deferments of non-critical arms purchases in 1986.

Recent estimates of how these labor force trends interact with military spending are uncertain, but it is clear that Iraqi military spending as a percent of GNP was over 50% in 1985 and 1986. Military spending as a percent of Central Government Expenditures was between 45 and 57%. The percent of total population in military uniform has risen from 1.1% in 1979 to around 4% by late 1986.[44]

These trends reflect the fact that Iraq has been forced to keep a steadily greater portion of its manpower at the front. Unfortunately, it is difficult to be accurate about the details. Western sources are far too casual about reporting Iranian build-ups of 300,000, 500,000, 700,000, or even a million men. The manpower numbers in such normally reliable sources as the IISS *The Military Balance* are valiant "guesstimates", but they are also extremely uncertain.

The nominal strength estimates issued by U.S. intelligence sources are no better. They tend to credit Iran with 1,250,000 men and Iraq with 750,000, but these estimates do not take meaningful account of the very different mixes of revolutionary, volunteer, and paramilitary forces on each side or the fact that Iran does not maintain anything approaching constant manpower levels in the field.

Iraq's need to both finance the war, and maintain civil economic standards at a high enough level to ensure popular support, have also virtually consumed Iraq's once massive foreign currency reserves. These reserves were still close to $20 billion at the start of 1981, but by 1982, Iraq had became a major borrower. By the end of 1986, Iraq's total foreign debts approached $45-50 billion in spite of major cutbacks in development and non-critical imports. This foreign debt would have been impossible for Iraq to finance and refinance if nearly half of this debt had not been to

Southern Gulf states who either did not expect repayment or were willing to defer repayment indefinitely.

Iran is also now feeling acute economic strains, but in a different way. Iran has had to generate high levels of military spending in spite of its on-going revolution, the collapse of much of its pre-revolutionary economy, and growing major difficulties in maintaining its oil exports. This need to finance "guns, butter, and rhetoric" has had a serious impact on the Iranian economy since the start of the war, and the situation has gotten much worse in the last two years.

Iran was able to obtain money to pay for the first few years of the war with past savings, by reallocating the money spent by the Shah on luxury imports of goods and services, by doubling the money supply, by cutting back on development, by using up much of its over $10 billion cash reserves, and through the sale of external assets. Iran was also able to help finance the domestic costs of the war by drawing on its population for contributions.[45]

Even so, Iran had only so much to sell and could only make so many economies. It has now probably exhausted many of its sources of hard currency except oil and still needs at least $6 billion a year simply to finance the basic military imports necessary to continue the war, and at least $2 to $3.5 billion worth of imported food. This means Iran needs a total of between $10 billion and $12 billion worth of imports to keep its civil economy and the war operating at levels which are likely avoid a major popular reaction. Iran, however, now has only one real export: oil and gas.[46]

The Impact of the Oil War

Iraq largely ignored the vulnerability of its oil export systems at the start of the war. As a result, Iraq suffered a serious strategic surprise when Iran destroyed Iraq's oil terminals in the Gulf, and most of its ability to export, during the first two weeks of the conflict. Iraq then saw Syria ally itself with Iran a year later, and cut off Iraq's main pipeline to the Mediterranean.

Iraq has, however, been able to gradually rebuild much of its export capability by expanding oil pipelines through Turkey, and by opening new links through Saudi Arabia. The Ceyan Terminal in Turkey averaged 975,000 barrels per day (BPD) of Ceyan crude in 1986, and Turkey consumed additional amounts of Iraqi oil. Saudi Arabia and Kuwait also responded to the initial cutoff of Iraqi exports by marketing up to 300,000 barrels a day of "war relief" crude oil under an agreement where Iraq is supposed to return the oil once the war is over. This arrangement still seems to be in operation. Further, Iraq now exports an average of 375,000 BPD of Basra crude through a new pipeline connection to the Saudi port of Yanbu, and Jordan has shipped some 70,000 BPD annually of crude and refined product which is trucked to its port at Aqaba, as well as has consumed some 20,000 BPD.

The economic benefits of this recovery of oil export capability, however, are now seriously threatened by the fall in world oil prices. These prices dropped from an OPEC average of $28.00 in late 1985 to around $11.00 a barrel in mid-1986 and then rose again to around $18.00 a barrel as OPEC and other producers cut production in late 1986.

To put this in perspective, one European source estimates that Iraq averaged about 2.0 million barrels per day (MMBD) during 1970 to 1979, with an average annual value of roughly $7 billion. It ran into serious production problems early in the war, but restored its average annual production to about 720,000 BPD in 1983, with a net value of around $9.7 billion. Its average annual production rose to about 856,000 BPD in 1984, with a net value of around $11.2 billion; its average annual production rose to about 1.1 MMBD in 1985, with a net value of around $12.5 billion. However, although its average annual production rose to around 1.8 MMBD in 1986, its annual income was around $7.0-7.5 billion. These estimates are controversial, and U.S. estimates of Iraqi production tend to be higher. Nevertheless, the limited current rise in oil prices still means Iraq is unlikely to receive more than $9 billion in export earnings in 1987, versus $11-12 billion in 1985.[47]

As a rough estimate, Iraq needs $12-$15 billion in foreign currency to maintain its civil economy and war effort at the 1985 level, creating a potential gap in foreign exchange income of about $5-$8 billion. While Iraq has evidently started a major new austerity program since early 1986, it has also become far more dependent on French and Soviet willingness to engage in deferred counter-trade for arms, on an increasingly uncertain Saudi willingness to allow it to ship oil through links to Saudi pipelines and ports, or direct and indirect Saudi and Kuwaiti aid, and on the willingness of Dutch, German, Indian, and Japanese lenders to roll over at least $10 billion in comparatively short term debt.[48]

The crash in oil prices in 1986 has also affected Iran, and its effect has worsened because of the cost of continuing Iraqi air attacks on Iran's oil facilities and shipping. Once again, estimates are uncertain, but European estimates indicate that Iran averaged about 4.4 million barrels per day (MMBD) during 1970 to 1979, with an average annual value of roughly $14 billion. Iran maintained its production levels early in the war, and exported about 1.7 MMBD in 1983, with a net value of around $19.9 billion. Iran's average annual production dropped to about 1.5 MMBD in 1984, because of the world "oil glut", with a net value of around $12.9 billion. Its average annual average exports rose to about 1.6 MMBD in 1983, with a net value of around $12.5 billion.

Although Iran's average annual exports rose to around 1.8 MMBD in

**Figure 7. Iranian and Iraqi Oil Net Exports Resulting in
Foreign Exchange Income: 1978-1986**
(Average In MMBD)

Year	Iran	Iraq
1978 (peak)	5.2	2.6
1980	1.7	2.5
1981	1.4	1.0
1982	2.2	0.7-0.9
1983	1.7-2.5	0.7-0.9
1984	1.5-2.2	0.9-1.2
1985	1.6-2.2	1.1-1.5
1986	1.5-2.0	1.7-1.8

Note: The Iraq's oil production dropped from around 2.5 MMBD in 1980, when the war began, to 1.3 MMBD when Iran destroyed Iraq's export terminals in the Gulf, and Iraq could only export through Turkey and Syria. When Syria cut off Iraqi exports, Iraq's exports dropped from 1.3 MMBD in the first quarter of 1982 to 800,000 BPD. Iraq's expansion efforts slowing raised this production to 1.2 MMBD during the second half of 1983. Iraqi production then slowly rose from 1.4 to 1.7 MMBD during April to October, 1985. Most of the data are taken from William L. Randol and Ellen McReady, *Petroleum Monitor*, Vol. 5, No. 3, December, 1986, pp. 14-15. The lower end of any range of estimates is a private European estimate.

1986, its annual income was around $7.0-7.5 billion. Once again, the limited current rise in oil prices in late 1986 and early 1987 would still mean that Iran is unlikely to receive more than $7-9 billion in export earnings in 1987, versus $11-12 billion in 1985. Iran's exports only barely paid for its foreign exchange needs in 1985, and some estimates indicate that Iran's net foreign exchange income from crude oil exports may have fallen below $6 billion in the first nine months of 1986. These revenues have risen since late 1986, but not enough to reduce the strain on Iran's foreign exchange holdings.

Iran will be almost completely dependent on its oil earnings to finance its future military and civil imports since it can only export less than $2 billion annually of other goods and services. While Iran's foreign debt is not as significant as Iraq's, it too is an important factor. Iran must also finance some $5 billion worth of foreign credits, including $3.1 billion from OECD non-bank sources.[50]

As a result, both Iraq and Iran may be approaching a rough balance in net foreign exchange income from oil exports during 1987 – at least if Saudi Arabia should fully reopen its pipeline links to Iraq and allow the second link to be opened. Much of Iran's initial advantage in export capability has vanished. This result is reflected in the oil production statistics shown in Figure 7. In spite of various Iranian attempts to pressure OPEC to limit Iraq's oil production, there is also little real prospect that anything will affect either nation's future exports except their physical ability to export. Both need the revenue too desperately, and no action by OPEC or any other body is going to limit their efforts to maximize their own oil revenues while reducing those of their rival.

Much thus depends on Iraq's future ability to attack Iran's oil exports. While Iraq may not be able to use its superior firepower to dominate the land fighting, it has been able to pose a continuing threat to Iran's oil exports. Iraq has also sharply reduced Iran's ability to meet all of its needs for refined product with its domestic resources.

Early in the war, Iraq reduced Iran's total refinery capacity from 1.32 MMBD to 670,000 BPD (Barrels Per Day) – largely because of the destruction of the Iranian refineries at Abadan and Bakhtaran. While Bakhtaran came back on line in 1984, Iran lost the use of its refinery at Masjid-l-Sulaiman, and total refinery output dropped to 615,000 BPD.[51]

Iraq has since increased its attacks on Iran's remaining refineries and has forced Iran to begin importing refined product – another drain on its scarce reserves of hard currency. The scale of this drain, however, is uncertain. Iran has solved some of its problems in the past by cycling its crude through the refinery in Aden in South Yemen. This has allowed it to minimize the financial impact of damage to its refineries.

Iraq has also steadily escalated its attacks on Iran's main oil export facilities at Kharg Island and struck at any shipping to and from Iran that its fighter aircraft could reach. While Iraq has never yet been able to close Kharg Island for any length of time, it has steadily increased its damage capability and the scale of temporary interruptions. Successful Iraqi attacks on Kharg were able to reduce Iran's total exports to about 800,000 BPD during the first weeks of 1986, and then again in several weeks in the winter and fall.

During 1986, Iraq also has expanded its attacks to cover Iran's "tanker shuttle" between its oil production and loading facilities in the upper Gulf and transhipment areas in the lower Gulf which it hoped were outside the range of Iraqi fighters. It has sunk or crippled many of these shuttle tankers. Further, Iraq has shown it can do more than damage Kharg and Iran's shuttle tankers. In mid and late 1986, Iraqi Mirages struck deep into the lower Gulf and hit tankers and facilities near Sirri, Larak, and Lavan – Iran's prime transhipment or oil export areas.

The net result of these Iraqi attacks is partially reflected in Figure 8, which shows the monthly trends in oil production since the beginning of Iraq's intensive oil strikes on Iran. It is important, however, that such estimates are uncertain, and that even the lower range of the estimates for Iran still indicates that Iran has never dropped its sustained total exports to the levels sometimes reported in the press, but Iran obviously did suffer in 1986. Further, as the following chapters describe, Iran has had to pay more

**Figure 8. Iraqi and Iranian Monthly Oil Production
During the Tanker War: 1984-1987**

Month and Year	Iran	Iraq
1984		
January	2.0	1.2
February	2.4	1.0
March	2.4	1.2
April	2.3	1.2
May	2.1	1.2
June	2.2	1.2
July	2.4	1.2
August	1.8	1.3
September	1.8	1.3
October	2.0	1.2
November	2.4	1.3
December	2.5	1.3
1985		
January	1.4	1.3
February	2.1	1.3
March	2.2	1.2
April	2.4	1.4
May	2.0	1.3
June	2.2	1.4
July	2.3	1.5
August	2.6	1.4
September	2.2	1.6
October	2.3	1.7
November	2.2	1.7
December	2.4	1.7
1986		
January	1.5-2.1	1.1
February	1.5-2.0	1.3
March	1.5-1.8	1.5
April	1.5-1.8	1.4
May	1.-52.1	1.5
June	1.5-2.2	1.6-1.8
July	1.6-2.2	1.7-1.8
August	0.9-1.7	1.6-1.8
September	0.9-1.5	1.8
October	1.2-1.6	1.6-1.9
November	1.6	1.7
December	1.9	1.7
1987		
January	2.0-2.1	1.7

Source: William L. Randol and Ellen Macready, *Petroleum Monitor*, New York, First Boston Corporation, various editions. The lower end of any range of estimates is a private European estimate.

and more for insurance premiums, its tanker shuttle, and alternative oil shipment facilities.

Oil exports are also important to Iran for political reasons. Iran faces an uncertain situation in regard to Syria. There is a growing risk that Syria will turn away from Iran and reopen its pipelines to Iraq. Iran's ties to Syria have already been strained by sharp differences over the future of Lebanon and Syria's support of a secular state. Iran virtually had to buy Syria's continued support in 1986 by sending Syria six million tons per year of oil on credit, and Syria has not paid the interest on its debt to Iran.

Neither Syria or Libya seem to be continuing significant arms deliveries to Iran – although some arms may still be coming from Libya. Saudi pressure on Syria to end its support of Iran and open its pipeline to Iraq continues. Iran faces the continuing threat of having to trade its potential oil revenue for support by an increasingly uncertain ally.

As Figure 9 shows Iran has sought to deal with this situation by creating new export facilities which are less vulnerable to attack, but Iran has had serious problems in financing any such pipelines, ports, and loading facilities.[52] Iran at first made extremely ambitious plans. The NIOC (National Iranian Oil Company) announced in late 1985 that it had designated three new terminals at Jask, Qeshem, and Lengeh, as well as new loading points at Ganaveh and Kangan/Asaluyeh. It also established a "ferry" of chartered tankers to move oil to transloading points near the islands of Sirri and Larak in the Eastern Gulf.

While the tanker ferry rapidly did become Iran's economic lifeline, Iran did not fare as well in creating alternative oil pipelines and loading facilities. While Iran could create new mooring points in the Gulf to reduce its dependence on its highly centralized oil loading facilities at Kharg Island, these new mooring points had to be dependent on facilities at Ganaveh about 40 km due north of Kharg, which proved vulnerable to Iraqi air attacks. Further, the almost inevitable starting point for any new Iranian pipelines to the east was Gurreh – about 80 km north of Kharg, and it too was vulnerable to air attack.

Each of the three major pipeline options Iran developed also presented problems. The first was a new set of facilities which would ship through a nearly 236 mile 42″ twin pipeline from Ganaveh to floating terminals off Asaluyeh on Iran's southeastern coast south of Kangan, and 186 miles southeast of Kharg. This pipeline was called the Moharram Project, and was to be built in two phases. The first phase was to create a pipeline to load offshore mooring buoys near Bushehr, and the second phase was to reach all the way to Asaluyeh.

Iran completed plans for the 1.5 MMBD twin pipelines, and got initial bids from Daewo of South Korea and JCG of Japan in October-December, 1985. However, Iran then came up against three major problems: the cost of the pipeline escalated to $1.2-2 billion, rather than

Figure 9. Iraqi and Iranian Efforts to Create Alternative Oil Production Facilities (Capacity shown in MMBD)

Pipeline	Current Exports	Status Capacity at End-1987	Capacity at End-1988	
IRAN				
Moharram Project (1.5MBD line from Ahwaz to Asaluyeh)	None	On hold indefinitely	On hold indefinitely	
IGAT-2 (Link from Gurreh to IGAT-2 gas pipeline running to Asaluyeh)	None	Uncertain	Uncertain	
Jask Line (745 mile 1.1 MMBD line from Gurreh to Jask just outside the Straits)	None	On hold indefinitely	On hold indefinitely	
Turkey Pipeline (1.5 MMBD line through Turkey to Mediterranean.)	None	On hold indefinitely	On hold indefinitely	
IRAQ			Probable	Maximum
Turkey Line	1.2	1.7	1.6	1.7
Saudi Kuwait Subsidy	0.3	?	0	0.3
Yanbu I	0.3	—	—	—
IPSA-2	—	0.6	0.6	1.6
Aqaba	None	On hold indefinitely	On hold indefinitely	
Syrian Line	—	0	0	0.8
Total	1.8	2.3	2.6	4.0

Adapted from See *The Middle East*, April 1986, pp. 7-9; Thomas L. McNaugher, "Pipelines and Power in the Gulf: Shifting Balances," CERA, December, 1986; and William L. Randol and Ellen Macready, *Petroleum Monitor*, New York, First Boston Corporation, various editions.

the $600-900 million originally estimated, the pipeline would take at least 12-15 months to build, and the collection and pumping facilities at its origin would still be vulnerable.

The second option was a pipeline from existing facilities at Gachsaran to the IGAT-2 pipeline which ran from Isfahan to Taheri. This line allowed Iran to convert an existing gas pipeline to the east of its oil facilities and offered minimum vulnerability – although it still meant using a link from Gurreh to Gachsaran about 40 km to the northeast. A $188 million contract was let for this pipeline in December, 1985, but little progress seems to have been made.

The third option was the Jask pipeline. This was an ambitious plan to create a 745 mile pipeline to bypass the Straits of Hormuz and reach a newly built terminal at Jask. This, however, was by far the most costly of all the options and it still meant relying on vulnerable facilities in the oil fields to the West.

There was a fourth pipeline option but it was far less serious. While Iran was able to get Turkish agreement to a counter-trade deal that called for Turkish imports of 100,000 BPD of Iranian oil, Iran had to defer the idea of a new high capacity pipeline to the Mediterranean through Turkey when it examined the costs of this option. The new pipeline had an estimated cost of over $10 billion.

Iran might have made more progress in spite of its cost, time, and vulnerability problems if it had not been confronted with the sudden crash in world oil prices described earlier. This price crash deprived Iran's exports of at least 50% of their value per barrel, and forced Iran to defer its plans for the Jask and Moharram pipelines indefinitely. Iran is now forced to rely on improving its air defences and retaliatory capability against shipping to Iraq, rather than on finding new ways to ship its oil.

In contrast, Figure 8 shows that Iraq has been able to steadily expand its own pipelines, and could approach its former peak export levels of 3.2 MMBD by late 1988. Iraq rapidly obtained additional funding for the further expansion of its pipelines through Turkey – an expansion which should increase their capacity by about 500,000 BPD during the course of 1987. It obtained Saudi aid and permission to link up with existing Saudi pipelines and to build a whole new pipeline to Saudi Arabia's Red Sea coast.[53]

Iraq has also obtained important aid in the form of oil exchanges from its neighbors. Saudi Arabia and Kuwait marketed 250,000-350,000 BPD of their oil for Iraq while these pipeline developments were underway. While they originally planned to suspend their shipments of oil for Iraq once the expansion of Iraq's pipeline through Turkey was completed, they responded to Iran's 1986 offensives against Iraq by restoring their agreement to market oil for Iraq on the basis of future exchanges.

The Kurdish Issue

The final wild card in this complex mix of variables is the Kurdish issue. If a shift in Syrian alignments could weaken Iran, the Kurdish problem has already weakened Iraq.

The Kurdish independence movement had virtually collapsed after 1975, when the Algiers agreement between the Shah and Iraq's Ba'ath Party led the Shah to cut off all aid to the Mullah Mustafa Barzani's Kurdistan Democratic Party (KDP), and to a halt to all U.S. covert aid. The Iraqi army destroyed all Kurdish villages within 20 km of the border and deported many Kurds to camps in southern Iraq. The elder Barzani had to leave the region and finally died in exile in the U.S.

The Kurds also did little to threaten Iraq early in the war. Iraq kept many of its troops in the area, and as many Kurds were fighting the Khomeini regime in Iran as the Iraqi government. After Iraq's military reversals in 1982-1983, however, the Kurdish independence movements begin to revive and Iran began an active campaign to create a Kurdish military opposition to Iraq while it consolidated control over many of its own Kurdish dissidents.

Iran helped the KDP rebuild itself into a major military element, under the leadership of Idris Barzani, the elder Barzani's son, into a major military element. While Idris Barzani died in early 1987, the KDP continues to remain the strongest anti-Iraqi group.[54] At the same time, it tried to win the support of the KDP's rival – the Patriotic Union of Kurdistan (PUK) – which was attacking both Iraq and Iran. Largely due to Iraq's refusal to grant concessions, Iran had considerable success.

The KDP built up a force of about 15,000 men in commands of about 1,000-1,500 men. These are organized into small raiding parties or *dasata* of about 12 men. Because they are so small and operate and supply themselves from sanctuaries in Kurdish areas or Kurdish homes and businesses, they are able to survive in spite of Iraq's relatively effective security forces.

Although Iraq still keeps over 100,000 troops, paramilitary forces, and internal security forces in the areas threatened by the Kurds, the Kurdish liberation groups have steadily expanded their operations since 1985. They have been able to temporarily occupy a few villages, drive Iraqi forces out of some of the countryside in the Northeast, and raid cities.

The KDP and other guerrilla groups are particularly strong along the Turkish border area, and are joined by a number of other guerrilla movements including some elements from Iraq's Communist party. They have received arms from Libya and Syria as well as Iran, and possibly from Israel. They present a continuing threat to Iraq's pipeline through Turkey.[55]

The Overall Balance of Vulnerability

This complex mix of trends does not favor either side. While both Iran and Iraq are under severe stress, and differ sharply in their strengths and weaknesses, each is a remarkably good political, economic, and military match for the other. They also are closely balanced in relative vulnerability and each has the capability to fight for at least another year.

As a result, much will depend on the outcome of future battles. While both sides have the resources to fight, either side can make a military mistake that could catalyze its internal political, economic, and social pressures into defeat. The key difference is that defeat for Iran is likely to mean ending the war, and defeat for Iraq could mean ending secular rule or even Iraq's current national structure and borders.

This balance of conflicting trends is why the future course of such fighting is so hard to predict. The most that can be said is that the analysis in the following chapters indicates that the fighting is likely to follow patterns first set in 1984, and which have evolved along similar lines ever since.

While the Iran-Iraq war has had several phases – including the initial Iraqi conquests in 1980, a stalemate in 1981-1982, and Iran's liberation of its territory in 1983 – it seems unlikely that further major changes will occur until one side is exhausted, Iran accepts a ceasefire, or Iraq is defeated.

In fact, the military issues are now relatively straight forward and simple. The issue for Iraq is whether Iraqi forces at the front can withstand Iran's superiority in manpower and ideological fervor long enough to force Iran into peace through exhaustion, and whether Iraq can find a way to use its technical superiority to cripple Iran's economy by cutting off its oil and damaging its economy. The issue for Iran has been whether it can take enough Iraqi territory, or inflict enough casualties on Iraqi troops, to bring down the government of Sadam Hussein and/or gain control of a major portion of Iraq.

While the risk of the war widening to include the Southern Gulf remains, neither Iraq or Iran seems to have the resources to produce a decisive result. The West might suffer a temporary oil shock, but it seems unlikely that Iran would be able to halt Saudi and Kuwaiti support for Iraq or obtain some other strategically important benefit. The question is not so much how the war will change, but which side will win.

As for the duration of the war, there is no clear way to predict when one side or both will be exhausted, any more than it is possible to predict defeat. It seems reasonable to assert that the war cannot last more than a few more years, but it seemed equally reasonable to predict it would be a comparatively short war when it began. It is also all too clear that several major Iraqi military defeats or the wrong kind of succession crisis in Iran could suddenly end the conflict. No one can credibly predict the timing or nature of the end of the conflict, and the practical problem for the West is not how to find the right prophecy, but rather how to live with uncertainty.

Notes

[1]Iraq's chemical complex occupies a 15 square mile area. Iraq can manufacture mustard gas, and Sarin and Tabin nerve gases. Syria has two nerve gas plants, one located near Homs and another near Damascus. BBC Television, November 25, 1986, and *Washington Times*, December 3, 1986, p. 1A.

[2]CIA, *World Factbook, 1986*, pp. 117-121. The manpower data on Iraq and Iraq are highly uncertain and should not be taken too literally. Different sources sharply conflict.

[3]Ibid

[4]Takrit is a small city in Northern Iraq which is the birthplace of many of Iraq's present leaders.

[5]The figures publicized by the Iraqi Ministry of Information are far more favorable. See the Central Statistics Organization, *Statistical Pocket Book*, 1984, for detailed trend data on the social and economic impacts of the war. The summary graphs give a good picture of the acute social impact of the war since 1982.

[6]CIA, *World Factbook*, 1986, pp. 117-121. The ethnic and religious data on Iraq and Iraq are highly uncertain and should not be taken too literally. Different sources sharply conflict.

[7]For good reporting on this issue, see the *Los Angeles Times*, April 1, 1986.

[8]At this writing, the scale of such deliveries is still very uncertain. The Chinese SA-2 is not regarded as a modern surface-to-air missile system.

[9]These cancellations included 160 F-16s, seven AWACS, two DD-993 guided missile destroyers, 500 Phoenix missiles, 16 RF-4Es, 200 Harpoon anti-ship missiles, 500 Gould Mark 46 torpedos, 100 Raytheon Improved Hawk Surface-to-Air missiles, armored personnel carriers and other vehicles. See Gary Sick, *All Fall Down*, New York, Random House, 1985, pp. 148-149.

[10]While the U.S. still holds some $261.8 million worth of arms that Iran had on order before the hostage crisis – including missiles, radar equipment, fighter parts, APCs, tank parts, C-130 aircraft, and Hawk missiles, – this has now aged under very poor storage conditions and most of it is useless. *New York Times*, December 10, 1986, p. A-21.

[11]Arms Control and Disarmament Agency, *World Military Expenditures and Arms Transfers, 1985*, Washington, GPO, 1985, pp. 134-135.

[12]U.S. Government sources.

[13]Joint Economic Committee, U.S. Congress, "The Soviet Economy Under a New Leader", Washington, March 19, 1986, p. 7. DMS, *International Defense Intelligence*, January 6, 1986, p. 1. CIA, *Handbook of Economic Statistics*, CPAS 85-10001, Washington, GPO, September, 1985.

[14]*Wall Street Journal*, January 30, 1987, p. 1.

[15]About $500,000 worth of F-14 parts stolen by a ring of corrupt U.S. civilian employees were smuggled to Iran. *Wall Street Journal*, January 30, 1987, p. 1.

[16]*New York Times*, February 2, 1987, p. A-1.

[17]Unless otherwise referenced, the estimates quoted here are based on Anthony H. Cordesman, "Arms Sales to Iran: Rumor and Reality," *Middle East Executive Reports*, February 1986, pp. 15-21, and discussions with U.S. officials in December, 1986.

[18]This agreement is thought to have been the formal outcome of an arms offer negotiated by Rafsanjani during a 1985 visit to Peking. *Aviation Week*, November 24, 1986, p. 29; *Economist*, November 22, 1986, pp. 41-42, and *Jane's Defence Weekly*, November 29, 1986, p. 1257.

[19]*New York Times*, November 25, 1986, p. A-1, and *Washington Times*, December 16, 1986, p. 10A. It is interesting to note that Iran received significantly better equipment from the PRC because of a covert trade in technology between Israel and the PRC. Israel has sold many of

its modifications of captured Soviet equipment to China, and an Israeli corporation, United Development Inc., acts as a major conduit between Israel and the PRC. Some technology transfer to the PRC also seemed to have occurred because of sales by Israeli Aircraft Industries.

[20]These were shipped in crates marked vehicle parts with the knowledge of the British Ministry of Defense. They were later rationalized as being unconnected with the "lethal systems of the vehicles". *Wall Street Journal*, January 30, 1987, p. 1.

[21]Ironically, Portugal refused to act as an agent during the U.S. covert arms sales effort to Iran and would not allow the transhipment of Hawk missile parts through Lisbon. *Washington Post*, January 31, 1987, p. A-19.

[22]*Washington Times*, February 10, 1987, p. 6A.

[23]The full value of the U.S. arms transfers is almost impossible to calculate. It initially appeared that they were worth only $30 million. Later reports, however, indicate that this includes only direct U.S. TOW and Hawk transfers and not parts or Israeli sales. The true value of U.S. arms transfers appears to be at least $64 million.

[24]It is still not possible to distinguish the size of officially tolerated U.S. arms shipments at this writing. There have been reports of shipments as large as 12,000 anti-tank weapons, $150 million in spare parts, and some 200 Phoenix missiles, but these seem false in the case of the Phoenix and to confuse U.S. shipments with those by Israel and other countries. Gorbanifar did try to obtain 200 Phoenix missiles and Harpoons for Iran in March, 1986, but these were not shipped as part of the covert U.S. arms deals. Similarly, Iran did not seem to have obtained the two Hawk missile radars and does not seem to have obtained some of the 234 types of Hawk parts it sought in mid-April 1986. U.S. Senate Committee on Intelligence, *Report on Preliminary Inquiry*, January 28, 1987, pp. 18-22 and 25-38. *New York Times*, February 2, 1987, p. 14; *Philadelphia Inquirer*, January 29, 1987, p. 14A.

[25]There are reports that Iran got critical spares for the APQ-120 radars on its F-4s from the U.S. during this period which allowed it to repair the Klystron amplifiers on the radars and use them to illuminate targets with the continuous wave beam needed to fire the Aim-7E radar guided air-to-air missile. Other reports indicated that Iran was dependent on covert Israeli arms sales to keep its entire F-4 force functioning which were tacitly tolerated by the U.S.. One of the other major uncertainties affecting the flow of arms to Iran during this period was the flow of parts for Iran's 250 Bell 214A and 40 214C transport helicopters and CH-47 heavy lift helicopters. While both Bell Textron and Boeing refused Iranian efforts to buy parts directly from U.S. companies, some parts seem to have been sold by firms in Israeli and Italy. *Washington Post*, August 26, 1986, p. 1; *Wall Street Journal*, September 5, 1986, p. 1; *Aviation Week*, November 17, 1986, pp. 16-17.

[26]Senate Select Committee on Intelligence, *Report on Preliminary Inquiry*, January 28, 1987, pp. 18-22. This report by the U.S. Senate indicates this deal would have been expanded to a total of 4,000 TOW missiles if the Iranian's had released all the hostages the U.S. expected. Also see *Washington Post*, January 11, 1987, p. A-1.

[27]See the *Report of the Select Committee on Secret Military Assistance to Iran and the Nicaraguan Opposition*, Senate Select Committee on Intelligence, Report on Preliminary Inquiry, January 29, 1987.

[28]*The Observer*, December 1, 1986, and the *Washington Times*, December 1, 1986, p. 9A.

[29]While Amiram Nir, Al Schwimmer, and Yaacov Nimrodi have received widespread publicity as Israeli agents as the result of the exposure of covert U.S. arms sales to Iran, Israeli intelligence officers and "quasi-official" agents have been selling arms to Iran since 1980. Israel has not only used retired military, but agents in Greece, Cyprus, the U.S., and Arab states. For example, a leading Saudi arms dealer, Adnan Khashoggi participated in Israel's covert shipment of arms to Iran for the U.S.

For typical reporting, see the *Washington Post*, January 31, 1987, p. A-17, and the *Philadelphia Inquirer*, January 31, 1987, p. 4A.

³⁰Sources differ sharply over the scale of U.S. and Israeli arms sales at this writing, but Israeli cargos continued to arrive in Iran as late as November, 1986, and after the reports of Israeli shipments had appeared in the papers. Israel conspicuously failed to deny Sick's report. (*Washington Times*, December 10, 1986, p. 8-A.) Also see *Washington Post*, December 5, 1986, December 6, 1986, p. A-13, December 9, 1986, p. B-8, December 16, 1986, p. A-1; *New York Times*, December 5, 1986, p. A-14 December 15, 1986, p. A-12, ; *Washington Times*, December 12, 1986, p. 9A, December 16, 1986, p. 8A; and *Los Angeles Times*, December 4, 1986, p. I-1.

³¹The exact proportion involving sales with connections to Israeli agents is unknown. *Wall Street Journal*, January 30, 1987, p. 1.

³²*Washington Post*, January 31, 1987, p. A-17.

³³*Business Week*, February 16, 1987, p. 27.

³⁴*Jane's Defence Weekly*, November 29, 1986, pp. 1256-1258; *Wall Street Journal*, January 30, 1987, p. 1.

³⁵*New York Times*, November 25, 1986, p. A-1; *Washington Times*, December 16, 1986, p. 10A, December 12, 1986, p. 8A; *Los Angeles Times*, December 12, 1986, p. I-23, December 10, 1986, p. 8A.

³⁶See Anthony H. Cordesman, "Arms Sales to Iran: Rumor and Reality," *Middle East Executive Reports*, February 1986, pp. 15-21, and discussions with U.S. officials in December, 1986, and Michael Brzoska and Thomas Ohlson, *Arms Production in the Third World*, London, SIPRI, 1986, pp. 147-161.

³⁷The first reports of these links were reported by Robert Woodward in the *Washington Post*. The U.S. has not formally reported on the nature of the data it has provided. In general, however, such data is provided selectively to deal with critical problems like warning of an attack, rather than released on a steady basis. All intelligence is generally altered to protect the source, and prevent hostile powers from determining the exact scope and nature of U.S. collection capabilities. This sometimes leads to reports of "disinformation", although raw intelligence is also filtered to protect the source when circulated to U.S. officials. The exact flow of data from the U.S. on the movement of ships in the Gulf and the E-3As in Saudi Arabia is uncertain. U.S. officials indicate, however, that Saudi Arabia has strictly complied with its agreement not to provide transfers of the data collected by the E-3As to third nations without the agreement of the U.S.

³⁸*Washington Post*, February 20, 1987, p. 1.

³⁹Issued in unclassified form by the U.S. Senate on January 28, 1987. Also see *New York Times*, January 12, 1987, p. A-1; *Baltimore Sun*, January 12, 1987, p. 1-A; *Washington Post*, January 13, 1987, p. A-1; *Wall Street Journal*, January 13, 1987.

⁴⁰*New York Times*, January 12, 1987, p. A-1; *Baltimore Sun*, January 12, 1987, p. 1-A; *Washington Post*, January 13, 1987, p. A-1; *Wall Street Journal*, January 13, 1987. The documents provided to Iran clearly exploited the fact Iran had executed nearly 200 Iranian Marxists and expelled 18 Soviet diplomats in the Spring of 1983.

⁴¹Robert Gates, then Deputy Director of the CIA and later Director, testified to the Senate Select Committee on Intelligence that both he and the CIA objected to the intelligence exchanges with Iran and to some of the data provided and were overruled by Colonel Oliver North of the NSC staff. It later became clear that North personnally released sensitive data to Iran without authorization. See the *Report of the Select Committee on Secret Military Assistance to Iran and the Nicaraguan Opposition*, Senate Select Committee on Intelligence, *Report on Preliminary Inquiry*, January 29, 1987. pp. 19-21, 23, 29-30, 37-39, 56, and *Washington Post*, February 20, 1987, p. A-1 and February 25, 1987, p. A-1. Another key uncertainty is the amount of intelligence that the NSC passed on to Iran in May and October, 1986.

⁴²According to sources at *Time* magazine, the U.S. failed to report that Faw, and the Iranian positions opposite Faw, were largely obscured by cloud cover during the period before the attack. This was part of standard U.S. procedures in protecting the details of U.S. satellite

coverage capability, but it helped lead Iraq to put too much faith in the U.S. estimate that the main Iranian thrust would come north of Basra.

[43]The estimates in this section are taken from various publications of the Economist Intelligence Unit, from Department of Commerce working data, and from the country chapters on Iran and Iraq in the Middle East Review, 1986, London, World Almanac Publications, 1986.

[44]Estimate based on data in ACDA, *Military Expenditures and World Arms Transfers, 1985,* Washington, 1985, pp. 66-67. Iraq had to refinance well over $5 billion in foreign debt in 1985, and now faces new strains because of the fall in oil prices and the high cost of re-equipping because of the 1986 offensives.

[45]The issue of Iranian foreign exchange and hard currency reserves is very uncertain. Reports that Iran has sold some 6 million ounces of gold seem to be untrue. Reserves have fluctuated up, as well as down, and Iran has paid off virtually its entire foreign debt.

[46]One of the many uncertainties affecting Iran's economic position is the extent to which it has actually received popular contributions and has been able to benefit from cheap conscripts. The Iranian method of obtaining volunteer and conscript manpower is sufficiently arbitrary and disruptive so it imposes significant loss of domestic and foreign exchange income. The "opportunity costs" or foregone revenue costs of the war may be extremely high.

[47]For excellent reporting on these trends, see William L. Randol and Ellen Macready, *Petroleum Monitor*, a monthly series of the First Boston Corporation.

[48]For sources on Iran and Iraq's economic problems, see the Economist Intelligence Unit, EIU *Regional Review: The Middle East and North Africa, 1985,* London, 1985, pp. 87-104; *Washington Post*, March 6, 1985, *Los Angeles Times*, April 1, 1986; Keith McLachlan and George Joffe, *The Gulf War*, EIU Report 176, London, 1985; William Randol and Ellen Macready, *Petroleum Monitor*, First Boston Research, Vol. 5., No. 3, New York, March, 1986; CIA, *Handbook of Economic Statistics*, CPAS 85-10001, Washington, GPO, September, 1985, and the *Middle East Economic Digest*, March 29, 1986, pp. 8-9.

[49]For excellent reporting on these trends, see William L. Randol and Ellen Macready, *Petroleum Monitor*, a monthly series of the First Boston Corporation.

[50]The statistics available on the Iranian and Iraqi economies are highly uncertain. This estimate is based on various publications of the U.S. Department of Commerce, the Economist Intelligence Unit, *The Middle East*, April 1986, pp. 7-9, and the *Middle East Economic Digest*, March 29, 1986, pp. 8-9.

[51]EIU, Annual Review: *Middle East and North Africa, 1986*, London, Economist Publishing, 1986, p. 97.

[52]See *The Middle East*, April 1986, pp. 7-9; and Thomas L. McNaugher, "Pipelines and Power in the Gulf: Shifting Balances," CERA, December, 1986.

[53]Ibid.

[54]He died in Oroumiyeh shortly after an Iraqi air raid. His death was, however, reported to be from a heart attack. *Washington Times*, February 2, 1987, p. 6A.

[55]For an excellent summary, see John Laffin, *War Annual 1*, London, Brassey's, 1986, pp. 89-91.

Chapter Three

The Fighting in 1984

The fighting that established the current pattern of the Iran-Iraq War began with the Iranian offensives of February, 1984. Iran had recovered most of its territory in 1983. It had won several massive victories over Iraq by exploiting its superiority in manpower, its knowledge of the terrain, willingness to take casualties, and ability to dominate in close infantry fighting in cities or near key terrain and water barriers.

As a result, Iran shifted in 1983 from defense of its territory to an effort to seize control of Iraq. It launched several probing offensives in the fall of 1983, and while none of these offensives made major gains, they were encouraging enough to lead Iran to conduct preparations for a full scale attack. Similarly, Iran conducted several small probing attacks against the Kurdish areas in Northern Iraq which seem to have been successful enough to convince the Iranians they could succeed in larger attacks in the south.

The Iranian Offensives of Early 1984

By early 1984, Iran decided it was ready to launch a full-scale invasion into Iraq. It had a force of at least 500,000-750,000 men along a broad 730 mile front which roughly paralleled the pre-war border, and had the ability to rapidly deploy another 200,000 reserves. It had also succeeded in building a 60 km canal eastward from the Karun River to check Iraqi efforts to provide a defensive water barrier and to create a capability to drown advancing Iranian troops by diverting the Tigris. Iraq restored much of this water barrier with a new set of large embankments – which ran in parallel lines along the front. Nevertheless, Iran responded by training and equipping its forces to cross these barriers as well as positioning its forces to bypass them.[1]   Iran launched its invasion in February. The invasion was led by a mixture of Pasdaran and Basij volunteers, with support from the regular forces. On February 14, 1984, Iran began a probing attack near the Shatt al Arab.[2] By February 16th, it expanded this attack into a helicopter and water borne assault which used rubber boats and small craft (the Fatima al Zahra attack) to attack the Iraqi marsh villages of Al Baydha and Sakhra.

This attack overran these Iraqi villages and Iran then attempted to cut the Baghdad-Basra road between Amara and Qurna. However, Iran only succeeded in advancing as long as its troops could take advantage of the cover of the marshes. Although some Iranian forces did reach the banks of the Tigris near the Baghdad-Basra road before they were thrown back, they could not survive when they attempted to advance across open territory where Iraq could bring its full weight of firepower to bear. By the time the attack ended, the Iranians had been forced out of Al Baydha and Sakhra, and had lost at least 3,000 men.[3]

The second phase of the Iranian offensive attempted to split the Iraqi 3rd and 4th Corps, and was led by the Pasdaran with the support of Iran's regular forces. These forces attacked along a 100 mile front in the area west of Meheran, and southeast of Baghdad, which aimed at taking Basra. This attack offered the potential strategic advantage of cutting Iraq off from the Gulf and easy access to Kuwait, the seizure of a major population center in a Shi'ite area, and control of roughly one-sixth of Iraq's proven oil reserves and of an area with potential reserves of up to 27 billion barrels.[4]

The two-pronged Iranian attack involved massive amounts of volunteer manpower and at least one regular Iranian armored division – the 92nd. It began on February 22nd, and lasted for roughly ten days. The attack was called the Val Fajr 6 offensive, and began in the Ghuzail area of the Kishk-Al Bakr sector – about 30 miles north of Basra.

Iran did make limited initial gains, and Iran claimed to take the key city of Qurna, at the junction of the Tigris and Euphrates Rivers, on February 23rd. However, Iraqi television coverage quickly made it clear that Iran was lying, and it later became clear that the bulk of Iran's attacking troops had been slaughtered near the edges of various water barriers or near Iraq's entrenched forward defense positions. Iran suffered five to seven times more casualties than Iraq, and may well have lost as many as 13,000 men.[5]

In spite of these casualties, Iran then reinforced its invasion by a total of at least five major combat formations. These forces attacked Iraq across the Hawizah marshes north of Basra on February 24th-27th. This new attack scored initial gains, and major battles continued during the next week. Iran could not follow-up its initial successes, however, and its invasion reached a bloody climax.

On February 29th, an Iranian force equivalent to nearly three divisions advanced over open desert in broad daylight. It attacked a prepared Iraqi defensive position that could concentrate massive firepower from Iran's flanks as well as against its center. Once again, Iranian forces found they could not substitute fervor for organization and firepower, and Iran was checked with heavy losses – up to 19,000 killed according to some estimates.[6]

The final major phase of Iranian offensive action in 1984 began on March lst. Iran attempted to salvage its attack through the marshes by attacking with two Pasdaran divisions reinforced with tanks and heavy engineering equipment. These forces attacked in the shallow lakes and reed filled Hawizah marshes east of Qurna, and near the junction of the Tigris and Euphrates rivers. Once again, however, Iranian troops advanced in exposed mass formations, and without adequate command direction. The Iraqis used helicopters, mass artillery fire, and mustard gas.[7] Once again, the Iranians took massive losses. By March 5th, Iraq had destroyed most of the new attacking formations.

Iran continued to attack through the rest of March. It tried to use the 92nd regular Armored Division in a battle at Ghuzail, but had no more success than with the Pasdaran. It tried human wave tactics to counter minefields and barbed wire, but with equally little success. By the end of March, Iran had lost up to 40,000 casualties versus a maximum of 9,000 for Iraq.

Part of Iran's failures during this invasion stemmed from making the same kind of mistake about Iraq's ethnic vulnerability that Iraq had made about Iran at the start of the war when it tried to appeal to the Iranian "Arabs" in Khuzustan. Iran's overall goal was to seize the key forward road in the southern front and to isolate Iraq's southern port city of Basra from Baghdad and the rest of Iraq.

While the exact role of Iran's religious leadership, Revolutionary Guards, and regular military in planning the attack remains unclear, it seems that the Religious Leadership and Revolutionary Guards reasoned that because the population of Basra and Southeastern Iraq was largely Shi'ite, an Iranian attack would trigger a popular uprising within Iraq. This may explain why Iran put so much faith in popular volunteers and in poorly planned mass infantry and human wave attacks. It threw thousands of "boy volunteers" into combat almost straight from their cities and villages. These volunteers had little military equipment and resupply capability, and few instructions – other than to advance to their primary objective and obtain supplies from the newly "liberated" Iraqi Shi'ites.

It may also explain why the attacks had relatively limited support from Iran's regular forces, armor, artillery, and combat engineers. The bulk of Iran's regular forces were not committed either in preparing for the battle or during. The main units in the attack were virtually all revolutionary infantry which were forced to fight without proper combined arms support.

This mix of strategic and tactical failures deprived Iran of the ability to use its infantry effectively, and gave Iraq a substantial advantage in using its superior mass of armor and artillery firepower. While the Iranians often scored impressive initial gains, they tended to bunch indecisively once they reached their first objective and they advanced into the killing zones established by Iraq's fixed defense positions and supporting artillery. Thousands of Iranians died pointlessly in this fashion between the first Iranian offensive in mid-February and the end of March.

The Iranian Success at Majnoon

Iran was only able to hold onto one significant piece of Iranian territory – the Majnoon islands – which it had taken on 25 February as part of its broader attack across the Hawizah Marshes. These "islands" consisted of a network of desolate mud and sand mounds, and two enclosed areas in the marshes east of Qurna and northeast of Basra, which Iraq had built up to help develop an oil field. There were nearly 50 wells in the area, but Iraq had capped these wells before the fighting began.

Iran held onto its initial gains in Majnoon because the islands were relatively deep in the Hawizah Marshes where Iran could take optimal advantage of its use of mobile pontoons, small craft, cross country motorcycles, and helicopters. Iran was equipped for warfare in the area while Iraq could not bring its artillery and armor fully to bear.

Iraqi forces could only counterattack along a narrow causeway and could not deploy massive amounts of armor and artillery – a tactical situation somewhat similar to the one Iraq faced during Iran's successful attack on Faw in 1986. Even so, Iran was only able to consolidate its positions on the northern island. This made it difficult for Iran to deploy for an attack from Majnoon's "lower" or "western" island against either Basra or the main Iraqi roads running north and south.[8]

Iran responded to these various defeats with steadily more vociferous charges that Iraq had made massive use of chemical warfare. Some of these charges were unquestionably valid. Iraq almost certainly used mustard gas and possibly primitive nerve agents in the battles near Hur ul-Hoveyzeh on 25 February, in the Shatt e-ali area on 26 February, in the Talayeh area on 2-3 March, in the Majnoon Islands on 9 March, and in the Jofeyr-Al Ba'iza and Kawther regions on 17 March.[9] Iran's tactics made Iraqi use of mustard gas particularly effective, since Iranian forces moved slowly and on foot. Mustard gas achieves maximum effect as a persistent poison.

The Reasons for Iraq's Success in 1984

It is important to understand, however, that the main reason for Iraq's victories in 1984 was the combination of Iraqi superiority in firepower, armor, and air power, and of Iran's failure to properly plan and manage its infantry attacks. Even if all Iranian claims are taken literally, Iraq's use of gas accounted for only 3-5% of Iran's casualties.

Further, Iraq could never have achieved its rapid victories simply on the basis of its superior firepower. Iran helped defeat itself by consistently exposing its manpower in direct "human wave" assaults on heavily held Iraqi positions, by attacking in broad daylight, by attacking without major artillery and air support, and by attacking without effective battle management.

By the end of March, these tactics had caused so many losses that Iran had reached the point where the Iranian Army had lost its offensive capabilities for several months to come. Iraq had inflicted massive casualties on Iran. Iraq also had inflicted major equipment losses on the Iranian Army. While considerable uncertainty existed about the size of Iran's operational equipment holdings at the beginning of the fighting in February, it was clear by late March that Iraq could deploy more than 3,000 main battle tanks to less than 1,000 for Iran, and that Iraq could deploy 1,800 artillery pieces to less than 600 from Iran.

Iraq had also clearly developed an edge in air power. While the Iraqi air force was not particularly effective, Iraq showed that it could fly well over a hundred sorties per day while Iran often flew less than 10. Iran's lack of any source for resupply of combat aircraft or major spares and repair parts for its existing fighters had crippled the Iranian air force. Iraq had at least 300 fully operational combat aircraft while Iran had less than 90 that it could fly for even a few sorties per week, and most of these Iranian fighters no longer had fully operational avionics and/or air-to-air missiles.

At the same time, Iraq was easing some of the economic strains caused by the loss of its oil loading facilities in the Gulf and pipeline through Syria. During 1983, Iraq had succeeded in expanding its pipelines through Turkey, and by March, 1984, it has succeeded in increasing its exports from a monthly average of 800,000 BPD to an average of 1.2 MMBD. Iraq was completing plans and contracts to establish new pipelines through Saudi Arabia. While this added capacity did not become available until late 1985, it was a powerful force in influencing Iraq's foreign creditors to refinance its debt and continue to make new short and long term loans.

Iraq's New Tanker War

In fact, it was Iran which now began to find its oil export capability was vulnerable. Iraq had shown even during Iran's offensives that it could use its air superiority to attack more than battlefield targets. Although a partial ceasefire affecting civilian targets went into effect on February

18th, Iraq conducted enough strikes before this time to demonstrate that its aircraft and missiles could strike with comparative immunity at Iranian towns, cities, and rear areas. The ceasefire on attacks on population targets also did more to redirect Iraqi strikes than it did to end them. The Iraqi Air Force soon began to strike at Iran's oil exports. While the exact details remain uncertain, Iraq seems to have hit seven ships in the Gulf between 25 February and 1 March.

On March 27, 1984, Iraq launched the first of a long series of Super Etendards strikes using Exocet missiles. Iraqi fighters hit two small tankers southwest of Kharg. This attack occurred just as the Iranian National Oil Company (NIOC) was beginning negotiations with Japanese traders for the renewal of a contract for 200,000 BPD of crude. Iran also seems to have been increasing production to try to recoup some of the costs of the fighting. It was exporting from Kharg Island at the exceptionally high rate of 3 MMBD in spite of an Iraqi threat on 27 February, that it would blockade Iranian oil exports.

This combination of events gave the initial Iraqi attacks exceptional political impact, and Iraq then began to attack shipping to and from Iran in real earnest. On April 18th, the Iraqis hit a small Panamanian tanker just outside Kharg. They then hit a large Saudi-owned tanker on April 26th, and another tanker on May 7th.

These attacks led Iran to try to respond in kind. Iranian fighters hit a Kuwaiti tanker near Bahrain on May 13th. This was the first major Iranian attack on commercial shipping, although Iran rarely acknowledged responsibility for this or subsequent attacks.[10] Within five weeks, eleven ships had been hit by both sides, ten of which were oil tankers.

The Iraqi and Iranian attacks then, however, began to lose much of their political and strategic impact. Neither side could or would inflict enough damage to affect world oil supplies in the facing of a growing world "oil glut". Even in the usually sensitive spot market, oil prices showed little movement. The only regional impact was that insurance rates rose sharply for ships going to Kharg, from 0.25% to 7.5% by the end of May. This translated into an increased cost ranging between $1.00 and $1.50 a barrel of oil, and Iran had to offer compensatory price discounts. While the volume of Iranian exports temporarily fell by about 50%, as customers diversified their supplies, it quickly recovered as other customers took advantage of Iran's discounts.

At the same time, Iraq's attempts to use its attacks to bring Iran to peace negotiations failed completely. Although Iraq coupled new peace initiatives to a five day suspension of attacks between 19 and 24 May, Iran simply chose to ignore them. It then became clear that five Iraqi fighters with Exocets might be able to harass Iran's oil exports but could scarcely halt them.

The "tanker war" did, however, escalate to include the Southern Gulf in early June. The Iraqis sank a Turkish flag tanker off Kharg Island on June 3rd. Two days later, Saudi jet fighters downed an Iranian jet over Saudi waters. Iran and Iraq resumed occasional air and missile strikes on population centers. On June 10th, a Kuwaiti tanker was hit near Qatar. This attack, which was probably by an Iranian aircraft, was the first in the lower Gulf.

These events helped trigger another new peace effort. On June 11, the day after the Kuwaiti tanker was hit, both Iran and Iraq accepted another UN initiated halt to attacks on each other's towns and cities. This ceasefire was gradually extended to include oil facilities. Iran's exports from Kharg reached 1.6 MMBD. On June 15th, the speaker of Iran's Majlis, Rafsanjani, proposed extending the truce to Gulf shipping as well. Iraq insisted, however, that any such truce must allow it to repair or replace its own export facilities in the Gulf – a proposal to which Iran made no response. It also rapidly became apparent that Iran's idea of peace was the departure of Sadam Hussein and his supporters and billions of dollars in Iraqi reparations.

The resulting failure of the new peace effort led to further escalation of the tanker war, although the U.S. and Saudi Arabia took steps to limit such escalation to the northern Gulf. On June 20th, U.S. officials announced with Saudi support that Saudi Arabia had set up an air defense interception zone (ADIZ) known as the "Fahd line" which extended beyond Saudi territorial limits. It was also announced that Saudi F-15s, guided by U.S. E-3A AWACS (airborne warning and control system) and refueled by USAF KC-10 tankers, would engage any aircraft threatening Gulf shipping in this region.

Iraq hit several more ships in the Gulf and on June 24th, struck at the Iranian oil export facilities at Kharg Island. The Iranians later confirmed that their loading facilities at the Western or Sea Island side of Kharg were damaged in this raid but it rapidly became clear that Iraq would not take the air losses necessary to destroy Kharg's ability to load tankers. Iraq instead escalated the war against shipping. Between June 23 and July 25, the Iraqis launched at least four different series of attacks against shipping in the Gulf. On July 5th, the Iranians responded by attacking and damaging the Primrose, a Japanese-owned super tanker sailing under Liberian registry.[11]

This constant – but low level – "tanker war" proved typical of Iraq's basic strategy for the rest of 1984. Iraq alternated strikes on Iranian cities, and attacks on shipping to Iran, with calls for ceasefires and peace talks. Iraq, however, lacked the combination of sensors, air, and missile power to inflict major damage on Iran's civil and economic centers and to sustain a blockade of Iran's export facilities.

This Iraqi failure was partly the result of a lack of the proper technology. Iraq's aircraft lacked adequate range and endurance, its anti-shipping missiles were not sufficiently lethal to score quick decisive ship kills, and it had no maritime patrol aircraft. Iraq's failure was also partly the result of a lack of adequate military organization and leadership. Iraq never committed its air power in mass on a sustained basis, and failed to exploit each successive improvement in its capability to strike at tankers or Iran's oil facilities. Iraq's attacks always came in brief bursts and with a flood of rhetoric which greatly exaggerated the military reality.

This Iraqi mistake is all too common in attempts to "manage" escalation. Attackers often assume that relatively limited levels of military escalation can be decisive in their effect, and can change the political and military calculations of their opponent, because of the potential for further escalation. In practice, efforts to achieve military or political goals through limited escalation, backed by implied threats, have virtually always failed to have their desired effect. The opponent has almost inevitably misunderstood the signal, or has reacted only to the size of the escalation and not to the implied threat. Such escalation has usually ended in doing little more than increasing an opponent's hostility.

Attempts to use air power as a substitute for victory on the ground have rarely had success except against the most unsophisticated or uncommitted opponent. While such air attacks may produce initial panic or disruption, the economic, political, and military structure of nations under air attack has always proved far more resilient than the advocates of strategic bombing estimate. Supposedly critical vulnerabilities have generally proved to be easily repairable or subject to substitution – particularly when the country under attack is given time to recover. Once again, the net effect has generally been to unite a nation in hostility rather than to intimidate it.

Further, Iraq's attacks lacked consistency and persistence. During this period of the war, Iraq gave Iran ample time to recover after each new round of Iraqi air attacks. Iraq may have chosen this pattern of attacks because each round of peace initiatives seemed to be on the edge of success. Each time, however, Iran ended in using the new peace initiative or cease fire to reduce the level of Iraqi attacks on its cities and shipping traffic. It then reiterated its demands for the removal of Sadam Hussein and for billions of dollars worth of reparations.

Iran's Shift in Land Warfare Tactics

As for Iran, its military strategy shifted from frontal assault to one of attrition. Iran occasionally maneuvered its forces in what seemed to be preparation for a new major offensive, but only made limited attacks designed to gain key terrain advantages near the front. Iran did conduct occasional air attacks on Gulf shipping, used its navy to harass cargo ships moving to Southern Gulf ports, and kept up its pressure on Iraq's supporters through a mix of threats, subversion, and terrorism. These Iranian actions, however, were designed more to limit the flow of aid to Iraq from the southern Gulf states than to halt the flow of shipping and trade. Iran always took careful account of the risk of provoking Western action, and kept its attacks at very low levels even if one considers its lack of aircraft and combat ready ships.

The pattern of land combat during the rest of 1984 did show, however, that Iran's leadership had begun to learn that ideological fervor was not a substitute for military reality. While the data involved are uncertain, Iranian official statements, and reports from within Iran, indicate that Iran's casualties in the 1984 spring offensives must have approached 30,000-50,000 dead.

Such losses must have shown Iran's religious leaders that Iran's ground forces could not succeed without far better training, leadership, and organization. They also indicated that direct mass infantry attacks on well positioned Iraqi defenders could not succeed without more armor, logistic stocks, mechanized mobility, air support, and air cover. Iran's leadership also seems to have realized that it had made Iran's defeats much worse by attempting to hold on too long to limited territorial gains without strategic meaning, and by committing untrained volunteer manpower with inadequate leadership and equipment to attacks with no goal short of total victory.

In any case, Iran used the period from May to September, 1984 to increase its efforts to obtain new heavy combat equipment, and to reorganize its popular and infantry forces to conduct more orderly and better structured mass attacks. Iran began to pay more attention to logistics and support, and built a series of improved military road and logistic storage areas, especially in the south. It concentrated on improving the training of its volunteers, and especially NCOs and junior officers.

Iran began to plan its assaults far more carefully and limited them to areas where it could infiltrate at night or take advantage of terrain and achieve limited gains. One typical instance was an attack on October 18th, when Iran tried to recover land on the Tigris plain that Iraq had taken at the start of the war. It advanced on a 12 mile front, and took full advantage of night and terrain. While Iraq retook some of the ground it had lost by October 20, this kind of Iranian attack gave the Iraqi serious defense problems because Iran could often seize a limited amount of territory and confront Iraq with the alternative of either ceding the loss or counterattacking and sustaining casualties for relatively unimportant objectives.

Iraq's Failure to Properly Improve Its Land Warfare Tactics

Iraq tried to counter these Iranian moves by continuing to build-up its fixed defenses, water barriers, cross-reinforcement capability, and logistic stocks. Iraq also made steadily better use of its massive superiority in firepower. In the process, however, Iraq made a major mistake. Iran's lack of success in its spring offensives convinced Iraq that Iran lacked the ability to score significant breakthroughs as long as Iraq could preserve its superiority in mass firepower and military technology.

While Iraq did launch some minor counterattacks during the remainder of 1984, most of these counterattacks were far more limited than Iraq claimed and few had more than minimal success. Iraq never came to grips with the problems inherent in using its superior firepower and mobility in offensive action or even large scale counterattacks. It also failed to improve its infantry assault, infiltration, and counter-infiltration tactics. Iraqi forces relied on fighting from fixed positions, and failed to improve its capability to fight and patrol in mountain areas and in the marshes in the South.

Iraq's fear of losses and over-confidence in its technology helped paralyze a critical part of Iraq's military development, and Iraq failed to exploit a key solution due to its lack of strategic depth. Iraq faced the strategic and tactical problem that it could not succeed in defeating Iran simply by staying in place, and could not force Iran to peace by taking Iranian territory. Iraq's only hope of defeating Iran on the ground was to inflict such massive casualties on Iranian troops that the resulting losses undercut popular support for continuing the war.

It is important to note that Iraq did not win the key battles in 1984, rather, Iran lost them. While Iran had suffered such losses in early 1984, they resulted as much from Iranian mistakes as from Iraqi tactics. Once Iran improved its tactics, Iraq could only inflict similar losses by using massive numbers of Iraqi ground forces. This meant Iraq had to conduct relatively deep counterattacks, and execute these counterattacks with great skill against Iranian land forces with a manpower superiority of 3-5:1. Iraq was not willing to take these political and military risks.

Iraq also failed to give the improvement of its infantry, rough terrain, and marshland/water barrier assault capabilities sufficient priority. Although Iraq did improve its ability to use its armor and helicopters in maneuver attacks during 1984, it still generally took casualties nearly equal to those of Iran whenever it attempted local counterattacks.

Iraq's Mixed Success In Improving Its Air War Capabilities

Iraq found its reliance on technology presented problems in other areas.

It lacked the numbers of modern Western fighters, the maritime patrol aircraft sensor and the target acquisition aircraft, and the fighter range and loiter capability to target and strike effectively at the high volume of shipping moving through Iranian waters. Less than 50% of Iraqi Exocet firings did serious damage to their target.[12] Iraq also found that while the Exocet was more lethal against ships than the AGM-65 Maverick air-to-surface missiles available to Iranian forces, the Exocet's warhead was still too small to do catastrophic damage to large tankers. This deprived Iraqi air-to-ship missile attacks of much of the shock value they might have had if entire ships and crews had been lost.

This experience was almost certainly a factor that led Iraq to increase its orders for additional Mirage F-1s equipped with extended range fuel tanks and capable of launching both Exocets and laser guided weapons.[13] However, Iraq also faced the problem that Iran was reducing its vulnerability. Iran started to tranship oil from Kharg Island to a loading point at Sirri Island, which was 250 miles southeast of Kharg and just northwest of Dubai. Iran also improved the tank farm on Sirri. Since the island was well outside the range of Iraqi aircraft, this reduced Iraq's ability to threaten foreign tankers.

In other areas of the air war, Iraq began to employ cluster bombs in close air support missions and steadily improved its sortie rates and mission effectiveness in support of its ground forces.[14] At the same time, Iraq did not improve the quality of its sporadic air and missile strikes against Iranian cities. This may have been because Iraq lacked the combination of aircraft and missile numbers, range, and payload to conduct successful mass attacks against the Iranian population and economic targets. Iraq also seems to have been unwilling to risk large numbers of aircraft in such attacks, however, perhaps because Iran could still fly fairly effective Combat Air Patrol (CAP) sorties and many Iranian targets had reasonably effective land-based air defenses.

Notes

[1] "Gulf War, Waiting for the Final Blow", *Jane's Defence Weekly*, October 18, 1986, pp. 848-849.
[2] Iranian reports sometimes refer to the Shatt as the "Arvand River" for propaganda purposes.
[3] *Observer*, 26 February, 1984, *Guardian*, *Telegraph*, March 2, 1984,
[4] "Gulf War, Waiting for the Final Blow", *Jane's Defence Weekly*, October 18, 1986, pp. 848-849.
[5] *Guardian* and *Times*, 2 and 3 March, 1984. *Observer* and *Sunday Times*, 4 March 1984
[6] John Laffin, *War Annual I*, London, Brassey's, 1986, pp. 80-82.
[7] By this time, Iran had been producing mustard gas at Samawah and nerve gas at Rutbah for about 18 months.
[8] *Times* 25 February, 1984; *Guardian*, 7 March, 1984; *Telegraph*, 12 and 26 March, 1986; and *Jane's Defence Weekly*, October 18, 1984, pp. 848-849.

[9] For an excellent and objective technical discussion see J. P. Perry Robinson, "Chemical and Biological Warfare: Developments in 1984", *World Armaments and Disarmament, SIPRI Yearbook, 1985*, Solna, Sweden, 1985, pp. 178-188 and 206-217. Also see Pearce Wright, Why Troops Still Have to Fear Mustard Gas", Science Report, *Times*, 6 March, 1984. Part of the confusion involved may have stemmed from the effects of mustard gas. Mustard gas or Lewisite often initially appears to be little more than a mild irritant because it acts as a vesicant or skin blistering agent. It sometimes takes hours before the lungs begin to blister and the skin deforms. Limited exposure produces very uncertain symptoms. Also see Gustav Anderson, "Analysis of two chemical weapons samples for the Iraq-Iran War," Peter Dunn, The Chemical War: Journey to Iran," and "Iran Keeps Chemical Options Open," *NBC Defense and Technology International*, April 1986, pp. 12-14, 28-38, and 62-65;

[10] See Jim Bussert," Iran-Iraq War Turns Strategic", *Defense Electronics*, September, 1984, pp. 134-136.

[11] Douglas Martin, "Iranian Jets Damage Japanese Tanker", *New York Times*, July 6, 1984, p. 3.

[12] See Nick Cook, Iraq-Iran The Air War", *International Defense Review*, November 1984, pp. 1605-1606

[13] Estimates of Iraqi Mirage F-1 holdings differ sharply. One French journalist estimated in October, 1985 that Iraq had taken delivery of as many as 87 regular Mirage F-1s by October 1, 1985, and was in the process of taking delivery on 24 more Mirage F-1s with extended range and the ability to use laser or optically guided smart bombs. This same journalist indicated that Iraq had ordered 24 additional such Mirages, and had take roughly four months of training and technical effort to learn how to use smart bombs before launching its August, 1985, attacks on Kharg Island. U.S. sources note that Thompson CSF has copied the laser illuminator and laser guided smart bomb technology the U.S. first employed in Vietnam, and that Iraq is now using this technology with one fighter illuminating the target and the other launching the laser guided bomb. This attack method is only highly effective because Iran lacks effective medium to long range air defense missiles and fighter cover.

[14] These seem to have been Chilean copies of U.S. bombs using stolen U.S. plans.

Chapter Four

The Fighting in 1985: Iraq's Improving Anti-Oil Capability, Iran's Improving Infantry Capability

These changes in Iranian and Iraqi tactics set the stage for 1985. Iran learned to conduct smaller offensives and accepted the need for careful planning of its major efforts. It stopped concentrating on a single part of the front, and deliberately struck at a wide range of areas – particularly in the North and South where the terrain and water barriers made it difficult for Iraq to achieve tactical warning or make use of its superior firepower. Iran also started to keep up constant pressure on Iraqi positions defending the Baghdad-Basra highway. The resulting fighting was particularly brutal in the Hawizah marshes, which cover much of the southern front above Basra.

Iran Resumes Its Major Offensives

On March 11, 1985, Iran attempted to take advantage of its improved training and preparations. It launched a major new offensive called "Fatima Zahra" north of Qurna.[1] This offensive was designed to seize Basra or cut it off from the rest of Iraq. The Iranian attack involved seven divisions and well over 100,000 men, including four-five divisions of Revolutionary Guards and volunteers.

Iran took full advantage of its growing experience in marsh warfare. During the previous six months, Iran had built up excellent lines of communication into the marshes, acquired large numbers of small craft, and systematically scouted out all of the routes through the marshes. It patrolled the marsh area aggressively, taking advantage of reeds that often reach 10 feet in height, and forced Iraq back to its fixed defenses on shore.

73

This improved preparation allowed Iran to succeed in crossing the Tigris in two places, and to briefly cut the highway from Basra to Baghdad nearest the border. Extremely bloody fighting took place on both sides. While the Iraqis never approached the point where they risked a major defeat, they fully committed their elite Republican Guard Division. Iraq also fully committed its air force for the time – flying as many as 150-250 sorties per day – and deployed massive artillery reinforcements. By the time the defensive battle was over, Iraq had committed a total force of roughly five divisions and 60,000 men. Both sides took very heavy casualties before Iran was driven back – Iraq lost up to 8,000-12,000 men and Iran lost 15,000-20,000.[2]

The net impact of this campaign was to reassure both sides that their land warfare tactics were successful. The Iranians were encouraged that they could overcome the effect of Iraq's lead in weapons and technology when they used proper tactics. While they did not see the offensive's failure as a victory, they did see it as successful in terms of relative attrition. They also became convinced that Iraq was vulnerable to small attacks which could maximize the value of night attacks, mountain warfare, or water barriers and rough terrain – the conditions where Iran could deny Iraq the ability to effectively use its armor, artillery, and sit behind its fixed defensive positions.

Nevertheless, serious divisions remained within the Iranian command. The regular forces tended to favor carefully planned offensives with systematic preparation, good logistic build-up, proper training, and limited tactical objectives. The Revolutionary Guards, and Iran's religious leadership, put more emphasis on surprise, ideological motivation, the use of popular volunteers, and human wave attacks. Iran's defeats of 1984 did not by any means create a unified view of how to fight the war, and the tension between the "professionals" and the "revolutionaries" was reflected in some of the statements of key Iranian commanders.

Iran's Chief of Staff, Colonel Ishmael Sohrabi, explained some of the rationale behind its new tactics as follows,

> Our blitzes are planned so as to make it hard for the enemy to redeploy its forces to the areas attacked. In our various operations, while we aim to avoid sustaining heavy casualties, we seek to surprise the enemy and to wear him out psychologically...We wish to render it almost impossible for enemy commanders to plan properly; our operations enable our men to fight an enemy with superior hardware.

In contrast, Mohsen Rezai, the commander of the Pasdaran stated,

> This tactic has not replaced our previous ones. It keeps the enemy constantly entangled. This strengthens our main tactic, which is launching big and determined operations[3]

The Fighting in 1985   75

Escalating Air and Missile Combat

Iraq, in turn, concluded that its basic strategy and tactics were correct, and that it could rely on technology and fixed defenses. This still reinforced Iraq's mistakes in interpreting the lessons of the fighting in 1984. Iraq continued to fight relatively passively, failed to increase its infantry and assault capability, and concentrated on increasing its reliance on technology.

Iraq stepped up its air strikes against urban and oil targets. Between January 1 and March 31, 1985 Iraq hit roughly 30 ships while Iran hit seven. This brought the total strikes in the "tanker war" to 65 Iraqi and 25 Iranian attacks since the March, 1984, offensive. Iraq also launched a series of large scale air and missile strikes against Iranian cities, launching as many as 158 air strikes over a three-day period in March, hitting nearly 30 towns and cities, and striking as deep as Tehran.

Iran retaliated with Scud B strikes against Iraqi cities, using Libyan-supplied missiles. While the Scud only had a 453 kg warhead, and was not particularly lethal in area fire against cities, its 300 km range did allow Iran to make at least symbolic strikes against Baghdad and Iran seems to have targeted most of the missiles against the Ministry of Defense.

As a result, most of the Scud hits did occur inside Baghdad, and at least some of the Scud attacks were lucky enough to hit targets. These attacks continued well into May, and killed up to several hundred people, but neither side's strikes at population centers had much political or economic impact once their initial shock wore off. Nevertheless, both sides continued their attacks on civil targets until yet another temporary ceasefire was declared on June 30th.[4]

Iraq launched another major raid on Kharg Island on May 30th. While Iraq did not repeat this attack for several months, and the attack seems to have done little more than start new fires in the Island's sixty square mile tank farm, the new strike was the first successful one since June, 1984.

Iraq also started to enjoy more consistent success in its few air-to-air encounters with Iran. Iraq relegated its Soviet aircraft largely to the bombing and close air support role, and relied on its Mirage F-1s. About this time, Iraqi pilots also began to make extensive use of Matra 530 air-to-air missiles in addition to the Magic 1. By mid-1985, Iraq claimed to have shot down 12-14 F-14 fighters, and while these claims were exaggerated, Iraq did find that its use of modern Western IR (infrared) air-to-air missiles allowed it to achieve reasonably high kill ratios.

The Beginning of Covert U.S. Arms Sales to Iran

Iraq did not, however, solve several basic problems in its use of airpower which continued to limit the effectiveness of Iraqi forces well into 1987. It rarely carried out proper reconnaissance and target analysis. It did not use its reconnaissance aircraft aggressively and was very slow to respond to either new photo reconnaissance data or to calls for battlefield and interdiction support from the army. It never really decided on the proper interface between artillery, attack helicopters, and fighters, and never demonstrated that it could mass its air strength against key strategic targets long enough and consistently enough to have proper effect.

It also could not cope with Iran's target mix. Iran conducted much of its exposed movement at night when Iraqi aircraft were "blind". It learned to create extensive shelters and dugouts and its troops learned how to "dig in" in virtually any terrain. It rarely massed conspicuous amounts of armor or other heavy equipment, and even its bridges consisted of easily replacable power pontoons.

These Iranian tactics sharply reduced Iraqi targeting opportunities and the value of armed reconnaissance flights over the battlefield. Much of the time, Iraq was forced to hazard its few experienced pilots, and fighters costing tens of millions of dollars, to try and find and kill a few exposed vehicles or infantry men. While Iraq was often criticized for not pressing home its air attacks, much of this criticism ignored the question of "With what value and at what cost?" Iraq never found an effective answer.

It was also during this period, that the U.S. quietly made a decision that was to eventually to lead to the Iranian arms sale scandals of 1986 and 1987. In a series of exchanges which have still not been fully explained, several Israeli officials and U.S. consultants outside the government helped persuade the senior officials of the U.S., and the Director of the Central Intelligence Agency, that it might be possible to rebuild American political ties with "moderates" in the Iranian government, and to free American's held hostage by pro-Iranian Shi'ite factions in Lebanon.

This followed a reappraisal of U.S. policy towards Iran that had begun in late 1984, when the National Security Council (NSC) issued a National Security Study Directive (NSSD). The resulting study concluded that there were no new options for rebuilding U.S. ties to Iran. Senior members of the National Security Council staff then sought independent advice. In May, 1985, this resulted in a five page memo from the CIA National Intelligence Officer on the Middle East that argued the U.S. should permit allies to sell arms to Iran to counterbalance Soviet efforts to gain influence in Iran.[5]

Using this paper, indirect inputs from Iranian middlemen, Israeli arguments, and the views of private consultants, two members of the National Security Council – Howard Teicher and Donald Fartier – staff then began to prepare a draft National Security Decision Directive (NSDD) arguing that the U.S. should take short and long term initiatives to reestablish relations with Iran to counterbalance what they felt was growing Soviet influence in Iran. These options included providing limited shipments of U.S. arms to Iran in an effort to open up lines of communication to the more "moderate" factions and deal with the hostage problem.

The background to the CIA paper and NSC action is complex and some aspects are still uncertain. The U.S. had long realized that Israel was making low level shipments of arms to Iran. The U.S. rejected quiet Israeli arguments that these shipments were of strategic value to the West, made some objections to these shipments. At the same time, U.S. officials tolerated them in part because of its hope that this might moderate Iran's conduct in sponsoring radical groups in Lebanon, and in part because it felt that keeping any line of communication open to Iran's leadership might be useful.[6]

Israel had resumed its efforts to persuade the U.S. to join it in such initiatives and capitalized on the seizure of William Buckley, the CIA station chief in Beirut on March 16, 1984. This provided what some NSC staff members regarded as further evidence that U.S. counterterrorism efforts could not suppress the activities of pro-Iranian groups in Lebanon or win the release of the U.S. citizens they had captured.

Michael Ledeen, a consultant to the NSC also visited Israel in 4-5 May, 1985 and talked to senior Israeli officials about Iran, including Prime Minister Shimon Peres and senior members of Israeli intelligence. It is still unclear whether Ledeen did this as the result of prior contacts with Israeli officials, or contacts with European intelligence officers, and whether he acted at the formal request of National Security Advisor Robert McFarlane.

The end result, however, was that Ledeen briefed McFarlane in mid-May, 1985 and that McFarlane tasked the intelligence community with producing a Special National Intelligence Estimate (SNIE) on Iran on May 20, 1985. While Secretary of State George Shultz formally objected to Ledeen's activities on June 5, 1985 – and McFarlane advised Shultz on June 14th that he had instructed him to discourage any arms sale initiative – the work on the NSDD still proceeded.

Then, on June 14, 1985, a TWA airliner, Flight 847, was hijacked. While President Reagan gave a speech calling Iran part of a "confederation of terrorist states" and "a new international version of Murder Incorporated," the NSC staff concluded that there was little punitive action the U.S. could take.[7] The resulting discussions of what Israel could do to help also brought the Iranian issue to the attention of President's Chief of Staff, Donald Regan. The whole issue of how Iran should be treated then steadily became one which was handled at the political level, as distinguished from the foreign policy level.

McFarlane transmitted the draft NSDD recommending both the option of arms sales and of intelligence to Secretary of State George Shultz and Secretary of Defense Caspar Weinberger on June 17, 1987.[8] Both

Secretaries rejected the NSC argument, which Shultz stated was "perverse" and contrary to American interests, and which Weinberger termed "almost too ridiculous to comment upon."[9] At this point, however, the problem of American hostages began to take steadily greater precedence over strategic considerations, a trend that was steadily reinforced by each hostage incident, particularly when Syria informed the U.S. in late 1985 that Buckley had been tortured and killed.

Israel also took several strong initiatives to support a U.S. initiative towards Iran. David Kimche, Director General of Israel's Foreign Ministry, had indirectly been pushing the idea of a U.S. initiative towards Iran since at least the early fall of 1984, and on July 3, 1985, he visited the White House and asked McFarlane to take up the proposal again, stating that his request was on the instructions of Shimon Peres. A "private emissary" from Israel visited McFarlane on July 13. The next day McFarlane sent Shultz another cable supporting the Iran initiative, and indicating that it might help the seven U.S. hostages in Lebanon. This led Shultz to immediately reply that the U.S. should show interest without formally supporting any action and that McFarlane should take the initiative.

While there are conflicts in the testimony, it was at this point (July 13-17th) that McFarlane visited President Reagan, who had just had an operation, in the hospital. This conversation was taken, rightly or wrongly, as approval of covert contacts with Iran. These contacts were simultaneously being supported by two private arms dealers, a Saudi named Adnan Khashoggi and an Iranian named Manucher Ghorbanifar – sometimes described as an advisor to Iran's Prime Minister. Further, an Israeli arms dealer, Al Schwimmer, was introduced to McFarlane by Ledeen at the suggestion of David Kimche.

This ultimately led Ledeen to meet in Israel in late July with Kimche, Ghorbanifar, Schwimmer, and another Israeli arms dealer, Yaacov Nimrodi – an ex-Israeli military attache to Iran.[10] The end result was to propose new contacts with Iran and trading the sale of U.S. TOW anti-tank and Hawk anti-air missiles for the U.S. hostages. This finally led to a meeting in the White House on August 6, 1985, where President Reagan presided. Although the details are unclear, it is clear that the key issue was whether to trade arms for hostages and that CIA Director William Casey, Donald Regan, and Vice President Bush supported the arms initiative and that Secretaries Shultz and Weinberger opposed it.

The meeting does not seem to have had a formal outcome, but the practical result was that Israel felt it obtained authority from the NSC on August 30th to sell 508 TOW missiles to Iran, which the U.S. would replace. The first 100 missiles arrived in Iran on August 30, 1985 and the remaining 400 on September 14, 1985.[11]

This arms transfer helped lead to the release of one U.S. hostage –

Reverend Benjamin Weir – on September 14th, but the sale did not lead to the broader release of U.S. hostages that the White House officials expected. In fact, Iran established a pattern that it was to repeat in 1986, when the U.S. shipped arms directly to Iran. Iran released one hostage, but kept the others to retain its leverage over the United States. Iran repeated this pattern when it released Reverend Lawrence Jenco on July 26, 1986 and David P. Jacobsen on November 2, 1986.

On each of these subsequent occasions, the pro-Iranian groups in Lebanon carried out only one-third to one-half the releases the U.S. expected, and Iran seems to have encouraged such groups to take new hostages in compensation. By the time the covert U.S. arms deals became public in early November, 1986, pro-Iranian groups had as many U.S. hostages as they did before the arms deal.[12]

Iran's Broader Problems With Military Supply

The covert U.S. sales to Iran did, however, do a great deal to reduce the impact of "Operation Staunch," the U.S. effort to restrict arms deliveries to Iran which the U.S. had made its declared policy in 1983. The covert U.S. sales began at a time when the Iranian leadership desperately needed some indication it could get the arms it needed to continue the war. Iran was no longer able to get as many U.S. parts as it had obtained in 1979-1981. Although it had spent some $7-8 billion on arms, Iran also could not get a balanced mix of U.S. supplies from the commercial or illegal arms markets. It was often short of critical parts and items for its U.S. aircraft, missiles, and armor that only the U.S. or a few other governments supply.[13]

There also were no easy or effective substitutes for such supplies. Iran had received some $1.5 billion in arms from the PRC between 1979 and the beginning of 1984. It also had spent billions of dollars on purchases from nations as diverse as Israel, North Korea, Taiwan, Ethiopia, Brazil, Syria, Argentina, Libya, Belgium, France, the Netherlands, Portugal, and Austria. Nevertheless, it could not get the U.S. parts and arms it needed for its largely U.S. equipped force structure.

In one case, Iran may even have been desperate enough to buy back arms that had been captured by Iraq. These arms consisted of M-48 tanks that Iraq put on the world market because it could not get ammunition and spares. Arab and Swiss arms dealers then sold them to Iran for $100 million, netting a $10 million profit on the deal. Iran also came close to buying 150 self-propelled 155 mm howitzers from Belgium, that were to be sold through Syria, at a cost of $800,000 a gun. According to some reports, Iran only cancelled the deal when the price rose towards $1 million. Iran was paying almost two and one-half times the world market price for most of its U.S. types of arms and ammunition.[14]

The one major deal that Iran was able to negotiate for U.S. weapons, aside from its purchases from Israel and the U.S., may have been with Vietnam. The government of Vietnam seems to have signed a $400 million deal with Iran in July, 1985, to sell 80 M-48 tanks, 200 M-113 APCs, 12 F-5 fighters, 12 Cobra Gunships, Sidewinder missiles, and large amounts of captured U,S. parts and ammunition it acquired as the result of its defeat of South Vietnam. Some of this equipment was new – the F-5 fighters were still in crates – but deliveries were slow and the Vietnamese sales could not provide the range and types of parts and equipment to repair and sustain most of Iran's U.S.-equipped forces.[15]

The covert arms deals thus gave Iran good reason to believe that U.S. policy was uncertain and opportunistic. Iran also found it could improve its access to other suppliers as they gradually became aware that U.S. controls were weakening. While the exact pattern in arms flows is uncertain, it is clear that Israel stepped up its other arms sales to Iran to the point where they totalled around $500 million in value by mid-1986. It is also possible that that other Western nations such as Greece, Spain, and Portugal became more willing to expand their arms shipments.[16]

Iraq's Improving Effectiveness in Attacking Iran's Oil Facilities

The arms transfer also signalled the beginning of a period in which U.S. policy towards Iran and Iraq was in nearly complete disarray. The regular U.S. foreign policy system continued to tilt towards Iraq, tried to halt arms transfers to Iran , and quietly gave Iraq intelligence. At the same time, a few officials in the NSC and CIA began to run a major covert operation tilting towards Iran that was implemented largely by middlemen and Israeli agents.

These events, however, did not have any apparent impact on the battlefield. The fighting on the ground died down to the levels which had been common in the latter part of 1984. This still meant serious clashes involving thousands of men. Low level fighting killed about 100 men a day on the southern front, much of it occurring in the marsh areas. Similar fighting occurred on the northern sector of the front, and one Iranian attack produced over 2,000 Iranian casualties in a single day in mid-July.

While Iran did not score any major gains in the south, Iran does seem to have gained about 80-140 square miles in the central and northern sectors by mid-August, most of it in small scattered attacks. Iran also began to patrol more aggressively in the Gulf, inspecting occasional freighters and making new threats to halt any traffic being transhipped to Iraq. Iraq responded with naval artillery fire against the offshore wells and facilities in Iran's Cyrus oil field.

The next major shift in the war occurred in mid-August and took the form of new Iraqi attacks on Kharg Island. The raids began on August 14th, with another major attack on August 25th, and set the pattern for consistent follow-on attacks throughout 1985. While the August attacks did not damage Iran's newly repaired Sea Island terminal, they did seriously damage the main offshore loading point or "T-Jetty". This temporarily cut Kharg's export capacity by about 30%.

The new series of Iraqi air strikes involved a change in Iraqi aircraft, tactics, and training. Indian and French experts had steadily improved Iraq's altitude attack training and planning. Iraq also took delivery of new versions of the Mirage F-1 which could launch the Exocet missile and which could be refueled over Iraq before they struck at Iran. This greatly extended the operational range of the Iraqi F-1s, and led Iraq to return the Super Etendards it had borrowed to France.

Every improvement in Iraqi fighter range proved to be important. Although Kharg is only about 140 miles south of the Iraqi coast, it is still close to the range limit of fully loaded Iraqi fighters flying low altitude attack profiles from Iraq's main air bases. (The total flight distance using Lo-Lo-Hi profiles is about 340 miles.) Sirri and Larak – the islands at the eastern end of Iran's tanker shuttle – are just barely within the range of Mirages flying fuel-saving high altitude profiles with maximum external fuel.

Kharg was also a particularly important target. Nearly 90% of Iran's wartime oil exports have been loaded from the island, but Kharg is a very difficult target to destroy. The island is comparatively large (20 miles wide by 40 miles long). It has good low altitude AA (anti aircraft) gun defenses and Hawk surface-to-air missile defenses. Its main pipelines and oil facilities are well dispersed, highly redundant, and often buried or sheltered. Oil flows to Kharg from the mainland through buried underwater pipelines and largely under natural pressure. Iran does not require the large vulnerable surface facilities like desalinization plants and gas-oil separators common in the Southern Gulf.[17]

As a result, only the tanker loading facilities on the Island present high pay-off air targets for attack by fighters. These facilities include the "T-Jetty" on the Island's eastern side, and the much smaller "J-Jetty" or Sea Island loading facility on the western side. Even these targets, however, are comparatively small and were well defended with Hawk and other surface-to-air missiles and AA guns. Accordingly, Iraq's only real hope of success was to commit large numbers of aircraft in the face of high probable losses, or to acquire modern fighters with sophisticated air attack munitions and to strike at the "T-Jetty" with considerable accuracy.

The precise munitions Iraq used in its August 14th and 25th attacks on Kharg are unclear. It is clear, however, that Iraq flew at least two comparatively large attack waves, and that its strikes were more accurate than in previous attacks. While some reports claimed Iraq used "some 100,000 pounds of bombs", Iraq did not have anything like this pay load delivery capability. There is also good reason to believe that Iraq may have begun to use the French AS-30 air-to-surface laser guided missile and radar homing missiles during this period.

Reports differ on whether the Iraqis attacked on 14 August using two or four waves of aircraft, but some reports indicated the first wave used a variety of French and Soviet ECM (electronic countermeasures) and anti-radiation missiles to suppress the Hawk and Shilka surface-to-air missiles. The succeeding waves seem to have launched stand-off missiles at ranges of 6-8 kilometers. Iraqi fighters also seem to have fired Brandt 68 mm pre-fragmented or dart rockets.[18]

One factor that makes it possible that Iraq began to use anti-radiation missiles is the exceptional lack of response from Iranian air defenses. The factors that indicate Iraq then used AS-30 missiles in its attacks on the oil facilities are the accuracy with which Iraqi aircraft hit the Western jetties and control facility, and the size of the explosions. The AS-30 has a 240 kg warhead, flies at less than 100 meters above the surface, and is much more effective against hard targets than unguided rockets. The AS-30 and its associated Atlis laser designator pods are known to have been delivered to Iraq in November, 1984, and Iraqi pilots were trained in France during this period.[19]

In any case, Iraqi fighters hit Kharg with a total four large scale raids between mid-August and the beginning of September, and Iran responded by stepping up its use of its navy to harass Gulf shipping. By early September, 1985, a total of more than 130 ships had been attacked by both sides since start of the "tanker war" in March, 1984.

Iran Makes Little Progress On the Land but Maintains Its Ability to Export

Iran responded with still more threats to attack ships going to Southern Gulf ports and then launched a new offensive against Iraqi positions in Majnoon. This attack took place early in the morning of September 11, 1985. Pasdaran forces took advantage of night and surprise, and special commandos forces were able to take control of the western sector of the Islands. Only a major counterattack by the Iraqi Third Corps and the Al-Hussein Corps, a special Presidential unit, kept Iran from seizing all of Majnoon and gaining a new foothold to attack Basra.[20]

Iran did, however, succeed in making limited gains in other small attacks to the north, in the Neimak region of Bakhtaran province. Iran captured part of a 180 square mile area in Iraqi Kurdistan, west of the Iranian town of Piranshahr, about 370 miles North of Tehran. Both sides lost at least 2,000 men during this fighting in the course of one 10 hour encounter, and Iraq and Iran may each have lost as many as 2,500 men a day during this period. The overall loses on both sides seem to have been about the same.[21]

Iraq continued its attacks on Kharg and Iran's oil exports in spite of the new Iranian offensives. Its attacks succeeded in reducing Iran's exports, but it did not halt them. Part of the problem Iraq faced lay in the number of loading points involved. Kharg was designed for a maximum loading capacity of 6.5 MMBD, and had actually loaded a maximum of 6 MMBD before the war.

By this point in the conflict, the "oil glut" was reducing Iranian daily loadings to 1.5-2.0 MMBD, and Iran had facilities for 14 small to medium sized tankers on the east side of the Island, and for 20 tankers on the Western side – including 3 supertankers. A well sheltered computerized switching facility allowed Iran to avoid oil spills and rapidly shift from one loading point to another. The loading points targets were also relatively easy to repair and this made it very difficult for Iraq to achieve enough damage to really halt Iranian exports.[22]

Nevertheless, Iraq kept up constant pressure on Kharg Island. On September 12, 1985 – the day after Iran attacked the Iraqi positions at Majnoon – the Iraqi air force launched its ninth major attack on Kharg since mid-August. Each Iraqi attack did, however, tend to become more difficult. Iran re-organized its air defenses on the Island, and shot down several Iraqi Mirage F-1s. Iraq also seems to have suffered higher losses because of the relatively low quality electronic countermeasure equipment it could obtain from the USSR and Western Europe.

Iraq had been able to benefit from surprise during its first major attacks on Kharg in 1985. Its fighters flew at extremely low altitudes and then suddenly popped up to attack Iranian air defenses. According to some Western sources, this allowed Iraqi planes to directly over fly Iran's surface-to-air missiles for optimal ECM effectiveness and to fire their ARMs (anti radiation missiles) against targets with fully active radars.

Iran, however, seems to have improved its ECCM techniques (the Hawk is a very difficult system to jam), and to have adopted radar emission tactics that made Iraqi ARM strikes more difficult to target. Iran also seems to have strengthened its SHORAD (short -range air defense) defenses in order to force Iraqi fighters to fly at higher altitudes, and learned to identify the flight profiles of the fighters illuminating targets on Kharg. This reflected Iran's comparatively high level of technical capability, something it had demonstrated earlier by using radar reflectors or decoys to discourage AM-39 attacks on ships at Kharg, and in modifications to some of its key oil facilities to reduce their radar return.[23]

This gradual strengthening of Iranian capabilities may also have been related to the covert arms shipments authorized by the U.S. However, the timing of any such impact is uncertain. A shipment of Hawk missiles and Hawk parts went by plane from Israel to Iran in November, 1985. The flight was authorized by Lt. Colonel Oliver North, of the NSC. Virtually all of the shipment seems to have been returned, however, because Israeli middlemen substituted older parts and missiles, and sent equipment for the regular Hawk missile, rather than the improved Hawks in Iranian forces.[24]

In any case, Iran's defenses did not improve enough to force Iraq to halt its attacks. Iraq continued its attacks on Kharg in spite of their loss in individual effectiveness, and in spite of new Iranian pressure on the Northern front, and new Iranian threats and naval maneuvers at the mouth of the Gulf. Iraq's persistence also paid off. While Iraq took added losses, it scored new successes in damaging the loading terminals on September 27th and October 3rd. By early November, Iraq had reduced Iran's shipments via its tanker shuttle to Sirri by 30-50%, and Iran had been forced to draw down on its limited strategic reserve (about 15 million barrels) in tanks on Sirri, and the 250,000 additional barrels it could ship from its southern fields at Lavan.

Iran responded by trying to find other means of exporting oil. It negotiated a new agreement with Turkey which was formalized on January 8, 1986. Turkey agreed to take deliveries of 100,000 BPD of Iranian oil for domestic use and to supply Iran with manufactured and agricultural goods. This agreement, however, could do little to provide the volume of oil trade Iran needed.

Accordingly, Iran bought new offshore mooring buoys to load 300,000-400,000 BPD at two points northwest of Kharg to ensure that it could continue to operate its oil "ferry" to Sirri Island. Iran also announced plans to open a new port at Ganaveh (northeast of Kharg), to build pipelines to Lavan Island or Jask near the Straits of Hormuz, and to rush efforts to build new pipeline links from the pumping station at Gurreh to Bushehr and Asaluyeh – although it later became apparent that such plans were far more costly than Iran had initially estimated and that Iran lacked the resources to finance such pipelines.[25]

One of Iraq's major strategic failings throughout the Iran-Iraq war was its failure to use its airpower long enough and consistently enough to have any real effect. This time, however, Iraq gave Iran no chance to recover. By late December 1985, Iraq had conducted nearly 60 major air strikes against Kharg. Iran could do little more than respond with more rhetoric about alternative methods of exporting its oil. It announced it was opening its new loading facilities at Ganaveh, and would soon issue contracts for a pipeline to Jask. Iran even went so far as to indicate it planned to "abandon" Kharg for the war's duration, although such plans were more ambitious than real.[26]

The "Year of the Pilot"

Iran had few military options. It could only retaliate against the shipping to Iraq in the form of harassment. It stepped up its search of ships moving through the Gulf in September. It intercepted nearly 300 cargo ships during the month of October, although this had little practical effect. While both sides continued to strike at the other's shipping, it was Iraq that scored virtually all the hits. This helped raised the number of ships hit, damaged, or attacked since the first attack on Gulf shipping began in May, 1981 to nearly 200 by the end of 1985. Over 150 of these attacks had occurred since the "tanker war" began, March, 1984.[27]

Iraq became so confident during this period that it declared that 1985 was the "year of the pilot". It claimed to have flown 20,011 missions against Iran, 77 destructive raids against Kharg Island, and to have scored 124 effective hits on "hostile" maritime targets. An Iraqi military spokesman also claimed that Iran had lost 38,303 dead.[28]

Iraq seemed to have reason for its confidence, particularly because the world oil market appeared to be giving its military efforts new impetus. Iran's oil exports not only dropped in size, but each barrel was worth less on the world market. By early 1986, Iraq's repeated raids on Kharg and Iran's shuttle tankers began to have a major effect on Iran's income. Saudi Arabia then increased its oil production in an effort to increase Saudi revenues. The resulting crash in world oil prices cut Iran's average oil income by nearly two-thirds.

As the year closed, Iraq seemed to have succeeded in both checking Iran's efforts at winning a war of attrition and in putting major financial pressure on Iran. Iraq then recaptured the southern half of one of the Majnoon Islands, and stepped up its use of helicopters and fighters in providing close air support. Iraq also seems to have begun to use a new air-to-surface rockets with anti-personnel bomblets.

On the surface, Iran's response to these Iraqi successes seemed limited. Iran did not launch any major new offensives. It instead again tried to put pressure on the southern Gulf states. In December, Iranian sponsored terrorists conducted a series of car-bombs against the U.S. Embassy and other targets in Kuwait. These attacks were part of a broader Iranian effort to persuade Kuwait to reduce its aid to Iraq. Kuwait, however, stood firm, and Iraq responded by launching a series of five missile attacks against Iranian towns. This led to a new series of air and missile exchanges against civil targets that lasted into February, 1986. Iraq was still launching missile strikes against Dezful on 11 February 1986.

Notes

¹ It is often difficult to be precise about the names of given attacks. Iran often gives names or numbers to relatively small attacks, or even to changes in a battle. It is quick to rename or renumber any attack that follows a tactical defeat.

² *Economist*, March 30, 1985, p. 47; *Jane's Defence Weekly*, March 30, 1985, p. 532 . Other sources report Iranian losses of 30,000 and Iraqi losses of 10,000. *Washington Post*, February 11, 1986.

³ *Middle East Review*, 1986, London, World Almanac Publications, 1986, pp. 110-111.

⁴ Ibid. Also see *The Middle East*, May, 1985, pp. 16-18; *Washington Post*, May 27, and July 21, 1985, *New York Times*, May 29, and June 13, 1985; *Economist*, June 22, 1985, p. 35.

⁵ Unless otherwise referenced, this and all the following references to the history of U.S. covert arms sales to Iran are based upon the chronology in the unclassified version of the *Report on Preliminary Inquiry* of the Senate Select Committee on Intelligence, January 29, 1987, and the *New York Times* edition of the *Tower Commission Report*, New York, Bantam and Times Books, February 1987.

⁶ McFarlane later testified that he had asked the CIA if Israel was shipping arms to Iran and that the CIA denied it. His Deputy, Admiral John Poindexter seems to have been fully aware of Israel's interests. *Report on Preliminary Inquiry* of the Senate Select Committee on Intelligence, January 29, 1987, p. 2; *Tower Commission Report*, pp.16-29 and 102-147.

⁷ *Washington Post*, July 8, 1985, and December 7, 1986, and U.S. Senate Committee on Intelligence, *Report on Preliminary Inquiry*, January 28, 1987, p. 4.

⁸ *Washington Post*, December 7, 1986, p. A-25.

⁹ *Report on Preliminary Inquiry* of the Senate Select Committee on Intelligence, January 29, 1987, pp. 1-2; *Tower Commission Report*, New York, Bantam and Times Books, 1987, pp. 23-26.

¹⁰ It later became clear that these later three individuals had been discussing and Iranian initiative since mid-1984.

¹¹ *Report on Preliminary Inquiry* of the Senate Select Committee on Intelligence, January 29, 1987, pp. 4-8; *Tower Commission Report* pp. 28-31.

¹² Fred Reed was abducted on September 9, 1986 and Joseph James Cicippio on September 12th. Edward Austin Tracy was taken on October 21, 1986. In all three cases the U.S. State Department identified pro-Iranian radical groups as being responsible. The net result neatly balanced out the total hostage releases. *Washington Post*, December 7, 1986, p. A-25; *Tower Commission Report*, pp. 153-334 for full details.

¹³ As later became clear, Iran often was getting obsolete parts from various suppliers. This contrasted sharply from 1981, when Israel was still afraid of an Iraqi victory and shipped up to $135 million worth of critical items. The *Observer* (1 December 1986) estimates that Israel signed a contract with Iran in July, 1981, that included such critical items as 40 155 mm field guns, 68 Hawk missiles, M-48 tanks, and possibly 50 Lance missiles and 3,730 Copperhead laser guided 155 mm artillery shells. *Washington Times*, December 1, 1986, p. 9A. Reports of these sales later led to claims that Secretary of State Alexander Haig at least informally approved the sale, although Haig denied that such advanced technology weapons were shipped and that he gave any "green light" to such sales.

¹⁴ James Bruce, "Iran: The Price of An Arms Embargo", *Jane's Defence Weekly*, November 29, 1986, pp. 1256-1258; and Elaine Sciolino, "Iran, in Six Year Search for Arms, Finds World of Willing Suppliers", *New York Times*, November 25, 1986.

¹⁵ *Jane's Defence Weekly*, November 29, 1986, pp. 1256-1258.

¹⁶ *Jane's Defence Weekly*, November 29, 1986, pp. 1256-1258 and *Washington Post*, December 7, 1986, p. A-25. France's Prime Minister Jaques Chirac later indicated that Iran had made somewhat similar arms for hostages initiatives, and had rejected them. Most French sales to Iran during this period seem to have consisted of large artillery shipments which were made before France's conservative government came back to power and which may have been

made without the full knowledge of the French government. *Washington Post*, December 1, 1986, p. A-7.

[17] *New York Times*, *Baltimore Sun*, and *Wall Street Journal*, August 16 and 17, 1985.

[18] See Gwynne Dyer, "The Gulf: Too Late for a Crisis", *Washington Times*, November 6, 1985.

[19] See Kenneth R. Timmerman, "Mirage Over Kharg", *Defense and Armaments*, No. 44, October, 1985, pp. 53-58.

[20] "Gulf War, Waiting for the Final Blow", *Jane's Defence Weekly*, October 18, 1986, pp. 848-849.

[21] *New York Times*, September 10, 1985, *Chicago Tribune* and *Christian Science Monitor*, September 9 and 11, 1985.

[22] *Chicago Tribune* and *New York Times*, September 3, 1985, *Washington Times*, September 4, 1985.

[23] Ibid, and *New York Times*, September 10, 12, and 21, 1985.

[24] *Washington Post*, December 7, 1986.

[25] As has been discussed earlier, the NIOC announced that it had designated three new terminals at Jask, Qeshem, and Lengeh, as well as new loading points at Ganaveh and Kangan/Asaluyeh. The problem Iran faced was that its new mooring points could not be installed with the speed it needed and would still be dependent on facilities at Ganaveh, which proved vulnerable to Iraqi air attacks. While Gurreh is the logical starting point for new pipelines to the east, it too is vulnerable to air attack.

This is why Iran was forced to consider a new set of facilities which would ship through a nearly 1,000 mile pipeline to the south eastern cost. Iran completed plans, and got initial bids from Daewo of South Korea and JCG of Japan in October-December, 1985. Iran then, however, faced three major problems: the cost of the pipeline reached nearly $1.5-2 billion, rather than the $700-900 million originally estimated, the completion time for the new line was at least 12-15 months to build, and Iran faced the risk that its collection and pumping facilities at the pipeline's point of origin would still be vulnerable.

In February, this mix of cost, time, and vulnerability problems combined with a new problems – the sudden crash in world oil prices triggered by a Saudi Arabia in an effort to stop acting as OPEC's swing state and to make massive increases in oil production in order to boost its oil income. This combination of problems forced Iran to indefinitely defer its plans for a new pipeline. Similar factors led Iran to defer the idea of new high capacity pipeline to the Mediterranean through Turkey, a pipeline which had an estimated cost of over $10 billion. In contrast, Iraq already had found funding for a further expansion of its pipelines through Turkey to increase their capacity by about 500,000 BPD during the course of 1986-1987.

[26] *Chicago Tribune*, December 30, 1985; *New York Times*, December 30, 1985.

[27] *Los Angeles Times* and *Washington Post*, September 7, 1985.

[28] *Jane's Defence Weekly*, 18 January, 1986, p. 43

Chapter Five

The Fighting in 1986: Iran Strikes Back

In spite of its reverses, Iran's ambitions to topple Sadam Hussein's regime had only increased. During 1985, Iran quietly bought large numbers of small boats, bridging equipment, and pontoons . In the late summer and fall of 1985, it began major amphibious training exercises in the Caspian. Iran also bought chemical defense equipment, and indications began to appear in late 1985, that Syria was providing Iran with aid in developing its own chemical warfare agents. The ground fighting remained limited through the end of 1985, but Iran sent more volunteers to the front in December. It called up at least 50,000 new volunteers and some estimates went as high as 300,000-500,000.[1]

Iran Prepares to Assault the Faw Peninsula

While Iraq's air strikes captured world attention during the latter half of 1985, Iran was conducting an impressive engineering effort in the south. Iran gradually built a major military road system on earth mounds through the marshes and flood areas along the Shatt al-Arab south of Abadan. It managed to make more of its helicopters operational, and began to use them more aggressively . For example, it set up a helicopter support facility on an oil platform in the Gulf at Rostam, about 75 miles east of Qatar and 30 miles north of Halal Island – where Qatar has an offshore crude oil processing plant and 50 miles from Dal Island, where the UAE (United Arab Emirates) has gas and oil installation. Iran used this platform for as many as 15 attacks on shipping during late 1985 and early 1986.[2]

Most importantly, Iran improved its amphibious capabilities south of Abadan and stockpiled large amounts of small craft and pontoon bridging equipment. It created amphibious commando units of roughly 1,000 men who were specially trained for amphibious assaults and fighting in wetlands, and which had an effective command structure similar to that of airborne or special forces units.

Iran also improved the training of its volunteer forces, gave them steadily more effective small unit leadership, and improved the battle management capability of its revolutionary command.

As early as mid-1985, Iranian troops began to systematically infiltrate the marsh area of the Southern Front, and gradually came to dominate the complex waterways and low "islands" of the marsh area. Iraq responded by trying to cut down the reeds in the marsh area to deny Iranian troops cover, and built 30-40 feet-high watch towers with night vision devices and acoustic sensors to try to provide warning of Iranian action.

Nevertheless, Iraq lost the battle for control of the marshes and waters of the Shatt al-Arab. The Iranians came to dominate the Hawizah marshes and increased their patrols off the Iraqi shore of the Shatt. As a result, Iran both improved its ability to attack north of Basra and developed the ability to support a major offensive south of Basra. By January, Iran was ready to launch a new series of offensives.[3]

Iran also outbid and outplayed Iraq in gaining the support of the Kurds. Iran had the manpower and ethnic unity to put down any Kurdish resistance. At the same time, it was more than willing to encourage Kurdish nationalism as long as its target was Iraq, and Iran's victories in the north had put Iran in the position to give the Barzani faction of Iraq's Kurds considerable military support. The Barzani-led KDP was able to steadily increase its raids throughout 1985 and early 1986, and its main rival – the PUK – finally decided not to reach a new autonomy agreement with Baghdad.

Only strong Turkish threats to cut trade kept Iran from exploiting Kurdish separatism in the areas near Iraq's pipelines through Turkey, and the Turkish Third Army was still forced to deploy some 20,000 men in the border area. Iraq withdrew some of its troops in the area in late 1985 to strengthen its position in the south, and its only option was to arm the Christian villagers in the area. This left Iraq increasingly exposed on its "Kurdish flank" during the course of 1986.

The Progress of Covert U.S. Arms Transfers

The covert U.S. relationship with the Iran also began to expand. The operation was now almost totally under the control of the NSC and the Director of the CIA, and the State Department, Department of Defense, and U.S. intelligence community were at best kept only partially informed. The issue was also primarily one of obtaining the release of U.S. hostages, although the NSC and CIA increasingly tried to use their contacts with Iran to feed it data on the Soviet threat and expand there contacts with Iranian "moderates."

The leading actors in the NSC were now McFarlane, his deputy John Poindexter, and Colonel Oliver North – a leading advocate of aid to the Nicaraguan Contras who had worked closely with Israel in prior covert operations. It also came to involve a retired U.S. officer, Major General Richard Secord, who was an ex-U.S. advisor to the Shah's military forces, and a leader of the covert private U.S. volunteer effort to aid the Contras. This involvement of North and Secord was eventually to lead to the illegal diversion of a significant amount of the money scheduled for the Iranian arms deal to the Contras and create a massive political scandal in the U.S. when the American dealings with Iran were exposed.

Israel continued to be a driving force behind this American effort, which was directly encouraged by Peres and Israeli Defense Minister Rabin. In the fall of 1985, Leeden continued to meet with Kimche, Gorbanifar, Schwimmer, and Nimrodi.[4] This led to expanded negotiations with Iran, with the Iranians pushing for the delivery of Hawk surface-to-air missiles and parts before the release of hostages, and the U.S. and Israel pushing for the release of the hostages before the shipment of arms.

The new arms deal was supposed to deliver 3,300 TOWs, 50 to 120 Hawk missiles, and the eventual delivery of two Hawk missile radars and some 234 sets of Hawk spare parts. It is unclear that the Americans involved knew or cared enough about the Iran-Iraq War to fully assess the impact of the proposed arms transfer, which Iran sought largely to counter the Iraqi threat to its oil exports. It is also still unclear exactly what arms Israel was providing on its own. Nevertheless, it is clear that both Shultz and Regan were informed and that the U.S. eventually authorized the shipment of some 18 Hawk missiles from Israel to Iran in late November. This flight operation was conducted by CIA officers, but without the permission of the Deputy Director of the CIA, John McMahon.[5]

The Hawk shipment created immediate problems. It seems to have included older types of missiles past their useful life, some of the funds involved seem to have been diverted and embezzled, it angered the Iranians, and no hostages were released. Further, sufficient objections to the legality surfaced from the CIA to force the issue of whether a formal Presidential Finding would be signed to authorize further arms shipments. This Finding was drafted on November 26, 1985.[6]

This draft was pushed forward from within the NSC which was now largely hiding the details of its operations from the other Departments of the U.S. government, and which recommended that the President conceal the operation from the Congress to protect the hostages. It also was increasingly becoming tied to a broader CIA operation that was trying to use intelligence transfer to Iran to minimize Soviet influence.

The actual arms for hostages initiative became so convoluted, that it is unclear that any of the actors involved – U.S., Israeli, or Iranian – could track the pace of events. McFarlane, who was about to be forced to resign as President Reagan's National Security Advisor, met with Kimche and Ghorbanifar in London in early December, 1985, over the mishandling of the Hawk shipments to Iran but it is unclear that anyone ever fully mastered the details of what quality and number of arms were being shipped, how the money was being handled, or how many hostages were to be released at a given time.

It has since become clear that neither President Reagan nor his senior advisors in the NSC ever really considered the strategic effect of their actions on the Iran-Iraq War or the near certainty they would become public. Even so, the U.S. could not make a formal decision on the need for such transactions. While the President, the Secretaries of State and Defense, McMahon, McFarlane, and Poindexter met on the issue on December 7th, there was evidently so much disagreement that the meeting evidently took no decision. Similarly, some members of the NSC staff later argued that the draft Presidential Finding approving the arms transfers with Iran was "approved" on December 5, 1985 – two days before the meeting – but the Senate Select Committee could not find a signed version.[7]

There is no way to tell the extent to which other nations were making similar mistakes. It is clear that Britain and France at least tolerated some covert arms transfers during this period, that France was accommodating Iran by limited anti-Khomeini activity in France, and that the USSR was at least considering a new initiative to improve relations with Iran that took practical from in 1986. Nevertheless, the U.S. was clearly becoming involved in potentially explosive operations. After meetings in London in early December, it largely dispensed with Israeli and Iranian middle men.

In fact, it again seems to have considered cancelling the entire operation. In early January, however, Israeli Prime Minister Peres, his terrorism advisor Amiram Nir, and Kimche all put pressure on the White House to go on with the deal.[8] The hostage issue was also becoming more sensitive, and this led the senior officials in the NSC to decided to advocate direct U.S. shipments to Iran.

On January 7, 1986 another meeting was held in the White House with the President, Vice President Bush, Shultz, Weinberger, Casey, Attorney General Edwin Meese, and Poindexter – who had replaced McFarlane as National Security Advisor on December 11, 1985.[9] Once again, the Secretaries of State and Defense objected to the U.S. initiative to Iran, but the hostage issue was given top priority. Although another meeting was held in the White House on January 16, 1986, President Reagan issued a formal finding authorizing arms shipments directly to Iran on January 17th. He had instructed the director of the CIA, William J. Casey to keep the information from the Congressional committees supervising intelligence.[10]

Iran Launches Its Attack on Faw

Meanwhile, Iran continued to build up a massive concentration of forces in the border area. It mobilized and deployed nearly two thirds of its elite Pasdaran Corps, including the Karbala 25th division, Najaf-Ashraf 8th division, Ashoura Division, and Special Martyr's brigade, and nearly half of the regular Army, including the Bakhtaran 81st Division, Mazandaran 30th Division, and the Khorassan 77th division. These forces were initially deployed between Ahwaz and Dezful, and especially in the Hoor-al-Azim and Hoor-al-Howeizeh regions.[11]

Iranian forces then divided into two major concentrations. One smaller concentration was to the north of Basra, opposite the flooded Hawizah marshes. The main concentration was to the south opposite the Faw Peninsula. This dual concentration of Iranian forces led the Iraqis to focus on the defense of the marshes, because much of the low level fighting during mid and late 1985 had been in this area.

Iran, however, directed its offensive thrusts in several directions, something for which Iraq was ill prepared. On February 9th, Iran launched the first phase of its three-pronged attack (the Al Dawa or Dawn 8 offensives) against the Iraqi 3rd Corps and the Iraqi 7th Corps. The new offensive involved over 150,000 men. The Iranian forces in the north launched two thrusts across the marshes. These attacks were repulsed, although it is unclear whether they were ever intended to be more than diversionary efforts.

The story was very different in the south. While some Iranian units like Iran's 3rd and 77th (Golden) divisions took heavy casualties, Iran was able to use its new lines of communication and improved amphibious capability to make significant gains. Iran first seized Umm al-Rassas Island in the Shatt al-Arab. Then, on the night of February 9th, 1986, Iran carried out a major amphibious landing near Iraq's largely abandoned oil port of Al Faw.[12]

Faw was about 50 miles from Basra and about 38 miles south of the nearest major Iranian facility at Khorramshar. While Faw was on a long marsh-ringed peninsula, and was relatively isolated from Basra and the main roads between Iraq and Kuwait, it was still of special strategic importance. The Faw peninsula juts out between the Shatt al-Arab and the Island of Bubiyan in Kuwait. A successful Iranian thrust thus offered Iran several benefits: (a) it cut Iraq off from the Gulf, (b) it positioned Iran to attack Basra from the South, and (c) it positioned Iran to cut off Iraq's main lines of communication to Kuwait.[13]

Iran took advantage of night and rain to launch its assault, and this gave it comparative security from Iraqi air power. It sent six different assault forces across the Shatt al-Arab. The Shatt was roughly 400 meters in the areas Iran chose for the attack, had a fairly strong current and some tidal action. Nevertheless, the Iranian landings were successful at all six points and Iranian troops began to move forward over a 40 mile front along the coast of the Faw Peninsula.

Iraqi planners do not seem to have fully considered the possibility of an Iranian amphibious assault in this area before the Iranian landings, and seem to have ignored Faw's strategic importance when the assault began – although this Iraqi failure was at least partly the fault of U.S. intelligence analysts which had given Iraq an assessment estimating that the main Iranian thrust would be north of Basra, but had neglected to inform Iraq that it had no coverage of the Iranian forces in the south because of cloud cover of the area.

The Iraqi commander in the area also failed to cope with the problem of simultaneously dealing with several small amphibious forces. At higher echelons, the Iraqi 7th Corps Commander does not seem to have realized the need to destroy an enemy landing force before it can secure a bridgehead. Iraq was far too slow to react, and kept its attention focused on the marshes to the north.

As a result, Iran was able to rapidly reinforce its original bridgeheads during the next few days. It erected a pontoon bridge which could be swung against the shore to reduce vulnerability to air attack and allow easy repair and service. This allowed to Iran to speed up its troop movements and resupply. The local Iraqi forces could not cope with multiple thrusts against them or Iran's ability to move over water barriers and by foot. As a result, Iraqi forces tended to panic. Iran continued to build-up its forces with only limited opposition, and succeeded in virtually routing Iraqi forces in Faw by February 10th.

Iran succeeded for several reasons:

- First, Iran achieved strategic surprise. Iraq, at least partially as the result of U.S. intelligence, prepared for an Iranian offensive north of Basra, and concentrated its forces accordingly.[14] Iran also may have had obtained U.S. intelligence on the weaknesses in the Iraqi position from Colonel Oliver North of National Security Council. The Iraqi forces around Al Faw, which had been largely abandoned once Iran destroyed Iraq's oil loading facilities early in the war, were unprepared for the rapid landing and infiltration of Iranian forces.

- Second, Iran exploited Iraq's slowness to react, and its inability to maneuver. Iranian forces penetrated deep into Iraqi positions during the initial hours of the attack. Rather than dig in, Iraqi units panicked and abandoned both critical fixed defenses and most of their heavy equipment. While estimates disagree, Iraq seems to have suffered about 4,000 casualties during the initial fighting versus 2,500 for Iran, and add to that about 1,500 men taken prisoner of war.[15]

- Third, although Iraq claimed to have flown up to 355 fighter and 134 combat helicopter sorties per day, the Iraqi air force did little to halt the Iranian advance. This initially was inevitable because heavy rain over the battle area made it almost impossible to fly effective attack sorties, but even when the weather improved, Iraqi fighters rapidly began to take losses without being able to find targets or achieve damage worth the cost of a several million dollar airplane. Iraq lost 15-30 aircraft, and found few exposed targets. Iran's infantry had learned to disperse, dig in and take cover, and move heavy equipment and supplies in small amounts or at night.[16]

  Iraqi air attacks were equally ineffective in destroying communications along the long causeway along the shore of the Shatt al-Arab from Khorramshar and Abadan city to the Iranian launch point on the southern tip of Abadan Island. Iraqi efforts to bomb the causeway were quickly repaired, and Iraqi aircraft failed to do consistent enough damage to any of the bridges across the canals or khors that cut through the main causeway to inhibit Iranian movements.

- Fourth, Iraq was not prepared or ready to counterattack. Its unit commanders in Faw had lied to their higher command during the initial critical attack period, and Iraq held back its reserves far too long because of its fear of an attack further north.[17] Iraq was still committing forces to a useless counteroffensive in the Majnoon islands as late as February 12th. Once Iraq did rush forces from the Majnoon front to the south, its initial counter attacks on 13 and 14 February were poorly organized and did not include elite infantry trained to fight on foot in the assault role. When Iraq did finally commit elite units like its 10,000-man Presidential Guard Brigade, these were not ready for infantry assaults, close fighting, or movement through the wet lands and marshes where Iraqi artillery and armor fire had only limited effect against well dug-in Iranian troops.

It is doubtful that the covert U.S. arms shipments to Iran had as critical impact on the fighting as the faults and misuses of U.S. intelligence, but it is important to note that by this time the U.S. had firmly linked direct control of the arms shipments to Iran to the intelligence operations discussed earlier, and the U.S. was considering trading some 4,000 TOW anti-tank guided missiles from the release of hostages and better relations with Iran[18]

The first 500 TOWs were shipped to Bandar Abbas in Iran on 18 February 1986. Another 500 TOW missiles, and possibly Hawk and F-4 parts as well, were flown to Bandar Abbas on February 27th.[19] Two Boeing 707s operated by Southern Air Transport, Inc., are known to have carried some 45 tons of cargo from an Air Force base in Texas to Tel

Aviv. These arms were paid for using a CIA-run Swiss account, and at least some of the receipts from Iran then went to illegally aid the Contra rebels in Nicaragua. Iran ended up paying as much as three times the regular price for TOW missiles.[20]

While the TOW was of great potential value to Iran's infantry dominated assault forces as a means of killing Iraqi tanks and hardened defense points, the deliveries probably arrived too late to influence the battle at Faw and at this point the U.S. has still not made any effective transfer of Hawk missiles or parts. While there were three Hawk sites covering Iranian forces in the area, only one was operational. Further, the new arms transfers did not produce the release of the hostages that the U.S. expected. In fact, the U.S. operation only continued after another letter from Israeli Prime Minister Peres to President Reagan.[21]

In any case, the fighting did clearly favor Iran. While Iraq did inflict serious casualties on Iran once it committed its reserve forces and firepower – Iran may have suffered some 10,000 dead and critically wounded by the end of the first six days of fighting – the counterattacking Iraqi forces took unacceptable casualties in return. While estimates are uncertain, Iraq seems to have lost at least 5,000 dead or critically wounded.

Iraq also expended massive amounts of ammunition in ineffective area fire against scattered infantry targets. It used up some 200 tank barrels. It fired up to 600 rounds per artillery weapon per day – usually without clear targets. In fact, Iraq used up so much of its artillery ammunition it had to scour the world for emergency purchases of new ammunition stocks.[22]

Even when Iraq finally did move its reserves and counterattacked, Iran was able to continuously resupply and build-up its forces in Faw, although it did fail to build a second chain of pontoon bridges across the Shatt to Al Faw until September, and had to rely heavily on small craft. Iran conducted most of its movements to and within Faw at night or during poor weather, and this further reduced the vulnerability of its forces to air and artillery attack.

Iran also benefited from its seizure of large amounts of Iraqi equipment and supplies, and from seizing many Iraqi defensive positions intact. This helped Iran compensate for some of its equipment shortfalls, and meant it did not have to expose as much of its heavy equipment to movement across water barriers.

By February 16th, Iran occupied over 300 square miles of the Faw Peninsula, although much of this was marshland. Iran had well over 20,000 men in Faw and a total of 85,000 men committed to the attack. At the same time, Iran kept up its pressure on the rest of Iraq's forces by maintaining a major force of several hundred thousand men positioned for attack in the central war zone north of Susangerd – a force which could attack across the Hawizah marshes without warning. Iran also increased its pressure on Iraq by launching a small diversionary attack about 25 miles north of Basra on the night of February 11th, and encouraged dissident Kurdish groups in the north to attack Iraqi positions and keep Iraq from shifting forces south.

The War Shifts Back Towards Stalemate

At the height of Iran's success, it threatened to break out of Al Faw. Iranian troops reached the Khaur Abdallah waterway opposite Kuwait, and there were even reports that Iranian forces had surrounded the Iraqi navy base at Umm Qasr. Iran also captured Iraq's main air control and warning center covering the Gulf, which was located north of Al Faw.[23]

By this time, however, Iraq was steadily improving its defenses. It replaced the commander of the defending 7th Corps, and began to have some success in its counterattacks after 15 February – although this success was so disguised by the constant series of false Iraqi propaganda claims that near panic continued in Kuwait and Saudi Arabia.[24]

The fear of an Iraqi defeat led to constant consultation among nearby Arab states, as well as a special Arab Foreign Ministers meeting. Iraq's success was also tenuous. Casualties continued to be high on both sides. Iran was losing at least 350 dead a day but Iraq was losing over 200.[25] Iraq continued to lose major amounts of armor, and suffered significant fighter losses to ground based air defenses. Iran claimed to have shot down roughly 7 Iraqi fighters a day, while Iraq claimed to have shot down several of Iran's remaining F-4s.

In fact, both sides began to discover the cost of their respective military limitations. Although Iran built up its forces in the Faw Peninsula to over 25,000 men, it was still pushed back. Iraq's three pronged counterattack down the center and sides of the Faw Peninsula advanced extremely slowly, at best, but Iran could not support its forces with adequate armor and firepower. Iran simply proved unable to deploy significant numbers of its remaining major weapons. It was forced to move back from any position that favored Iraq's armor and artillery, and to dig into the marsh areas and wetlands above Faw.[26]

After February 17-18th, Iraq was able to fully deploy its superiority in air power, firepower, and armor. The slow, grinding Iraqi assault largely halted Iran's attempts at rapid frontal assaults. Iraq also began to make much more effective use of multiple rocket launchers for area fire, and reduced its use of largely ineffective tube artillery weapons – which simply could not deliver the required mass of fire within a sufficiently short time period.

The Iraqi air force kept up a high sortie rate of several hundred sorties per day, and while it had little killing impact, it did force the Iranians to dig-in and largely paralyzed rear area activity and daytime infantry attacks during fair weather daylight hours. Iraqi forces even scored some minor gains in the Majnoon area, and Iraq showed that its air force could continue to pound at Iran's oil facilities and shipments in spite of the pressure of the Iranian offensive. Iran's oil production occasionally dropped to 800,000-900,000 BPD.[27]

Iraq's Continuing Military Problems

Iraq, however, found that it was paying an unacceptable price for its lack of infantry assault and infiltration capability. Even though Iraq committed major further reinforcements from its Third Corps area on February 21st, Iraq could not fight or maneuver as effectively as Iran through the wetlands. Many of its gains during the day were lost at night – when Iran could make use of its superior ability to fight on foot.

Iraq also gained little from its attempts to use gas warfare, evidently because it could not develop effective area concentrations. Weather and water effects robbed Iraqi nerve agents, cyanide agents, and mustard gas of much of its impact. While up to 8,500 Iranian soldiers were affected, only 700 were killed or seriously wounded – a poor return in casualties for the Iraqi effort and worldwide criticism of Iraq's use of poison gas.[28]

Iraq continued to take very heavy losses even after it slowed its efforts at direct assaults, and lost nearly two battalions in one such attack on February 23-24th. Iraq's clumsy attempt to launch a small amphibious flanking attack on 9-10 March cost it several battalions, and it lost the equivalent of another brigade trying a three-pronged counterattack against dug-in Iranian troops.[29]

While Iraqi pilots continued to press their attacks at unusually low altitudes, and took the losses inevitable in flying more effective attack sorties, Iraq found that its air superiority could not be used effectively as a killing mechanism without excellent targeting, precision munitions, high risk attack sortie profiles, and effective damage assessment.

The Iraqi Air Force could sometimes inhibit Iranian movement, but it usually flew too few sorties per strike to have more than a harassing effect, and generally failed to kill even one infantryman per sortie. Eyewitness press reports indicate that even attacks by Iraq's Blinder bombers generally did not produce enough lethality over areas occupied by Iranian troops to produce one kill per sortie because such troops were dug in and well dispersed.[30]

Iran continued to pour in manpower regardless of its losses and called up a whole new wave of Basij volunteers. It continued to prove that it could exploit its advantage in manpower more effectively than Iraq could exploit its advantage in technology. Further, while Iran took significantly higher losses, Iraq was losing skilled manpower[97] that took years to train and its losses had far more domestic political impact.

Low Level Land Warfare Continues

Further, Iraq found that it could not substitute firepower for mass attack in other areas of the front. Iran succeeded in several limited attacks in the north. On February 24th-25th, Iran launched an eight brigade attack (Al Dawa 9) in the northern border area in Kurdistan, about 170 miles north of Baghdad, 60 miles northwest of Kirkuk and 14 miles from Sulaimaniya. This Iranian attack seems to have been directed at seizing the high ground above the Sulaimaniya-Chwarta road, and took place in areas with mountains over 6,600 feet and involved about 120 square miles of Iraqi territory.

Although most Iraqi villages in the area had already been abandoned, Iran took the town of Chorta. Further, Iran showed it had the active support of the Barzani faction of the Pershmerga, although it is unclear how important a role such Kurdish rebels played. While the new Iranian attack was largely a spoiling attack and had limited strategic value, and with Iraq succeeding in forcing Iran to give up some of its gains, Iran's new success did reinforce the political impact of its gains in the south.[31]

By early March, a pattern of fighting was established in Faw that lasted for the rest of 1986. Iran retained about 120 square miles of the Faw Peninsula, and managed to keep a light pontoon bridge operating across the Shatt al-Arab. Iran used this bridge, powered floating bridges, and small craft to reinforce the bridgehead.

In spite of losses and casualties that now approached 20,000 men, Iran maintained an active force of 25,000-30,000 men in the Faw Peninsula. Iran also kept several hundred thousand more men along the border in positions where they were ready to attack Iraq above or below Basra. Iran did not succeed in bringing many added heavy weapons into Faw, but it brought artillery forward elsewhere along the front and started to shell Iraq's main air base near Basra at Shuabia.

Iraq, however, proved able to contain Iran. Iraq steadily increased the firepower it could bring to bear in Faw to the point where further reinforcement of its heavy weapons strength became impractical because of the terrain. Iraq reestablished solid defensive positions, and had the option of launching a major counterattack into Faw. Moreover, Iraq succeeded in creating a more effective command, control, communications, and intelligence system, built up extensive ammunition stocks, and had a massive superiority in firepower. It also gained a much better idea of where Iranian targets were located as the front stabilized into fixed positions.

As a result, Iran's forces focussed on digging in and holding their existing gains, and Iraq's artillery, air, and firepower did not have enough effect to support a counterattack. Iraq lacked the assault skills to capitalize on any shock effect from its superior firepower and armor.

Further, Iran's lines of communication were too easy to repair for Iraq's air forces and artillery to do more than temporarily damage a few bridges, and a combination of rain and seasonal flooding channeled the Iraqi armored attacks to the point where Iranian forces could dig in and halt them with anti-tank weapons. Iraq could not advance without taking nearly equal casualties and these were simply too high for Iraq to pay the cost.[32]

By late April, both sides were locked in a new stalemate. Iraq succeeded in pushing Iranian forces out of much of their initial gains in Kurdistan, had checkmated Iranian efforts to advance in the Hawizah marshes, and had some positions within ten miles of the city of Faw. Iraq's air force also scored more successes as the weather improved, and as Iran had to regroup its forces and expose more targets.

The Iraqi Air Force seems to have carried out a particularly effective strike against a clumsy Iranian concentration of armor in the central front near Ahuaz, about 100 km east of the Gulf battle front. While the details of this attack are unclear, it seems to have involved more than 30 MiG-23BM ground attack aircraft sorties which hit an exposed Iranian concentration of M-60s, M-113s, and BM-21s which was preparing to reinforce the central front forces or Faw.[33]

Iraq did occasionally try more counterattacks, but took more losses than it could afford. Iraq's 28th and 704th brigades took severe casualties while attempting to advance on Faw in mid to late March. Iraq lost as many as 8,000-12,000 dead during its counteroffensives, and was forced to organize special trains to carry its wounded. Iraq went to such extremes as forced blood donations, trying to mass recruit the staff of some leading tourist hotels, and forcing empty taxis going north from Basra to carry corpses inside the vehicle and on their roof racks. Iran was also able to keep up its manpower levels in Faw in spite of Iraqi claims to have flown 18,648 sorties over Faw between February 9th and the 31st of March.[34]

Other factors discouraged Iraq from launching more counterattacks in spite of the fact that changes in the weather gradually dried out the terrain in Faw, and gave Iraq a steadily improving capability to use its armor. Iran continued to keep at least 300,000-400,000 men in positions along the 730 mile front where they were constantly ready for another attack, and Iran definitely had the edge in terms of strategic position.

To the north, Kurdish rebel groups were extending the areas within their control and Iranian troops were within ten miles of Sulaimaniya. In the center, Iranian troops were in the Meimak hills about 70 miles from Baghdad. Major concentrations of Iranian troops were in position to attack across the Hawizah marshes to reach the Baghdad-Basra highway, and Iran remained in Faw with the equivalent of two full divisions. It could concentrate its forces at any point, and take advantage of Iraq's lack of strategic depth, while Iraq had no major objective in Iran that its forces could credibly seize.

Iran, however, could not launch major new assaults. It did not have armor and firepower in Faw to capitalize on its strategic position and infantry capability. Iran also was obviously coming under growing financial pressure. It began a new and harsher series of threats to Iraq's financial backers in the Southern Gulf, and pointedly reminded Kuwait that Iraq's loss of Faw had left Kuwait far more exposed to Iranian military action.

This helped lead Iran to try to improve its relations with the West and USSR. Iran made new political and trade initiatives to the USSR and France, and continued its covert discussions with the U.S. It limited its military activity to a few helicopter attacks in the Southern Gulf, although it kept up terrorist pressure on Kuwait and it may have released some mines as a harassing gesture.[35] Equally significantly, Iran began to heavily discount its oil at a time when it already was getting only $11 a barrel, cut back on domestic uses of foreign exchange, began to delay low priority arms purchases, and quietly sought added short term credit.

Iraq chose to deal with this situation by publicly declaring it would not counterattack immediately because it wished to limit its losses. Rumors also repeatedly surfaced during this time, however, that Sadam Hussein met with his senior commanders, including Iraqi Air Force Commander Air Marshal Hamid Shaaban, and reorganized the Army and Air Force command to give them more freedom of action and removed himself from day to day direction of the war. Hussein was also reported to have allowed the Iraqi Air Force command to risk using larger numbers of aircraft per strike and to take higher losses in return for greater effectiveness.[36]

Iraq Attempts to Use Air Power to Break the Stalemate

In any case, Iraq stepped up its air attacks. In early May, the Iraqi air force launched a major raid on Tehran. This raid left Iran's biggest oil refinery in flames and damaged one of its processing units, although it missed both catalytic crackers in the 254,000 BPD facility. Iraq also resumed strikes against targets like trains and some civilian targets. The Iraqi air force increased its attack on the Iranian tanker ferry to Sirri, and succeeded in hitting two large tankers – the Superior and Energy Mobility. This led the chief of Iraq's Navy, Rear Admiral Abed Mohammed Abdullah to claim that Iraq had destroyed 58 Iranian tankers, 85 other merchant ships, and 40 supply ships since the beginning of the war in September, 1980.[37]

Iraq was particularly concerned with reasserting its strength during this period because Iran had followed up its victory at Faw with a new set of threats about a "final offensive" and May 19th was the anniversary of the death of the Prophet's nephew, Ali.[38] This may also explain why Iraq chose to launch a counterattack into Iranian territory in mid-May.

The Iraqi Attack on Meheran

This attack surprised Iran, which was then concentrating more on threats and protests relating to Iraqi air action than the risk of an Iraqi assault. Several divisions of the Iraqi 2nd Corps, totalling about 25,000 men, began to attack the Iranian border "city" of Meheran around the 10th of May. Meheran was a virtually abandoned town, about one third of a mile inside the border, about 106 miles east of Baghdad. It also was located in an area defended by only 5,000 low grade Iranian troops. As a result, it offered Iraq a cheap potential victory and the ability to conquer Iranian territory with none of the risks inherent in counter -attacking Faw.

By May 17th, Iraqi forces overran Meheran and five neighboring villages in Iran, fought their way through the initial hills in the border area, and inflicted heavy casualties on the poorly prepared Iranian troops. Iraq made effective use of its multiple rocket launchers and was able to drive Iranian troops out of virtually all the lower ground. Iraq did not, however, succeed in taking the high ground, and mountains ranging up to 1,500 meters, to the east of Meheran.[39]

The results of the fighting were more mixed in the north. While the Kurds in the KDP scored minor victories against Iraq at Mangesh and Dahok in northern Iraq, Iraq scored another minor victory at Fakkeh in the south and vowed to stay in Meheran until the end of the war. Iraq also succeeded in destroying the satellite dish at Assadabad, which knocked out much of Iran's overseas telephone and telex links for nearly two weeks.[40]

It spite of these minor victories, Iraq had clearly been thrust back upon the defensive. It called up its university students and their professors for rear area duty for the first time in the war. It required all civil servants to serve on the front during part of the year, and insisted that taxis delivering corpses move at night. At the same time, Iraq kept pounding away at Iran's oil traffic and facilities at Kharg. It launched nearly ten major air raids a month on Kharg during May and June, and kept up its air raids on Iran's border cities.

Iran's Covert Relations With the U.S. and Other Arms Deals

Iran responded with more threats about final offensives, and a new series of threats against the U.S. It launched occasional raids against tankers in Saudi and UAE waters, and pressured the GCC states to end their ties to

Iraq and the U.S. It also, however, began to expand the scope of its talks with France and the USSR – both of which were impressed by Iran's victory at Faw, and carried on with its secret contacts with the U.S.

Iran was unsuccessful in demands for Harpoon anti-ship missiles, reconditioned Hawk radars, and 200 advanced Phoenix air-to-air missiles for its F-14As; it did obtain U.S. agreement to provide more TOWs and critically needed Hawk parts. Two more Southern Air Boeing 707s flew from Texas to Tel Aviv in May, 1986, carrying the Hawk parts and TOWs. Then, on May 28, McFarlane, Lt. Col. North, of George Cove, a CIA official, and Amiran Nir flew to Iran in a plane carrying an initial load of spare parts for the IHawk missiles Iran needed to help protect its oil facilities. The rest of the Hawk parts and the 500 more TOW missiles were kept back in Israel awaiting the release of the U.S. hostages.

The U.S. officials were supposed to see President Khamenei, Prime Minister Musavi, and Majlis Speaker Rafsanjani, but McFarlane and the rest of his party got little results from their arrival in Tehran. They spent several days waiting in the Tehran Hilton, and talking to low level officials, before being asked to leave. At this point, McFarlane seems to have recommended against any further contacts, but Rafsanjani made a guarded speech on June 10, 1986, discussing improved Iranian relations with the U.S., and Iranian officials sent signals they wanted improved relations through two other countries. Finally, one hostage – Father Jenco – was released on July 26th.

Although this hostage release fell far short of U.S. expectations, it still sent Iran the rest of the Hawk parts on August 3rd. Further, Iran pressed for Hawk radars, Hawk missiles, Hawk electron tubes, and 1,000 more TOWs and military intelligence on Iraq. By late August, after discussions of returning the body of William Buckley for burial, the U.S. began preparation for the shipment of 500 more TOWs. After some complex delays, the 500 TOWs were delivered to Iran on October 28. Another hostage, Peter Jacobsen, was released on November 2, 1986. To all intents and purposes, the White House staff had become fully committed to the covert U.S. initiative in Iran, largely undercutting the overt official efforts of the State and Defense Departments.[41]

Further, Iran ensured at least temporary Syrian loyalty by offering easy terms for Syria's $2 billion oil debt – neatly cancelling the efforts of King Hussein of Jordan to bring a rapprochement between Iraq and Syria. Iran resumed its oil shipments to Syria in spite of the fact that Syria could not meet its debt payments or even fully pay for current shipments.

This Iranian action was critical to counter the effects of King Hussein of Jordan to restore good relations between Iraq and Syria. Iraq had offered Syria some 150,000-180,000 BPD as an inducement to reopen its 600,000 BPD pipeline to Iraqi oil shipments, and Saudi Arabia and Kuwait had offered Syria some $700 million in additional aid. Syria was then in serious economic difficulties, and if Iran had not made a counteroffer, King Hussein's initiative might well have been successful.[42]

Iran Retakes Meheran

Iran also secretly prepared for a counteroffensive to retake Meheran. The Iraqis had made the mistake of trying to hold the area in spite of the fact they were exposed on several sides and Iran held critical portions of the high ground in the area. At the beginning of July, Iran was ready and launched its " Kerbala 1" attack. Iran took advantage of the fact that the Iraqi commander who had led the original attack had been replaced because of ill-health and the new commander never patrolled more than 12 miles outside the city, and stopped below the first ridge in the nearby Poshtkuh mountains. This allowed Iran to build-up a major attack force without detection.

As a result, Iranian forces rapidly overran the positions of the two Iraqi brigades defending Meheran, killing one brigade commander, and causing 1,200-2,000 Iraqi casualties. Once again, command and control problems inhibited the Iraqi Air Force. The command to provide full-scale air support came far too late, and Iraq only flew 33 helicopter sorties during the critical phase of the Iranian assault, versus a capacity of over 500, and only 100 air support missions versus a capacity of over 300.

By the 3rd of July, Iraq was forced to admit that Iran had liberated Meheran. Iran not only took back the five heights Iraq had captured, it took four new minor hill positions in Iraqi territory. While it is unclear whether U.S. arms shipments played any direct role in this victory, it is important to note that the TOW anti-tank weapon was well suited for striking bunkers and weapons located in mountain cover and for stopping any Iraqi armored counterattacks.[43]

Iran loudly proclaimed its victory at Meheran on July 10th. It held a conference in Tehran of some 8,000 commanders to head what it claimed would be 500 new battalions of Basij forces. These units were to include conscripts for the first time, and the speaker of Iran's Parliament, Ali Akbar Hashemi Rafsanjani was careful to state that they might require up to a year of training...."Three months is not enough." These new forces were to be given Revolutionary Guards commanders with experience as company or platoon commanders. The battalions were to be subordinated to the Islamic Revolutionary Guards Corps – the command of the Basij – and have a nominal strength of 300 men each, with three companies of 100 men divided into platoons of roughly 22 men each.[44]

Iraq tried to respond with a low level, but unsuccessful attack on Iranian positions at Majnoon.[45] Rumors also began to surface of new internal political problems in the Ba'ath leadership. This led Iraq to turn again to airpower. Iraq launched a new wave of bombing directed at area targets in Iran after a three month lull. Between July 20th and 30th, Iraq hit at targets as diverse as a sugar factory, military camps, an oil refinery, and urban targets in Arak, Marivan, Sanandaj. Iraq also stepped up its attacks on tankers in the Gulf.[46]

New Developments in the Oil War

Iran, in contrast, seemed to shift its focus to OPEC. Rafsanjani issued new threats against the southern Gulf states, including the first public confirmation that Iran had deliberately sunk tankers and ships operating in southern Gulf waters[47] Iran loudly denounced Saudi Arabia for its increased oil production levels and its impact in lowering oil prices at the OPEC meeting in Geneva on July 28th. It also demanded a quota twice that of Iraq.

The Iranian oil minister, Gholam Reza Aghazadeh, claimed Iran was producing 2.2 BD, and would raise this level to 3-4 million barrels if Iran did not get its demands. The end result of this pressure was inconclusive. OPEC did increase Iran's quota to 2.3 MMBD – roughly what it was already producing. However, the OPEC meeting did not give Iraq – then producing about 1.8 MMBD – any quota at all. While Saudi Arabia reduced its production from 5.8 to 4.4 MMBD, this seems to have been the result of its conclusion that its levels were too high to maximize its oil revenues, and not because of Iranian threats.[48]

The fighting during August consisted of repeated Iraqi air strikes against strategic targets in Iran and Iran's oil export capability, coupled to constant low level Iranian attacks and threats regarding a final offensive. By August 8th, Iraq succeeded in hitting five tankers out of Iran's fleet of eleven tankers ferrying oil from Kharg to Sirri, but Iran rapidly found other tankers and few of the ships were destroyed.[49] Further, Iran replied by repeated artillery barrages of Basra and other Iraqi border towns and military positions.

Growing Internal Strains in Iraq and Iran

Meanwhile, both nations desperately sought new sources of arms and financing. Iraq and Iran cut back steadily on civilian imports, and Iran sold off the remaining overseas holdings of the Pahlavi Foundation. The cut in oil revenues left both nations with only about 40-50% of the revenues they had earned during 1985, and Iraq's debt was reported to have reached $45 billion.[50]

More rumors surfaced of internal unrest in Iraq and Iran. Iraq had continuing problems with its Kurds, and Iran seemed to experience a new wave of problems with its regular military, particularly in the Air

Force. Rumors that Revolutionary Guards units had shot some of the Iranian regular army commanders that failed to defend Meheran seemed to be confirmed, and clashes between the regular armed forces and guards seem to have taken place at Khatam war headquarters and the Anzali naval base.[51]

On July 14th, Colonel Ali Sayyad Shirazi, the commander of the regular army may also have been "kicked upstairs" into to a meaningless position in the Supreme Defense Council. Shirazi was relieved of his duties as ground force commander on August 4th, amid widespread rumors that he and the regular military felt that Iran's religious leadership and Revolutionary Guards were substituting ideology for tactical planning and insisting on tactics that resulted in higher casualties in both defensive and offensive combat even though this did not produce useful military results.

Although Shirazi was considered to be loyal to the revolution, and had been promoted up from the rank of a junior artillery officer in Shiraz, he evidently was felt to be too committed to the regular armed forces. At the same time, it is important to note that Shirazi was replaced with Colonel Hossein Hassani-Sa'di. Although Sa'di was a Khomeini loyalist, he was also a mature commander of 45 years of age who directed much of the Faw operation and who was former Southern Front commander.[52]

While probably unrelated to the preceding events, it is interesting that several Iranian pilots flew their aircraft to Iraq following this period. These defectors included at least three senior F-4 pilots. These defections symbolized the steady decay of the professional cadre of pilots, ground crews, and other technicians within the Iranian air force. This situation was not helped by the fact that experienced Iranian pilots were being forced to fly while still injured or in aircraft without functional IFF systems. Several Iranian fighters were lost to "friendly fire" for this reason and morale steadily deteriorated. Iran began to have almost as many problems in fielding experienced pilots as it did it keeping its aircraft operational. Similar problems seem to have occurred in Iran's ground based air defense forces and Navy.[53]

Iran also experienced a new wave of bombings by the Mujahideen Khalq. At least seven major bombings occurred in Tehran and Qom between January and mid-August. The Mujahideen Khalq had emerged as the most active of the Iranian exile groups. Ironically, its leader – Massoud Rajavi – had been forced to relocate from Paris to Baghdad in June. This expulsion occurred as part of France's balancing act to improve its relations with Iran, and solve a growing internal political crisis over the rescue of its hostages in Lebanon.[54]

The end result of France's action, however, was to give Rajavi much better access to arms, training facilities near the border, and much larger financial resources. While many of the agents responsible were captured in late August, and the Mujahideen Khalq scarcely threatened the survival of the regime, it was clear that Khomeini still had a significant opposition. Further, at least some elements of the anti-Iranian Kurdish Democratic Party of Iran (KDPI) attacked Iranian positions in the Dalam-Par hills in the northeast – demonstrating that Iran had not totally succeeded in dominating the Kurdish national movements.[55]

Iraq's Long Range Air Attacks Change the Oil War

Iraq also extended the range of its air strikes. On August 12, it raided the Iranian facilities at Sirri Island for the first time. This was a considerable achievement because Sirri is about 400 miles from Iraq and only 150 miles from the Straits of Hormuz. Iraqi Mirages fired Exocet air-to-ship missiles and hit three tankers loading at the terminal. Iraq may have used converted Antonov tankers to refuel the Mirages, or even have staged out of a friendly Gulf country. Other sources indicate, however, that Iraq simply took the risk of flying at very high altitudes – knowing that if its fighters had to engage in air-to-air combat they would probably use too much fuel to return.

The attack on Sirri had special importance because Iran was now transhipping virtually all of its oil exports from Kharg. Iranian efforts to set up an alternative 1.5 MMBD terminal called Val Fajr II at Larak Island, about 130 miles east of Sirri, failed because of weather and porting problems, and the five mother tankers or transfer ships at Larak had moved back to Sirri.[56]

Iraq followed up this strike on Sirri with repeated raids against the key oil shipping facilities on the mainland and against Kharg, and with attacks on Iran's refineries. By late August, it had flown 120 sorties against Kharg alone in the preceding twelve months. Iran responded by moving its tanker transfer loading site to a position about 15 miles northeast of Sirri, which placed its tankers closer to its coastal air defenses. The Iraqi strike also forced Iran to relocate three major transfer ships back to Larak.

Iran had to raise its shuttle tanker fleet from 11 to 20 ships, and chartered the world's largest tanker – the 564,739 ton *Seawise Giant* – to try to provide a stable loading platform at Larak. These charters cost Iran some $60 million annually, excluding rising insurance premiums, the cost of replacing combat losses, and $20,000 per day per tanker in operating costs. Nevertheless, Iraq's air strikes continued to be effective. Iran's average exports dropped from around 1.6 MMBD to $1.1 million.[57] Iraq also flew an unusually aggressive number of sorties against Iranian forces at the front, averaging 45-75 sorties per day.

Iran replied by firing its first Scud missile at Iraq in thirteen months, evidently targeting the Iraqi refinery at Dowra.[58] It again used the annual pilgrimage to Mecca to have its pilgrims cause unrest in Saudi Arabia, and launched a conspicuous attack on a tanker loading at the Fateh oil field terminal in UAE waters south of Sirri.[59] This brought the annual total number of attacks on Gulf shipping up to 59, versus 46 in all of 1985, and 40 in 1984.

Iran lacked the air and sea power, however, to retaliate effectively against the shipping that aided Iraq. It sent out daily patrols by P-3 Orion and C-130 Hercules aircraft from Lavan Island to try to plot tanker movements, and had a limited capability to strike with its remaining F-4s and Maverick missiles. Tankers and other ships were generally safe, however, if they could transit between anchorages in the area around Dubai to anchorages west of Qatar.

The Iranians did not acquire even a limited night warfare capability until June, 1986 when they obtained delivery of night vision goggles for their helicopter pilots, and subsystems to allow their AB-212 helicopters to fire short range wire-guided AS-12 missiles. While they hit a Greek freighter off Dubai in August and the UK-registered tanker *Pawnee* on September 25, 1986, they had very limited range and endurance. This was true even though Iranian helicopters operated from forward areas in the Gulf like the offshore oil platform at Rostam and the Iranian-held island of Abu Musa near Dubai.[60]

According to the U.S. Mideast Task Force commander, these strikes raised the total number of attacks on Gulf shipping since the "tanker war" began in March, 1984, to 144. They also led Iran to start examining tanker protection systems such as systems firing canisters of aluminum chaff, reflecting nets to be draped around tankers, and painting crew quarters with dull non-reflecting paint to weaken radar detection.[61]

Iran continued its political offensives in other ways. On August 18, it announced it had resumed gas exports to the USSR, and had signed an agreement to steadily expand them over the next five years. This resumption of economic relations, after the hostility following the Iranian crackdown on its communist party in 1983, was the outgrowth of a visit to Tehran by Soviet First Deputy Foreign Minister Georgy Korniyenko in February, 1986.[62]

The USSR also agreed to cut oil production to support OPEC's attempts to raise oil prices and indicated it would return its economic advisors to Iran. At the same time, Iran encouraged French efforts to improve relations, and the covert U.S. efforts to establish ties to Iran's "moderate" factions by selling token amounts of arms. Further, Iran made its first overt threats to Turkey in an effort to stop Turkish attacks on Kurdish movements friendly to Iran.[63]

Iran could not, however, easily solve its financial and arms problems. While it did obtain a growing number of Western arms, and got additional covert shipments of arms from the U.S. in August and late

October, it could not obtain enough arms and parts to bring its U.S. and European supplied arms to the level of readiness desirable for major combat operations.[64]

Iran's other sources of arms also continued to present problems. Iran was able to obtain some $4 billion worth of arms from North Korea and $230 million from the PRC between 1980 and 1985. Iran signed a new agreement for $1.6 billion worth of PRC-designed fighters, tanks, anti-ship missiles. Iran also may have gotten delivery on the first of some 50 J-7 (F-7 or MiG-21 variant) fighters, Chinese made SA-2 surface-to-air missiles, and Chinese SS-N-2 naval surface-to-surface missiles.[65] It also got some 20 Contraves Skyguard antiaircraft fire control systems from Switzerland.[66]

Nevertheless, Iran simply could not get enough high technology arms from such sources to convert from Western to Soviet and PRC-supplied arms, or to give Iran confidence that it could strengthen its air defenses and sustain any breakthrough it made in some "final offensive" attack on Iraq. The PRC deliveries also came slowly and often at rates that indicated they were being delayed until payment was received.

Equally importantly, Iranian foreign exchange reserves sank to about $43.5 billion – barely enough to fund its essential military imports – and could not meet its loan payments to critical foreign lenders like Japan.[67] Nevertheless, Khomeini made it clear that no peace settlement was possible as long as Sadam Hussein remained in power. Rafsanjani made claims that implied the war would be settled by the next Iranian new year, on March 21, 1987, and Iran took a hard line at a new series of meetings with Syria and Libya.

Iran Combines a New Military Build-Up With Pressure on the Gulf

Iran repeatedly briefed reporters that it had 350,000 new troops to join the Revolutionary Guards at the front for the final offensive, and now talked about 1,000 new battalions of volunteers. At the same time, Iran attempted to exploit any divisions within Iraq. It made a token release of Iraqi POWs and Iranian officials made speeches indicating the fact that a new government in Baghdad might not have to pay reparations in the event of an Iranian victory.[68]

As the war continued into September, Iraq made new peace initiatives without success. Iran launched another series of small offensives early in the month and scored some gains in the Haj Omran basin near Kurdistan. Both sides made the usual conflicting claims regarding gains and losses during these offensives, but Iraq flew over 100 sorties per day in support of its defensive actions, and it was clear that the local fighting was relatively intense.

Iranian naval brigades of the Revolutionary Guards also seem to have taken at least temporary control of the Al Ummya and Al Bakr oil platforms in the Gulf, and to have destroyed a radar facility on Al Bakr that Iraq was using to locate Iranian shipping targets in the Gulf. Further, Iran stepped up its naval intercepts of shipping through the Gulf to 15-20 inspections a day, and even briefly detained a Soviet cargo vessel, the Pytor Yemtsov. This was enough to start new rumors that Iran planned to launch its full final offensive on September 15th, the day of Ashura, when Shi'ites celebrate the martyrdom of Imam Hussein.[69]

This Iranian pressure seemed to have a growing impact on the GCC states. Saudi Arabia and Kuwait had pressed for agreement to extend the patrols by U.S. E-3A AWACS to cover the entire Gulf at the GCC meeting in August, 1986, but Qatar, Oman, and the UAE refused. They did so at least partly in response to Iran's growing power. The new Iranian victories also led to more reports that OPEC was increasingly being influenced by Iranian pressure and acting in a way that would help restore Iranian oil revenues. While the validity of these reports is uncertain, it is clear that mini-states within the UAE, such as Sharjah and Dubai showed an increasing tendency to quietly support Iran.[70]

Iran continued to delay its "final" offensive, although it did get additional arms from the outside. Total deliveries from the PRC between March and August, 1986, rose to $300 million. The deliveries included such key items as 12 Chinese F-7 fighters, T-59 tanks, anti-ship missiles, and possibly more Scud B missiles. Shipments from other sources, including Greece, provided more spare parts for its U.S.-made F-4 and F-5 aircraft, including vitally needed F-4 engines.[71] The USSR also quietly increased the arms flow to Iran from Czechoslovakia.[72]

Iraq's Expanding Oil War Does Not Relieve the Pressure

Iraq continued to fly long range air attack missions. Iraq hit the Iranian refinery at Tabriz on August 10, 1986, and then attacked the Iranian oil loading points at Lavan on September 7th. Iraq then launched a highly successful series of raids on Kharg Island, on the 16th of September.[73]

These raids forced Iran to rely more on Larak Island, and made significant temporary cuts in its average oil exports. The Iraqi air force also continued to hit at ammunition dumps and other Iranian military targets along the border, and struck at border towns like Marivan, Mosk, and Rabat. While Iran launched another Scud missile at Baghdad, it could do relatively little in the air. Aside from a limited number of attack and air defense sorties, and a few successful kills of Iraqi aircraft, Iran had to passively accept the Iraqi air strikes. More and more, the war became a struggle between the ability of Iraq's more effective air power to weaken Iran's economy and the ability of Iranian ground forces to invade Iraq.

Like Iran, however, Iraq was coming under steadily /increasing internal strain. Some estimates indicated that roughly one out of every ten regular soldiers on the front had received at least some form of combat injury. It was also clear that Iraq lost at least 2,500 officers during the first six month of 1986. The total of Iraqi dead lost in the war rose to over 100,000, and Iraq was forced to expand its six month draft affecting 110,000 male students and 15,000 teachers who had formerly been exempt.[74]

Iraq also extended liability to military service to 50 years of age, and accepted several thousand women for military training. It even assigned several for training as jet pilots. This call up of women symbolized an important side effect of the war, since women have steadily had to assume more and more managerial responsibility in Iraq, and the number of women in managerial positions in factories has risen by 25% since the war began.[75]

Iraq was at least $15 billion in debt to non-Arab states and owed them $1.5 billion annually in interest. This included $5 billion in debts for Soviet arms, $6.8 billion to international banks, $3.9 billion to import export banks, and $6 billion in unguaranteed debts to Western companies. This burden was so high that Iraq was increasingly unable to even meet its rescheduled debt payments, and had $285 million in outstanding payments of principle in October, 1986.[76] For the first time, it was forced to cut back on essential consumer goods like fish, chicken, and butter.[77]

Iraq's debts to the Arab world totalled as much as $30 billion, and some estimates went as high as $60 billion. Iraq even owed Jordan some $525 million for food and trade goods, a sum representing nearly two years worth of Jordanian -Iraqi trade and far larger than Jordan's $300 million in foreign exchange holdings. In spite of increasing oil exports, the decline in oil prices meant that Iraq was only earning about $11 billion a year. Given the fact that Iraq still needed some $6 billion annually in civil imports, and $8 billion to finance the war, Iraq was adding over $3 billion annually to its trade deficit.[78]

Iraq attempted to maintain morale by offering its troops rotational leave and by maintaining exceptionally good rations and privileges for its front line troops. Nevertheless, there were increasing reports of desertions. More and more reports surfaced of arrests and executions within Iraq. These were said to include up to 40 officers in an Army plot against Hussein; Naim Haddad, a member of the Revolutionary Council, and General Omar Haza, who was said to have attacked Hussein's policy regarding the war when Hussein visited him to console him for the loss of his son.

The Seventh Corps Commander, General Aziz Jaboumy, was said to have taken his family on a working visit to Pakistan and then to have defected to Iran. Further, the Iranian-backed government in exile – the Higher Council of the Islamic Revolution in Iraq led by a Shi'ite cleric, Mohammed Bakr Hakim – stepped up its propaganda activities.[79]

Iraq, however, was more concerned with external threats than internal tensions. Senior Iraqi officials like foreign minister Tariq Aziz continued to warn that the Iranian "final offensive" might come at any time, and that Iran might attack in more than one sector and attempt to exhaust Iraqi reserves.

This helps explain why Iraq continued to stress the expansion of its ground forces in spite of its financial problems. It expanded its Presidential Guard from 6 "brigades" to 16 to 17 mechanized "brigades" totalling about 25,000 men which were equipped with armor, including some T-72 tanks. Total army manning rose to around 700,000 men, and Iraq succeeded in filling out all seven active corps along the 730 mile front with Iran, and in creating a total of nearly 46 major combat units. While Iraq called these units "divisions", they were only manned and equipped to the size of reinforced brigades, by Western standards.[80]

Iraq also continued to strengthen its forward defenses. It added more barriers, minefields, and barbed wire, and increased the number of dug-in tanks. It increased the amount of artillery in each defense zone, and put more emphasis on preregistered target coordinates, and immediate response with mass fire.[81]

Iran Faces Internal Divisions and Growing Oil Export Problems

Iran, however, did not immediately launch a major offensive. It confined itself to small actions that nibbled away at Iraq's positions and morale. It kept up sporadic artillery barrages against Basra, and sponsored a series of combined Iranian and Kurdish special forces and commando raids on key targets like the major refinery at the Kirkuk oil field and the Iraqi military bases at Koi Sanjaq and Altun Kopru, although these commando raids had comparatively little initial success.

Iran instead seemed to·concentrate on its various political offensives. It held new talks with France, and announced that Soviet economic advisors would return shortly. It also continued its pressure on OPEC, and its mixture of overtures and threats to the GCC states in an attempt to weaken their ties to Iraq.

Iraq responded by continuing to strike at Iran's oil targets. It hit at Iran's gas compression facilities, the refinery at Shiraz, industrial centers in Isfahan, the Rustam and Sasan offshore oil fields, and at the oil pumping stations at the Marun and Ahvaz oil fields. Iraq continued to strike at tankers, and even hit a newly acquired Iranian shuttle tanker before it could even reach Larak. This tanker had just been converted for oil transloading at the drydock in Dubai and had some $500,000 in defense equipment. This included non-reflective paint, radar reflectors at either end of the vessel, chaff launchers, and an electronic decoy system.[82]

Iraq also launched exceptionally successful raids on Kharg on September 29 and October 6, 1986 – the latter of which temporarily closed the last two functional terminals in all of Kharg's fourteen tanker berths.[83] The new Iraqi air offensive cut Iranian oil shipments to about 800,000 BPD – or about half of Iraq's current export level – and delayed shuttle shipments to the point where 25-30 long haul tankers were normally waiting off Larak and waiting to load.

Iran was forced to try to rush full operational capability for the two mooring buoys it had bought in 1985 to try to provide a survivable capability to load its shuttle tankers without sending them to Kharg. Iraqi raids on Iran's refineries also forced Iran to start importing about 100,000 BPD in refined product, and led to still further increases in tanker insurance premiums. Iran had to introduce petrol rationing.[84]

These Iraqi attacks occurred at a time when growing tension emerged within Iran. Iranian officials like Rafsanjani increasingly appeared on television to justify continuing the war.[85] Iranian pilots continued to desert to Iraq, and Iranian unemployment rose to around 6 million. Casualty estimates rose to 250,000 Iranian dead and 500,000 wounded. Even conservative estimates put Iran's oil income at only $4 billion per year, versus $16 billion the preceding year. There were reports of mandatory conscription sweeps through the streets of Iranian towns and cities, and of some 100,000 desertions from the Iranian Army, and a later report to by the UN indicated that the number of political prisoners in Iran that had been executed since Khomeini came to power rose to 7,000 during this period.[86]

The Khomeini regime also seemed to be experiencing growing internal problems. New rumors surfaced that Khomeini was seriously ill. More importantly, an open political struggle took place over the way in which radicals loyal to Khomeini's designated successor, the Ayatollah Hussein Ali Montazeri had detained a Syrian official, Ayad Mahmoud, the charge d'affaires in Tehran. This struggle eventually led to an investigation of the conduct of some of Montazeri's key subordinates by Mohammed Mohammed-Reyshahri, the head of Iranian intelligence, and to the arrest of Montazeri's son-in-law and one of his most senior assistants and chief of staff, Mehdi Hashemi.

Hashemi was then the head of Iran's Global Islamic Movement – one of the organizations responsible for exporting the Iranian revolution, but also one which competed with similar initiatives by Rafsanjani. Other arrests then detained Montazeri's son-in-law Hadi, his son Saeed, two members of Parliament, and the Iranian government publicly acknowledged the arrest at least 41 others.[87] The arrests clearly had

Rafsanjani and Khamenei's backing, and later received Khomeinei's open support.

While Khomeini denied any power struggle was underway, the arrests and attendant publicity clearly seemed to be designed undercut Montazeri's authority. It is also a fact that Montazeri's public statements regarding the need to preserve private enterprise, to allow the "Bazaari" to conduct trade, to safeguard legal rights, and to minimize casualties were consistently more moderate than those of Rafsanjani or those around him. There also were many reports of a serious split between supporters of Rafsanjani, who favored active efforts to exploit Iran's contacts with the outside world and a major effort to obtain arms even from nations like the U.S., and supporters of Montazeri, who seemed to favor a much harder line towards relations with outside states, and much greater reliance on exporting a "pure" revolution.[88]

The Covert U.S. Arms Sales Become a Public Scandal

These open attacks on Montazeri's supporters were particularly striking because one of the main reasons for designating Montazeri as Khomeini's successor was to demonstrate the solidarity of the regime and its continuity even if Khomeini should die. Further, Montazeri initially seems to have deliberately played the role of a "moderate", as a man who was more concerned about casualties, the social impact of conscription, and the other human costs of the war. This offered the people at least some hope of a softer regime in the future

Yet, the revolution simply does not seem to have been able to tolerate any alternative to Khomeini and the leaders actually running the war and the nation's political development. Further, Montazeri seems to have become a magnet for various elements within the Iranian revolution who disagreed with the leadership around Khomeini. While these disagreements do not really seem to have reflected major differences in ideology, over the conduct of the war, or over the nation's internal development, they do seem to have reflected a significant set of rivalries for control of the revolution, and it was this – not relations with the outside world – that seems to have triggered the wave of arrests.

The fighting on the ground continued virtually unchanged through October and late November, 1986. The internal struggle for power between Montazeri and Rafsanjani , however, helped lead to the exposure of the covert U.S. shipments to Iran which had begun in 1985, and to a major scandal in U.S. domestic politics. *Shiraa*, a pro-Syrian magazine in Lebanon, announced McFarlane's visit to Tehran in its November 4, 1986 issue.[89] Its editor, Hassan Sabra, later stated that the source of his story was Montazeri's office.[90]

Rafsanjani officially confirmed the story on November 5, 1986, and again on November 24, and December 5th.[91] The broad outlines of the U.S. transactions with Iran became public by the end of the first week of November, and one leak after another then led to the disclosure that the U.S. had shipped at least 2,008 TOW missiles and 235 Hawk assemblies. It also became clear that Israel had provided much larger shipments of U.S. parts and arms than had previously been believed.[92]

Iraq Reaches Out to Hit Larak

The only major developments in the fighting during November were in the air and tanker wars. On November 25th, Iraqi Mirage F-1EQ5 fighters hit Larak. While two Iraqi fighters ran out of fuel during the raid, and had to land in Saudi Arabia, the raid on Larak took Iran by surprise. Several ships were hit and the raid was considered a significant strategic success. The raid demonstrated that Iran lacked any options that could protect its oil export facilities other than rebuilding its air defenses. It also raised the number of tankers struck in 1986 to 90.[93]

While the exact timing of Iraq's upgrading of its refueling capability is uncertain, the Larak raid also demonstrated that Iraqi Air Force now had greater range than ever before. Iraq had modified 10 Soviet AN-12 Cub transports for use as tankers. These carried a palletized air-to-air refueling system that trailed a drogue from the rear ramp. Iraq also had the ability to use a "buddy-buddy" refueling system developed by the French air force which allowed one Mirage F-1 fighter to refuel another from a 2,300 liter centerline tank on the "mother" fighter.

While these refueling systems were difficult to operate and were unsuitable for mass long distance raids, they did bring Larak within Iraqi fighter range and gave the Iraqi Mirages the nearly 1,400 km range Iraq needed for such strikes.

Iraq also kept up its strikes on Kharg. On November 27th, it announced its 250th strike on the Island and claimed there was not a single jetty still operating. It also continued to hit at the Iranian refineries in Tehran, Isfahan, and Tabriz, and at hydroelectric facilities and power plants. Iraq claimed it was able to reduce the Sirri island ferry fleet to only five ships.[94]

Further, Iraq made better use of its laser guided bombs and had improved its evasion tactics. It also flew much larger overall numbers of combat sorties. On the same day Iraq first struck Larak, it flew a total of 164 combat missions, including many over the front – where it often used its Soviet-made Sukhoi Su-20s and MiG-21s as well as its Mirages.[95]

Iran's Growing Problems in the Air

In spite of all its arms deals, there was little Iran could do about war in the air. By the winter of 1986, Iran seems to have been reduced to as few as 40 fully operational fighters, and a total of 80-100 aircraft capable of some kind of operations. It no longer was able to operate the avionics on its P-3C maritime reconnaissance aircraft.

Some sources indicated Iran had only seven operational F-14s, none with functioning radars.[96] A defecting Iranian Air Force Colonel also claimed that Iran's F-5 force was at 10-15 fighters and the F-4 force was down to 20, and he claimed that Iran now had no operational RF-4 reconnaissance aircraft, had lost three C-130s because of a lack of spare parts, and could only operate about 10% of its 17 B-707s, seven B-747s, and remaining C-130s.[97]

Iran did, however, manage to improve some of its land based air defenses. It claimed that surface-to-air missile forces and ground based air defenses scored as many as 10 kills in November, and that nine out of ten of these missiles scored kills.[98] These claims were almost certainly exaggerated, but Iraq did lose 5-12 fighters during the fall and early winter – this was enough to start considerable speculation that the covert U.S. arms shipments may well have allowed Iran to make its Hawk defenses more effective in at least a few selected areas like Kharg Island.

Iran also used its surface-to-surface missiles. It continued sporadic Scud strikes against Baghdad, one of which killed 48 Iraqis, and wounded 52, when it hit a crowded apartment complex.[99] Further, Iran continued its pressure in other ways. In late November, Iran seems to have conducted a demonstrative raid on the Abu Boosk offshore field about 100 miles north of Abu Dhabi.

While this Iranian raid may have had some political impact on the GCC states, it scarcely matched the impact of Iraq's strikes deep into Iranian territory.[100] Nevertheless, Iran issued a new set of threats against the GCC states that Iran would "remember" their actions if they continued to back Iraq. These threats were particularly hostile to Saudi Arabia, which Iran claimed had aided Iraq in a strike on Larak.

Meanwhile, the "Tanker War" continued its grim process of slow and steady attrition. While fighter and helicopter attacks only threatened during daylight hours, this situation changed in September. On October 17, 1986, Iran also began night attacks with its Saam-class surface ship. It hit the Five Brooks, a tanker with what turned out to be Sea Killer missiles. The ship was only five miles off Oman and suffered five dead and 13 missing. It then hit two more ships – the Sham and August Star in November.

By early December, some 50 seaman had died in attacks on tankers in 1986, versus 50 in all of the preceding five years. Insurance rates continued to rise, and nearly a ship a week was being lost. According to Lloyd's, there had been 97 attacks on cargo ships and tankers during the first nine months of 1986, with 17 total losses. This compared with Lloyd's estimates of 259 attacks during the entire war. In a separate count, U.S.

Figure 10. Attacks on Ships in the Gulf: 1984-1986

	By Iraq	By Iran
1984	27	16
1985	40	13
1986	65	41
Total Number of Attacks	132	70
Ships Destroyed/Heavily Damaged	40	11

Source: Statement of George B. Crist, U.S. Marine Corps, Commander in Chief, U.S. Central Command before the Senate Armed Services Committee on the Status of the U.S. Central Command, January 27, 1986. p. 16.

intelligence produced the estimate shown in Figure 10 for the total attacks during 1984-1986. These figures show that Iran struck more than three times as many ships in 1986 as in 1985, while Iraq's attacks in 1986 greatly exceeded their previous total.[101]

The premiums for a six-month charter in Iranian waters had reached the point where they equalled 60% of the value of a vessel. Iran had been forced to insure such ships on its own, but would only cover 15% of the ship's value. By this time, Iran had to buy at least 10 VLCC (very large cargo carrier) and several ULCC (ultra large cargo carrier) tankers for the shuttle service between Kharg and Sirri and Larak islands.[102]

At the same time, Iraq kept up its air strikes on Iran's cities and economic facilities although Kharg Island's improving Hawk and other air defenses seem to have led Iraq to limit its attacks on the island. In a typical exchange, Iraq hit the oil center at Ahwaz, the Dangha power station near the Iranian-Soviet border, and a shuttle tanker on December 6th. According to some reports these strikes raised Iran's dependence on oil imports from 200,000 to 300,000 BPD. Iran replied by bombarding Basra on the 8th, and followed up with artillery attacks along a 50-mile front that included the logistic areas of the Iraqi III, IV, VI, and VII corps.[103]

In spite of these Iranian barrages, Iraq continued to fly daily MiG-21 and Su-20 attacks against Iranian cities and oil targets, and used its Mirages with laser guided bombs to hit high value economic targets. On December 13, Iraq hit a power plant and antiaircraft system in Tehran — its first attack on Iran's capital in seven months.[104] Similar raids against Iranian towns and cities continued into late December, killing a number of civilians, although Iraq generally claimed its aircraft were hitting at major economic or military targets.[105]

Notes

[1] "A New Gulf War Offensive?", *The Middle East*, February, 1986, pp. 10-12. *Washington Times*, October 26, 1986, p. A-9.

[2] *Washington Times*, April 3, 1986

[3] *Economist*, November, 2, 1985, p. 36; *Washington Times*, November 6, December 9 and 21, 1985; *Wall Street Journal*, November 15, 1985; *New York Times*, December 13 and 30, 1985; *Chicago Tribune* and *Washington Post*, 7 January, 1986.

[4] For a detailed chronology of these events, see the Senate Select Intelligence Committee, *Report on Preliminary Inquiry*, January 29, 1987, p. 10.

[5] Ibid, p. 11-13 and *Tower Commission Report*, pp. 32-35.

[6] *Report on Preliminary Inquiry*, p. 13 and *Tower Commission Report*, pp. 36-38, 154-164.

[7] Ibid.

[8] Ibid.

[9] Ibid. McFarlane was forced to resign on December 11, 1985 because of internal political differences with the White House. He continued to be involved in the arms deal as a private consultant.

[10] *Washington Post*, December 7, 1986, p. A-25. Senate Select Committee Report, pp. 15-18.

[11] *Jane's Defence Weekly*, 8 February 1986, p. 177.

[12] This attack took place on the day of the seventh anniversary of the Iranian Revolution. *Jane's Defence Weekly*, 13 February, 1986, *Los Angeles Times* 12 February, New York Times, 13 February, 1986.

[13] *Washington Post*, February 11, 1986; The *Economist*, 15 February, 1986.

[14] Although charges have been made that this was the result of U.S. disinformation, the main cause for the mistakes in the U.S. estimate seems to have been the fact that Faw was covered in clouds for the three critical days before the attack. The U.S. does, however, seem to have failed to inform Iraq about the limits in its intelligence coverage for security reasons.

[15] *Washington Times*, February 13, 1986. *Los Angeles Times*, February 14, 1986.

[16] *Jane's Defence Weekly*, 19 February and 1 March, 1985, *Washington Post*, February 14, 1986.

[17] U.S. intelligence sources provided U.S. newspapers with analysis based on satellite photo data during this phase of the fighting. For example, the *Washington Post* reportedon February 14, 15, and 16, 1986, that satellite photos clearly showed Iraq had failed to mass forces for a counterattack during the first three days of the fighting.

[18] Senate Select Intelligence Committee, *Report on Preliminary Inquiry*, January 29, 1987, pp. 18-20; *Tower Commission Report*, pp. 34-49, 227-334.

[19] The same plane that delivered the missiles picked up the 18 defective Hawk missiles shipped earlier. Senate Select Intelligence Committee, *Report on Preliminary Inquiry*, January 29, 1987, p.20; *Tower Commission Report*, pp. 40-43

[20] *Jane's Defence Weekly*, November 29, 1986, p. 1257; *Washington Post*, December 7, 1987, p. A-25.

[21] Senate Select Intelligence Committee, *Report on Preliminary Inquiry*, January 29, 1987, p. 22.

[22] *The Middle East*, April, 1986, p. 7-9, *New York Times*, February 14,15, and 21, 1986. Iraq bought hundreds of millions of dollars worth of ammunition from South Africa, Egypt and other sources. It also had to buy barrier equipment on a panic basis to make up for the barbed wire, mines, and other material lost in Faw. The Iraqis did not help things by telling a long series of lies about repulsing the attack and successful counterattacks, all of which proved false. For example, Iraq denied losing Faw until February 16. These lies did much to further discredit Iraq's political and military credibility.

[23] *Washington Times* and *Christian Science Monitor*, February 16, 1986.

[24] The commander, Major General Shawkat Ata disappeared after being recalled to Baghdad. *Washington Times*, September 19, 1986, p. D-6.

[25] *Washington Post*, 13, 14, 15, 16, and 17 February, 1986 ; *Economist*, 22 February and 1 March, 1986.

[26] The *Washington Post* reported this was confirmed by satellite photography on February 19, 1986.

[27] *Washington Post*, 19 February, 1, 3, and 4 March, 1986. *Baltimore Sun*, February 20, 1986. In spite of various press reports, eye witnesses in Faw indicate that Iraqi fighters did not go back to their normal mode of relatively low exposure munitions delivery during this period, and pressed their attacks home. *Washington Post* and *Washington Times*, February 20, 1986, and *Los Angles Times*, February 21, 1986.

[28] John Laffin, *War Annual I*, London, Brassey's, 1986, p. 87.

[29] *New York Times* and *Washington Times*, February 25, 1986.

[30] *Los Angeles Times*, February 20, 1986.

[31] *Philadelphia Inquirer*, *New York Times*, *Baltimore Sun*, February 25 and 26, 1986; *Washington Times*, February 26 and 27, 1986, *Washington Post*, February 28, *Washington Times*, March 4, 1986.

[32] *Economist*, March 15, 1986; *New York Times*, March 6, 1986; *Washington Post*, March 7 and 9, 1986.

[33] *Jane's Defence Weekly*, 29 March 1986. Page 561.

[34] *Washington Post*, March 4, 26, 1986; *Washington Times*, 26 March, 1986.

[35] *Philadelphia Inquirer*, March 3, 1986; *USA Today*, March 13, 1986, *New York Times*, March 15, 1986, *Washington Post*, March 4, 11, and 17, 1986.

[36] *Jane's Defence Weekly*, December 13, 1986, p. 1373.

[37] *Washington Times*, July 2, 1986, p. 5B.

[38] The refinery was supplying about 45% of Iran's refined product. *Financial Times*, May 8 and 9, 1986, *Times*, May 9, 1986, *Guardian*, May 9, 1986. Also See "Can Iran hold its bridgehead?", *The Middle East*, April 1986, pp. 7-9.

[39] *Financial Times*, May 19, 1986.

[40] The Kurdish Democratic Party claimed to have overrun an Iraqi battalion of some 800 men, and to have captured Mangesh --a town near Mosul. These claims later proved to be exaggerated. The Iraqis did, however, arrest the local village chief (a Kurd) for refusing to support the Iraqi counteroffensive and it was clear that the KDP's strength in the area was growing. *The Guardian*, May 19, 1986; *Financial Times*, May 28, 1986; *Washington Post*, August 8, 1986, p. A-15.

[41] The Iranians were evidently charged $16,000 for each TOW missile versus a regular price of around $6,000. The surplus funds were diverted to arms dealers and to the Contra rebels. *Washington Post*, December 7, 1986, p. A-25. By this time, the flow of arms from other sources had also broadened significantly. The led to later reports from the Mujahideen that a U.S. arms shipment had landed on Tehran airport on July 4th. The Mujahideen reported the aircraft was a Race Aviation B-707-331C, registration N345FA, and that the flight had been arranged by Rafsanjani and Col. Javidana of the Defense Ministry's logistics department. *Jane's Defence Weekly*, November 22, 1986, p. 1205. For overall reporting on events, see the Senate Select Intelligence Committee, *Report on Preliminary Inquiry*, January 29, 1987, pp. 20-30 and 32-39.

[42] *Chicago Tribune*, June 27, 1986, P. I-5.

[43] The confusion in reporting on the war is typified by the fact that Iran originally claimed to have overrun the 443rd and 705th brigades and then to have captured the deputy commander of the 71st brigade and to have broken the 71st, 72nd, 93rd, and 113th brigades in the fighting. Iraq in turn claimed to have wiped out a major portion of the Fifth, 10th, Lord of the Martyrs, 17th, 25th, 27th, and 41st Revolutionary Guards Divisions and the 2nd Guards or Imam Riza Brigade. Iran claimed to have killed 2,000 Iraqis and Iraq claimed to have killed or wounded 10,300 Iranians and captured 1,303 between June 30 and July 10, 1986. The real casualties seem to have been about 500 Iraqi killed, 1,500 wounded, and 1,100 taken prisoner. The Iraqi commander on the scene during the defeat, Major General Adin Tawfiq, was recalled to Baghdad and disappeared. *Los Angeles Times*,

July 3, 1986, p. I-5; *Washington Times*, July 4, 1986, p. 8A; *Washington Times*, July 9, 1986, p. 7A, and September 19, 1986, p. 6D; *Chicago Tribune*, July 10, 1986, P. I-6.

[44] *Washington Times*, July 10, 1986, p. 32.

[45] Reports that Iraq attempted to use poison gas at this time seem to be incorrect. Timothy Renton, British Foreign Office Minister speaking at Geneva, did announce, however, that Iraq was expanding its poison gas facilities and that poison gas attacks had produced up to 10,000 casualties during the course of the war.

[46] *New York Times*, July 25, 1986, p. A-5; *Washington Post* July 30, 1986, p. A-16.

[47] *Washington Times*, July 28, 1986, p. 7A.

[48] *New York Times*, July 29, 1986, p. D-1, and August 9, 1986, p. 32.

[49] *Baltimore Sun*, August 9, 1986.

[50] *Washington Times*, August 11, 1986, p. 3A.

[51] *Jane's Defence Weekly*, August, 16, 1986, p. 238.

[52] *Washington Times*, December 10, 1986, p. 8-A.

[53] Ibid and *Washington Times*, August 12, 1986, p. 1A.

[54] *Washington Times*, August 21, 1986, p. 4D.

[55] At this point in the war, the Kurdish movements were divided into three main factions. The Kurdish Democratic Party of Iran was headed by Dr. Abdel Rahmen Qasemlu, and claimed a strength of 10,000. The anti-Iraqi parties included Masud Barzani's Kurdish Democratic Party and Jalal Talabani's Patriotic Union of Kurdistan. The total Kurdish population in the region was estimated at about 16 million, nearly half of which lived in Turkey. About 20% of Iraq's population was estimated to be Kurdish. Iran's Kurds were estimated at less than 10%, but nearly half of Iran's total population was non-Persian. The Iranian Kurds were experiencing severe financial problems, and inflation and reports of clashes with the Pasdaran were common. The KDPI had built bases in caves in the cliffs near Kurdish towns like Sardasht, and often controlled small towns and cities in the Northeast at night. *Washington Times*, August 22, 1986, p. 6A, and *Wall Street Journal*, August 29, 1986, p. 16.

[56] *Jane's Defence Weekly*, 23 August, 1986, p. 268; *Washington Post*, August 13, 1986.

[57] *Washington Times*, August 13, 1986, p. 8C, and 15 August, p. 7; *Wall Street Journal*, August 22, 1986, p. 21; *Economist*, August 23, 1986, pp. 33-34.

[58] As usual, the missile missed and fell harmlessly in suburban areas near the refinery. Iran had only received about 20-30 Scud missiles from Syria and Libya and could not sustain a high fire rate. *New York Times*, August 13, 1986, p. A-3.

[59] *Washington Post*, August 18, 1986, p. A-14.

[60] Rupert Pengelley, "Gulf War Intensifies", *International Defense Review*, Vol. 20, No 3, 1987, p. 279.

[61] *Washington Post*, August 21, 1986, p. A-22; *Washington Times*, August 25, 1986, p. 8A.

[62] *Washington Times*, August 19, 1986.

[63] *Washington Times*, August 25, 1986, p. 8A. *Washington Post*, August 23, 1986, p. A-1; *Philadelphia Inquirer*, August 27, 1986, p. E-1.

[64] The arms shipments in August evidently included some 1,500 TOW missiles. *Washington Post*, December 1, 1986, p. A-1 and December 7, 1986, p. A-25.

[65] This agreement is thought to have been the formal outcome of an arms offer negotiated by Rafsanjani during a 1985 visit to Peking. *Aviation Week*, November 24, 1986, p. 29; *Economist*, November 22, 1986, pp. 41-42, and *Jane's Defence Weekly*, November 29, 1986, p. 1257.

[66] This I/J band radar is normally used to control the Oerlikon 35mm AA gun and AIM-7 Sparrow or Selenia Aspide missile.

[67] *Christian Science Monitor*, August 27, 1986, p. 1; *Philadelphia Inquirer*, August 27, 1986, p. E-1; *Wall Street Journal*, September 4, 1986, p. 3; *Washington Times*, September 4, 1986, p. 5B.

[68] Reports of Iranian land strength were issued of 20,000-250,000 Revolutionary Guards and 250,000-400,000 regular army. Iraq's strength was estimated at 700,000-1,000,000. Iran released 200 POWs. It claimed to have released 650 since the start of the war, and to

have 52,000 still under detention. *Washington Post*, August 27, 1986, p. A-7 and August 31, P. A-1.; *Baltimore Sun*, August 31, 1986, p. 6A.

[69] *Washington Post*, September 2, 1986, p. A-20, and September 4, 1986, p. A-1.

[70] *Christian Science Monitor*, September 3, 1986.

[71] There are some reports that Iran got critical spares for the APQ-120 radars on its F-4s from the U.S. during this period which allowed it to repair the Klystron amplifiers on the radars and use them to illuminate targets with the continuous wave beam needed to fire the Aim-7E radar guided air-to-air missile. Other reports indicated that Iran was critically dependent on covert Israeli arms sales to keep its entire F-4 force functioning. One of the major uncertainties affecting the flow of arms to Iran during this period was the flow of parts for Iran's 250 Bell 214A and 40 214C transport helicopters and CH-47 heavy lift helicopters. While both Bell Textron and Boeing refused Iranian efforts to buy parts directly from U.S. companies, some parts seem to have been sold by firms in Israeli and Italy. *Washington Post*, August 26, 1986, p. 1; *Wall Street Journal*, September 5, 1986, p. 1; *Aviation Week*, November 17, 1986, pp. 16-17.

[72] *Washington Times*, October 1, 1986, p. 9A.

[73] *New York Times*, September 17, 1986, P. A-15.

[74] There is some uncertainty regarding this. The students were called up in June. Sadam Hussein later announced they would be released early. *Jane's Defence Weekly*, November 1, 1986, p. 998.

[75] There have also been some interesting educational effects. Women tended to place better than men in university entrance examinations in Iraq before the war because they had fewer social outlets. The war has led to a still further increase in university education of women, and women will now compose the majority of a next generation of Iraq's university graduates.

[76] *Wall Street Journal*, October 14, 1986, P. 37.

[77] *The Economist*, December 20, 1986, p. 47.

[78] Iraq had cut its civil imports from $11 billion before the war to $6 billion in 1985. During 1986, it cut its total number of Egyptian workers from 1 million to 800,000 and deported some 1,000 Filipino and Thai bar girls the government originally hired to entertain soldiers on leave. *Washington Times*, September 19, 1986, P. 1A; *USN&WR*, September 15, 1986, p.42.

[79] Iraq also confirmed in October that it had hanged the junior oil minister, Abdel Monaem Hassen Aluan and six others for corruption. *Los Angeles Times*, September 11, 1986, p. I-65; *Washington Times*, September 15, 1986, p. 12A, and October 3, 1986, p. 6A.

[80] *New York Times*, September 26, 1986, p. A-10, and October 12, 1986, p. 3. *Washington Post*, October 12, 1986, p. A-22.

[81] *New York Times*, October 12, 1986, p. 3.

[82] Defense Analysts, a British consulting firm, had been aiding Iran to protect its tankers using radar-absorbent materials and reflectors to change the radar image of the ship, simple ECM gear to attempt to prevent a radar lock-on, and boiler protection systems. Four Iranian-chartered tankers – Pegasus 1, Achilles, Free Enterprise, and Lady A were given this equipment by the end of 1986. The Achilles was hit once by Iraqi Exocets, as was the Free Enterprise. Neither ship suffered serious damage, however, which was unusual given the damage to other vessels. At least one ship owner purchased MEL Matilda passive warning radars so his crews would know they were under attack, trigger their ships' automatic fire suppression systems, and take shelter. Another group, a consortium of Gulf Agency, Hotforge of Aberdeen and Special Projects Consultants of Aberdeen, offered similar protection systems for all tankers moving through the Gulf plus training in maneuver and minimizing secondary damage. This led to some changes in attack tactics. The Iraqis started firing AS-12 missiles from their Aerospatiale helicopters at the super structure and hull to affect ship control and the crew, rather than try to sink the ship. The Iranian's changed their tactics to fire without overflight to minimize warning and the use of countermeasures. *Jane's Defence Weekly*, October 25, 1986, p. 932; Rupert Pengelly "Gulf War Intensifies" *International Defense Review*, Vol 20, No.3, 1987, p. 297.

83 *Washington Times*, September 30, 1986, p. 8C, October 7, 1986, p. 4D, and October 8, 1986, p. A-21.

84 *Economist*, October 18, 1986, pp. 46-47. *New York Times*, October 19, 1986, p. E-3.

85 *Washington Post*, October 23, 1986, p. A-23.

86 *New York Times*, October 1, 1986, p. A-27 and February 13, 1987, p. A-13; *Economist*, November 1, 1986, pp. 43-44.

87 Reports from emerged from opposition groups like the Mujahideen that up to 650 people associated in some way with Montazeri or his associates were arrested by January, 1987.

88 It is extremely difficult to determine the facts and any such struggle involves great uncertainties. The revolutionary group around Montazeri and the pragmatists around Rafsanjani, President Khamenei, and Foreign Minister Velyati seem to split over Montazeri's objections to any contacts with "evil" foreign nations and desire for "Islamic" land reform.

89 *Washington Post*, December 7, 1986, pp. A-30 to A-31. Al Shiraa (Ash-Shira) announced that an American envoy had visited Tehran, and had shipped key tank and radar parts in four C-130 cargo planes from the Philippines. See *Washington Post*, November, 1986, p. A-15; *Newsweek*, November 17, 1986; *Time*, November 17, 1986, pp. 49-52; and *Aviation Week*, November 17, 1986, pp. 16-18. Senate Select Intelligence Committee, *Report on Preliminary Inquiry*, January 29, 1987, p. 38, and *Tower Commission Report*, p. 51, and 414-449.

90 The editor of Al-Shiraa later declared that the story had been leaked to him by a member of Montazeri's staff. He stated that the story was not Syrian inspired and that issue of the magazine had been suspended in Syria. *Washington Post*, December 7, 1986; *Baltimore Sun*, December 14, 1986, p. 18A; *Economist*, November 1, 1986, pp. 43-44; *Washington Times*, October 29, 1986, P. 6A; Barry Rubin, "My Friend Satan," *New Republic*, December 15, 1986, pp. 14-15.

91 *Washington Times*, November 25, 1986, p. 5A, and *Washington Post*, December 6, 1986, p. A-13.

92 *Washington Post*, December 7, 1986, p. A-25.

93 The aircraft were originally denied permission to land, and were given landing rights only after they insisted that the alternative would be to crash over Saudi territory.

94 *Jane's Defence Weekly*, August 16, 1986, p. 232.

95 This helped lead to reports that Iraq was using mercenary pilots from Egypt, France, or Belgium. *Baltimore Sun*, December 16, 1986, p. 6A. These reports were not confirmed at this writing.

96 *Jane's Defence Weekly*, December 12, 1986, pp. 1372-1373.

97 Ibid.

98 *Jane's Defence Weekly*, December 6, 1986, p. 1323.

99 Ibid.

100 *Washington Post*, November 26, 1986, p. A-14.

101 Statement of George B. Crist, U.S. Marine Corps, Commander in Chief, U.S. Central Command Before the Senate Armed Services Committee on the Status of the U.S. Central Command, January 27, 1986. p. 16.

102 *Christian Science Monitor*, December 4, 1986, p. C-13.

103 *Washington Post*, December 7, 1986, p. A-37; December 22, 1986, p. A-20, December 14, 1986, p. A-52; *New York Times*, December 9th, p. A-8; *Washington Times*, December 12, 1986, p. 6A.

104 The most recent previous attack had been on May 7, 1986, when Iraqi aircraft seriously damaged the Shahr Ray oil refinery.

105 *Washington Post*, December 22, 1986, p. A-20.

Chapter Six

The Fighting in 1987: Iran's Search for a Final Offensive

In what was in many ways a repetition of the Faw offensive of 1986, the character of the fighting changed radically just before the beginning of 1987. Iran launched a series of land offensives which responded to both its internal political pressures, and the Iraqi threat in the air. Like Iran's attack, these new offensives suddenly shifted the military balance between Iraq and Iran and showed Iran was still fully committed to winning the war.

Iran Rushes a New Land Offensive: Kerbala Four

The first attack came on the night of December 23/24th, 1986, and was called Kerbala Four.[1] While this attack involved exceptionally rapid Iranian mobilization, and Iraq was not fully prepared, it did not come as a complete surprise. Iran had announced in early December that 100,000 new Basij troops were leaving for the Gulf front.

These troops were said to have received three months of training in small arms and combat techniques, and to have a three month tour of duty. At this point they were said to have the option of re-enlisting or returning home to the front. The monthly pay of such soldiers was reported to be the equivalent of $262 a month while training and $524 while at the front. This was far more than most young workers could hope to receive from civil sector employment in Iran's depressed economy.[2]

Iran also somewhat paradoxically claimed during this period that it had now trained some one million women Basij since September, 1980, and had 90 training camps for women. It stated that nearly 1,000 women had earned a combat instructor's rating and that women were trained to use RPGs and machine guns. Iran claimed five divisions of women volunteers marched past the past Majlis building in Tehran on November 30th.[3]

It is unclear whether these announcements were intended to create the propaganda climate for a new offensive, or were directly related to actual mobilization. In any case, Iranian forces thrust across the Shatt al-Arab on an exceptionally wide 25-mile front and against some of Iraq's best defended positions. This new offensive extended from Abu al Khasib, south of Basra, to the island of Umm al Rassas near Abadan. It was directed against the Iraqi 3rd Corps forces in the area east of Basra and the Iraqi 7th Corps in the area near the Faw Peninsula.

The Kerbala Four attack was the largest since the Iranian attack on Faw, and Iran's media claim that it was in revenge for the 311 civilians Iran claimed had been killed in recent air raids. In fact, however, it seems to have had Rafsanjani's personal support, and may well have been triggered by his need to counter the internal impact in Iran of the disclosure of his covert dealings with the U.S. There were significant new signs of strain within the Iranian revolution in the weeks before the new Iranian attack. Rafsanjani made repeated defenses of the covert arms deal with the U.S. while stridently denouncing the U.S. and justifying the sales as a step towards victory.

On December 10, 1986, Iranian state radio announced that Mehdi Hashemi, who had been arrested on charges of murder and treasons on October 12th, had confessed to "gross deviations," "standing up against the Imam of the Islamic nation," and engaging in "underground operations." It also announced that all charges had been proven against Hashemi and his collaborators, except one. While the exact number that were convicted with Hashemi was unclear, nearly 200 of Montazeri's supporters had been arrested in October.[4]

While Khomeini had called for a halt to all new criticism on November 20, and singled out Montazeri for praise as a "noble treasure" – and Montazeri stated that Hashemi had "abused his confidence," and "was in no way involved in my office or schools affiliated to me" – the results of the December trials led to growing suspicion that the arrests reflected a power struggle between Montazeri and Rafsanjani. It seemed more and more likely that if Khomeini died without some new power alignment, Iran would be governed by a triumvirate of Montazeri, Rafsanjani, and Khamenei, with Montazeri increasingly restricted to a ceremonial role.[5]

This political background may also explain why Kerbala Four proved to be the worst managed Iranian attack since Iran's major offensives in 1984. The Pasdaran and Basij had minimal support from Iran's regular forces, which were concentrated in positions in the Central Front and opposite Baghdad, and there was little of the systematic preparation characteristic at Faw. The attack had much of the character of the hopeless mass infantry assaults that Britain, France, Germany launched against well entrenched defenses in World War I, and the Iranian infantry had exceptionally poor support from artillery and other combined arms.

The attack was led by the so-called "Division of the Prophet Mohammed", which was the name given Iran's efforts to mobilize 100,000 more popular volunteers in a 500 battalion forces. While the attacking force did not total more than 100,000, up to 60,000 Pasdaran and Basij crossed the Shatt al-Arab at a point where it was about 480 meters wide and had relatively slow moving current, and tried to dig in on the Iraqi side of the Shatt. While this minimized the impact of the water barrier, it also meant a direct assault on fully ready and well positioned Iraqi forces which had full artillery and air support. Another assault force of up to 15,000 men tried to secure the islands of Umm al Rassas, Umm Babi, Qate, and Sohial – which form a kind of strategic "bridge" across the Shat.

The resulting fighting showed just how much Iran could still suffer when it made the mistake of a head-on attack against well prepared Iraqi positions. The Iranians not only assaulted fully prepared Iraqi positions; they made no real attempt to use complex infiltration tactics, aside from using the cover of night at the beginning of the attack. Once they committed their forces, they also launched direct mass infantry assaults against fully prepared Iraqi positions. Iran took massive casualties from the start of the attack, and although the attack lasted two days, the major fighting was over in about six hours.

If the attack was some kind of political or military test of Iran's ability to win with pure revolutionary forces, it failed almost dismally as Iran's offensives of 1984. While experts disagreed over the size of the attack, Iran lost at least 6,000-12,000 dead in the fighting. Iraq claimed there were 100 Iranians killed for every Iraqi and that there were some 60,000 killed and wounded.[6]

While Iraq may have suffered casualties of 2,000-3,000 dead and wounded, Iran's claims that there were 9,500 Iranian killed and wounded were clearly ridiculous. Iran did not achieve any gains from the offensive, and the only positive result it could claim was its ability to inflict at least some casualties on even the best held Iraqi positions.[7]

Iran Responds With Political Attacks and Kerbala Five

Iran did not, however, accept its military reverses. It took the offensive politically, and attempted to use the OPEC meeting in late December to force Iraq to accept new oil quotas of 1.46 MMBD, roughly one-third less than Iran's quota of 2.25 MMBD, and then attempted to get support for ousting Iraq for refusing any quota as part of the new OPEC attempt to raise prices to $18 per barrel.[8]

While these efforts did not succeed, the broader problems within OPEC forced a 7.25% cut in OPEC production. This began to increase the financial pressure on Saudi Arabia – which continued to act as OPEC's de facto "swing" producer. While Kuwait and Saudi Arabia still continued to market 300,000 BPD for Iraq, Saudi Arabia responded by beginning to block as much as 350,000 barrels per day of the oil Iraq was shipping through Saudi pipelines.

The Saudis were caught in a dilemma between trying to increase their own revenues and keep Iraq from suffering a defeat. The end result, however, was to cost Iraq up to $1,000,000 a day in badly needed oil revenue, and the Saudi government indicated in February, 1987 that it was under so much financial pressure that the cuts would continue until June. This threatened to reduce Iraqi oil revenues by $300 to up to $730 million during the first six months of 1987.

Iran also held a meeting of some 200 foreign supporters in Tehran during the last week of December. The meeting included Hussein Mussavi, the leader of the Hezbollah Shi'ite group in Lebanon, senior Syrian and Libyan officials, a few Iraqi dissidents, anti-Iraqi Kurdish groups, and pro-Iranian groups from Bahrain and the UAE. Iran took an exceptionally strident line regarding the threat of the war broadening to include other states. It was clear that Iran was attempting to strengthen its efforts at political intimidation and to broaden its pressure on the Arab world.[9]

Ironically, popular morale seemed to improve in both Iraq and Iran as 1986 ended, and did so in Iran in spite of the failure of the new Iranian attack. The lack of a "final offensive," Iraq's mobilization of additional manpower, Iraq's successes in the air, and its successful land defense on December 25, had restored at least some of Iraq's popular confidence in the war and that of the military as well.

While Iran's latest offensive had failed, the casualties had been limited and the failure was largely unknown to the Iranian people. Although Iran faced stringent rationing, and suffered from low oil production and revenues, the impact of Iran's victory at Faw still had a powerful effect on Iranian public opinion. The vast majority of the Iranian people seemed ready for another year of fighting. Iran's pontoon bridges to Faw remained intact, and its forces remained ready along the border. Popular demonstrations in favor of the war continued in Tehran, and Iran continued to enjoy at least some political success in OPEC.[10]

Behind the scenes, however, Iran was preparing for far more than political warfare. It was regrouping for another attack. Iran prepared for two new thrusts: one directly against Basra with support from Iran's forces in Faw, and another thrust by its regular forces in the area north of Baghdad between Qasr-e-Shirin and Sumar.

Roughly 200,000 Iranian troops were deployed in the southern front, roughly the same number as their Iraqi opponents. The pool of attack forces, however, did not exceed 120,000, and they were largely Pasdaran and Basij. The force in the Sumar Basin totalled roughly 80,000, many of whom were "regulars", and had most of Iran's remaining armor and self-propelled tanks. U.S. experts estimated that Iran had nearly 1,000 tanks in the region.[11]

Iraq almost certainly detected Iran's preparation for this attack, but does not seem to have anticipated its direction or timing or to have received warning from the US, as it did during Iran's build-up for its December 24 assault. Although King Hussein of Jordan had flown to Iraq especially to warn it against complacency, a number of Iraq's key defensive brigades were out of position and did not have their forces committed at the front. [12]

Iraq seems to have relied on the fact that it had built up massive rings of defenses around Basra beginning in 1981, and had created a "moat" along the north-south stretch of the border opposite Basra, just near the 'corner' where it suddenly turns 90° to the east. It used earthern barriers to keep the marsh area along the border from draining. It also built up a large man-made lake at the southern end of this moat called Fish Lake. This created two lines of water barriers to protect Basra. The roughly 120-square miles of water barriers making up the moat and Fish Lake were nearest to the border with the Shatt-al-Arab just behind them.

The Shatt curves sharply to the east just south of Basra and the territory on both sides of the Shatt is relatively marshy. Iraq had strong defenses along the border north of the Shatt, but it tended to rely on the marshes to help provide a defensive buffer. Its positions on both the north and south sides of the Shatt near the border were not properly manned and ready, although it had strong forward defenses on the southern side of the Shatt to the east of Abu al Khasib, a refinery not far from the corner in the border and about 10 kilometers from Basra.

Iraq seems to have felt its forward defences would prevent Iranian forces from quickly crossing the water barriers north of the Shatt and Nahr el Khaiin River, which is the boundary line just above the Shatt at the point where it turns the corner until the Shatt itself becomes the border just east of Khorramshar. [13]

Iraq does not seem to have learned from its experiences in marsh warfare in 1985, or from its loss of the Faw Peninsula early in 1986. Iraqi forces simply were not ready for the Iranian assault, and then moved too slowly once it started. This made Iraq vulnerable to the Iranian thrusts in the south when they came. Iran was fully prepared for a major attack across the Shatt from Basra and simultaneously launched a flanking move along the upper side of the Shatt.

Iran gave the new offensive in the south the name of Kerbala Five, and it was to last until February 25, 1987. The precise goal of the offensive is unclear. It could have served several purposes, and the Iranian leadership may have speculated that it was certain to meet at least some of them. The possible objectives were (a) seize Basra and create an alternative pro-Khomeini capital in the south, (b) destroy the Iraqi army in the south and bring down the Ba'ath government, (c) weaken the Iraqi army through sheer attrition, and/or (d) lay siege to Basra while providing a further political lesson to the southern Gulf states.

Regardless of these uncertainties, it is clear that the new offensive was much better planned and structured than Kerbala Four. Iran committed some 50,000-75,000 troops to the initial attack with some 55,000-70,000 in reserve. These troops were well-armed and equipped and had very clear tactical objectives. Their overall battle management was good and seemed to include much larger cadres of experienced Pasdaran officers, NCOs and troops than were used in Kerbala Four. The initial Iranian assault took place on January 6, 1987. This was a good time of year because the water in the marshy area near Basra was not at its peak, but was high enough to allow powered boats to move freely and to make armored movement difficult.

Iran's forces started their advance at night at about 1:00 am. They moved across the border at the Jasim River and took the small border town of Duayji. During these attacks, waves of Basij volunteers attacked Iraqi positions, who were then followed by Revolutionary Guards. The Basij forces, which included a significant element of young volunteers of 14-15 years of age, took the initial shock of combat and more experienced Guards then moved forward against the remaining Iraqi troops.

In spite of Iraq's attempts to use firepower, air power and poison gas to halt a breakthrough, Iranian forces captured significant positions near the border. About four hours after the attack began, Salamcheh (about 22 miles south of Basra) and the first two Iraqi defensive lines near Kusk, about 40 miles north of Basra, were taken.[14]

The Iranians quickly established a "bridgehead" across the Iranian border and up the eastern side of the Shatt al-Arab about 12 miles south of the outer suburbs of Basra. This "bridgehead" rapidly built up to about 30,000-40,000 men, and exploited the awkward terrain between the Fish Lake and Shatt al-Arab. Iranian forces took positions on both sides of the lake, although they were not able to cross the Shatt or bypass Fish Lake to the northeast.

Iraq launched counterattacks and air strikes in support of its ground forces while it conducted longer range air strikes and fired surface-to-surface missiles against Iranian cities like Qom, Nahawand (southwest of Tehran), Ramhormoz, Isfahan, and Dezful. Nevertheless, Iran held on to a four mile strip of land between Fish Lake and the Shatt, and across from Basra. Massive artillery exchanges took place on both sides, and Iran fired missiles at Baghdad and at Basra – still populated by at least one million Iraqis.[15] Iraq made little initial progress, however, and quickly began to talk about the risk that this might be the "final offensive" the Iranians had promised before March.

The Political Developments Surrounding the Fighting

The USSR attempted to capitalize upon the U.S. arms scandals by issuing its strongest statement to date in favor of Iraq since the beginning of the war. Not only did Moscow blame Iran for continuing the war, but the chief Soviet delegate to the UN, Alexander M. Belonogov, attacked Iran for its anti-Soviet attitude.[16] Further, it was at this time, that reports began to surface that Iraq now had more MiG-27s and MiG-29s – making Iraq the only Third World country aside from India to have such weapons. Interestingly enough, the USSR took this action on the day the *New York Times* broke a story implying that the U.S. had sent disinformation on the USSR as part of its covert initiatives in 1986.[17]

The Growing Military Costs of Kerbala Five

It quickly became apparent Iraq needed weapons more than rhetoric. It suffered serious tank losses, some of which may have been to U.S.-supplied TOW missiles, and heavy air losses during its close support sorties.[18] It also continued to experience major problems in using both artillery and air power. While it had cluster bombs, its conventional fragmentation ordnance lost much of its effectiveness because the soft or marshy terrain absorbed much of the force of the explosion and offered a relatively high degree of shelter.

Both sides, however, took increasingly heavy casualties, and each made increasingly strident claims. By January 11, Iran claimed to have killed or wound 14,000 Iraqis and Iraq claimed to have destroyed 11 Pasdaran divisions and four additional brigades totalling some 60,000 men. Nevertheless, at least 30,000 Iranian troops continued to hold positions near Fish Lake. Iran also announced on January 12 that it would boycott the Islamic conference to be held in Kuwait because of Kuwait's support for Iraq.

These political actions did not mean the fighting on the ground had halted. Iran committed more popular volunteers into the front near Fish Lake. Khomeini emerged from three months of silence to declare that the war was a "holy crusade" and would continue until "victory". Iran also began a build-up of a force of another 100,000 "volunteers" for a Division of Vali Asr (Mahdi). Iran, however, made little further progress. While it occupied positions in a wide arc only 10 to 18 miles from Basra it could not move out of the narrow strip between the Shatt and Fish Lake, and many of its troops were concentrated in a narrow area about three miles long and $\frac{1}{2}$ mile wide.

Iran's troops did succeed in driving Iraqi forces out of many of their defensive positions in the rings or "Iron Citadel" around Basra. In fact, some of Iraq's secondary positions were virtually abandoned, along with large stocks of equipment and munitions, although Iraqi forces generally fought hard before they were driven out of their initial positions.

Iran faced a different situation, however, when its relatively lightly armed Pasdaran and Basij came up against Iraq's main defense positions, which included massive earth berms, bunkers, and concentrations of weapons. The Iranian troops lacked the weight of firepower and the mobility it needed and may have begun to have problems with supplies and in moving sufficient ammunition forward.

Iran also began to suffer internally as Iraq revived the "war of the cities". Iran could do little more than fire an occasional Scud missile at Baghdad or Basra while the Iraqi Air Force bombed Iran's cities day after day. These air attacks rarely caused serious strategic damage, although they did affect Iran's production and distribution of heating oil and fuel. They did, however, bring the war home to the Iranian people and casualties began to rise steadily in Iran's capital and western cities.[19]

Kerbala Six: Iran Tries a Thrust to the North

Iran then launched its attack to the north. This took place in the midst of the heavy fighting around Basra and was unusual because Iran was attacking on two different fronts at the same time. The Iranians, concentrating up to 60,000 "regulars" for the attack, began their advance on the night of January 13. The attack was called Kerbala Six, and took place near Qasr-e-Shirin in the central sector of the front.

The northern attack, however, was a relatively limited operation and not the kind of full scale thrust that might have exploited Iraq's commitment of its reserves to the front in Basra, some 250 miles to the south. It is unclear whether this had any relationship to the fact that most of the Iranian forces involved were "regular", but the fact is that they did not press hard enough to penetrate the major defensives of the Iraqi II Corps, much less threaten Baghdad, some 90 miles to the southwest.

The Iranian forces instead halted after what Iran called a "limited operation," and what seems to have been a somewhat half-hearted effort which resulted in significant casualties. Iran only took some of the hill positions near the border, and about 65-100 square miles of territory – much of which was Iranian land that Iraq had captured in 1980.

The Kurdish rebels which launched new raids in the far north above Kirkuk during this period also achieved comparatively little. The Kurdish attacks were not well coordinated, had little practical effect, and did not force Iraq to divert manpower to the region.[20]

The Land War Continues and the Air and Missile War is Intensified

Kerbala Six did not bring a halt to the fighting around Basra. Kerbala Five continued and the fighting became exceptionally brutal. The U.S. estimated that some 40,000 Iranian and 10,000 Iraqi casualties had occurred by January 16, 1987.[21] On the worst days, the Iraqi mortuaries near Basra were processing well over 1,000 bodies.[22] The Iranian forces also stopped their previous patterns of assaults on Iraq's forward

positions, and began to dig in in the face of Iraqi counterattacks. While
the Iraqi 3rd and 7th Corps had been mauled, they had not been split or
broken, and Iraqi forces began to slowly advance.

The best Iran could do between January 16 and January 19, was to
edge forward a few positions near Basra. Iran did launch a new attack
against the islands in the Shatt such as Bovarian and Umm al Rassas; and
lay siege to Basra by shelling the civil areas of the city, and firing more
missiles.

Even a new wave of infantry attacks on 19 and 26 January did not add
significantly to the 60 square kilometers of ground that Iran had already
captured. Iran was never able to repeat its rapid gains during the first 24
hours of Kerbala Five, and advanced by meters instead of kilometers –
when it advanced at all. The Iranian activity in late January did
penetrate three or four of the five main Iraqi defensive lines in some areas,
and was close enough to Basra to force further evacuations from the city,
but did not really succeed in threatening the main Iraqi defenses. Iranian
troops remained some nine miles east of Basra and about two miles from
Iraq's main defenses defending the port city at Abu Khasib.[23]

Iran did, however, force Iraqi to commit more of its few reserves from
the five brigade Presidential Guard and redeploy forces from its 7th
Corps. The exact size of the reserves Iraq committed is unclear, but it is
clear the 7th Corps forces – which normally were responsible for
defending the area east and northeast of Basra – had to aid the 3rd Corps,
the forces responsible for defending the area east and northeast of Basra.

Further, the fighting seemed to expose the fact that problems continued
to exist in Iraq's high command. Sadam Hussein seems to have distanced
himself from immediate responsibility for the fighting, and only rarely
visited the front – a marked contrast to previous battles. His speeches also
emphasized Iraq's five point peace plan as well as calls for victory. At the
front, the political situation was more dangerous. General Abdul Jawad
Thanoon, Iraq's Chief of Staff, seems to have fallen into disfavor, along
with General Talia Khalil Douri, the commander of the 3rd Corps. A
number of officers in the 3rd and 7th Corps were relieved from duty and
several were shot.[24]

Quite aside from politics, Iraq lost significant numbers of officers,
NCOs, and trained personnel and had at least one general captured. It
again expended tens of millions of dollars worth of ammunition and it lost
at least 500 major armored vehicles – some of which were lost to
wire-guided missiles that may well have been the TOWs supplied as part
of the covert arms shipments to Iran.[25]

For all this effort, Iraq could not dislodge Iran's troops from their
forward positions, and performed badly every time it tried major
counterattacks – just as it did at Faw and in earlier fighting. Iraq was far
better at static, rather than mobile defense. Iraq's only successful
offensive action were its daily air attacks on Iranian cities, which Iran

announced had killed or wounded some 2000 civilians. By the end of January, the Iranian offensive attacking Basra had turned into a siege, although casualty estimates had been raised to around 17,000 Iranian dead and 35,000-45,000 wounded and 6,000 Iraqi dead and 12,000-15,000 wounded.[26]

Iran also seemed to have some internal problems. It continued to successfully call up new volunteers, but the popularity of this effort was unclear. While popular marches and demonstrations in favor of the war occurred in several cities, some of the new volunteers evidently had to be obtained by forced quotas on the Pasdaran in various towns, regions, and government offices.

While reports conflict, Iran's Basij units seem to have run sufficiently short on trained combat troops that it recalled "volunteers" that had already served at the front. Other volunteers may only have done so because nearly one-third of the work force was unemployed due to the impact of the war and the revolution on the economy. Rafsanjani also made an unusual number of visits to the front, although this may have been as much to reassert his credentials as an advocate of the war after the U.S. arms sale scandal as because of problems of morale.

Iran reported that the number of Iranians hurt in Iraqi air raids was more than 1,800 killed and 6,200 wounded, and that there were as many as 202 killed and 644 wounded on a given day.[27] Iraq continued to conduct its strongest and most consistent bombing effort against Iranian cities since the start of the war and led to new conflicts over the size of Iraq's air losses. On January 22nd, Iran reported 57 Iraqi planes shot down and Iraq admitted to 15. Meanwhile, Iran kept up its artillery attacks on Basra and Scud missile strikes on Baghdad and Basra. Six Scud missiles hit Baghdad during the first 11 days of the new offensive.[28]

The relative capability of the air units on both sides at this time is unclear. It is interesting to note that many observers of Iraqi air raids reported that Iraq's aircraft were able to overfly Iran's cities without any sign of Hawk missile activity, although at least one Hawk kill of a MiG-23B may have occurred when the fighter overflew positions near Basra. The report of the Tower Commission later provided indications that Iran was able to reactivate its Hawk units as a direct result of the covert arms shipments it had received from the US and Israel. It concentrated these units in Kharg Island and to the rear of Basra.[29]

It is also clear from Iraq's behaviour that it felt the losses were serious. They were, after all, at least 5% of Iraq's operational force and perhaps as much as 10-15%. More importantly, many of the losses cost Iraq much of its small cadre of high quality pilots. While the USSR agreed to provide rapid replacement of the aircraft losses, the experienced pilots were critical. Iraq only had experienced pilots for 15-25% of its aircraft and only a much smaller number were top quality by Western standards. Many outside criticisms of the Iraqi air force ignored this fact, but Iraq simply could not commit irreplaceable pilots and aircraft at a cost of $15-$25 million to close support, interdiction or low pay-off strikes on oil facilities if these meant substantial losses. The average value of the target being destroyed was generally less than one-thirteenth of the cost of the plane, and its tactical and strategic impact was usually limited. Iraq was forced to strike at targets where most of its planes could survive, and where it felt the strikes were desperately needed or had major strategic impact.

At the same time, Western intelligence experts reported unusually high activity by Iran's F-5s, F-4s, and F-14s, and felt Iran had succeeded in obtaining new parts and technical aid in servicing its planes. Many experts felt that while Iran often flew only four to eleven sorties a day, it now had 80-100 operational fighters. Similar increases took place in Iran's use of its U.S.-made AH-1 Cobra gunships. However, most experts felt Iraq retained a massive advantage in the air.[30]

New Developments in the "Tanker War"

The shipping war also accelerated in the Gulf. Iraq continued to pound at Iran's shuttle tankers and oil facilities. Iran sent another purchasing mission to Greece, London, and Norway to buy 15 more tankers. While it claimed it wanted these for its shuttle to Sirri, some experts feared Iran was buying old tankers to use as blockade ships to attack Gulf ports.

At the same time, however, Iran demonstrated that it had a greatly improved capability to conduct an oil war of its own. Iranian ships began firing missiles much more aggressively at the cargo ships and tankers in the Gulf, often at night. Confirmed attacks included missile strikes on the *World Dawn* on January 8, the *Atlantic Dignity* on January 12, the *Saudiah* on January 14, the *Isomeri* on January 23, and the *Ambia Fortuna* on February 4, and the *Sea Empress* and *Wu Jiang* later in the month.[31]

This time the missile involved was clearly identified as the Italian-made Sea Killer, and on at least one occasion in early March it showed it could do catastrophic damage. It hit the small 998-ton tanker *Sedra* in a vulnerable area and turned the ship into an inferno, killing at least seven crewmen.[32]

The Sea Killer became operational in 1984, and was sold to Iran before the fall of the Shah. It is a relatively light missile only about 1.01 meters long and 20.6 cm in diameter. It weighs 300 kilograms and has a small 70 kilogram high explosive semi-armor piercing warhead. It has a maximum air-to-surface range of 25 kilometers and a minimum range of six kilometers. It is a sea skimmer which flies at a height of three to four meters.

The Sea Killer is deployed in both a helicopter launched and deck mounted configuration. The deck mount is a five round trainable launcher which can be integrated with the existing X-band radars, conical scan radars, and shipboard computers on many small combat ships. It rides the radar beam to the target, although it can be radio directed in a heavy jamming environment.

The helicopter systems includes an MM/APQ-706 tracking radar, a missile control console, guidance computer, command link, optical tracker with joystick, pilot display, and Sea Killer/Marte missile. The system weighs 865-1,165 kilograms with 300-600 kilograms for one to two missiles, 400 kilograms for the launch console, 143 kilograms for the radar, and 22 kilograms for the optical sight. The unit can either be fired directly from a helicopter firing at medium altitude or the helicopter can acquire the target on its radar, pop down to fly under a ship's radar and then pop up to fire the missile.[33]

Although none of these ships were sunk or seriously damaged, insurance rates continued to rise, and 16 ships had been damaged by early February – raising the total hit since the war began to 284.[34] The USSR went so far in mid-January as to send a Krivak-class missile frigate to escort four Soviet ships carrying arms to Iraq from the Straits to Kuwait. This was only the second Soviet warship to enter the Gulf since 1982 – the first had been sent when Iran detained two Soviet ships in September – and was clearly intended as a signal to Iran.

The U.S. did not increase its 6 ship force in the Gulf but it did send patrols further north into the Gulf – increased its force in the Indian Ocean to a full carrier group including the 85,000-ton carrier *Kitty Hawk* and eleven escort ships – and deployed the carrier task force just east of Masirah, off the coast of Oman. The US also sent F-111s to an "exercise" in Turkey.

Britain and France increased their ship activity, and the British Armilla or Indian Ocean squadron began to spend roughly 50% of its time in the Gulf. The squadron then consisted of the air defense destroyer *Nottingham*, the frigate *Andromeda* with the Sea Wolf anti-missile defense system, and the support ship *Orangeleaf*.[35]

It soon became clear that this activity was not simply the result of Iranian use of the Sea Killer. In mid-February, the US detected that Iran was deploying a much heavier coastal defense missile near the Straits of Hormuz and that there had been at least one test firing of the missile.[36]

The new system was a Chinese version of the Soviet Styx anti-ship missile which the Chinese designate as the HY-2 or Silkworm. The missile is not particularly sophisticated, and Western warships can jam it or shoot it down, but it is very effective against tankers and cargo vessels.

The Chinese version of the Styx missile is most effective at ranges under 40 kilometers, although it can fly further. The missile is 6.5 meters long, and has a diameter of 75 centimeters. It weighs 2,500-3,000 kilograms and has a 500 kilogram or 1,100 pound warhead. This warhead is about seven times the weight of that on the Sea Killer and three times the weight of that on the Exocet. The system has two or four missile launchers. It uses a mix of guidance systems including midcourse programmed autopilot, radio command, final command, or IR. It has a sea skimming option but normally flies at constant altitude and dives in. It is a slow subsonic missile which first entered service in 1959.

Nevertheless, the combination of the Sea Killer and Silkworm missiles gave Iran a powerful capability to strike at tankers and cargo vessels in the Gulf, a growing capability to sink ships rather than damage them, and even a limited ability to close the Straits of Hormuz.

Further, Iran was continuing to buy more of the outboard motor powered aluminium small craft it had begun to use in the summer of 1986 to mine the waters off Umm Qasr. Iran had used these to sow coastal mines in waters up to 60 feet deep, and had the capability to launch free floating mines that could at least harass traffic in the Gulf.[37]

Finally, it also became apparent that China had transferred enough technology to Iran to allow it to begin assembling or coproducing the Chinese variant of the Frog and Scud missiles. While these did not threaten shipping, they did give Iran another way of offseting Iraq's advantage in the air. While the Frog variant only had a range of about 40 miles, it could reach Basra. The Scud variant had a range of up to 180 miles and giave Iran the potential ability to fire at large area targets in Kuwait and the southern Gulf states.[38]

This led the US to issue a new series of declarations, beginning on February 25, 1987, that it would use armed force to secure the passage of cargo ships through the Gulf. The US also offered Kuwait US naval escorts to protect shipping to Kuwait, although Kuwait eventually refused the offer when the US made it clear that it would not operate as part of a joint task force with the USSR.

Kuwait was in a particularly sensitive position because it wished to avoid the domestic and political backlash from any overt dependence on the US. Kuwait had been forced to dissolve its Parliament in July, 1986, and police officials had announced in November, 1986, that some 26,898 people had been deported during the previous year. Informed sources put the true figure at 40,000, including many Iranian Shi'ites and large numbers of Palestinians. Even then, Kuwait's native population was still under 22% of the total population in country.[39]

Iran Adds Political to Military Intimidation

Iran simultaneously launched new political intimidation efforts direct against Iraq and the Gulf. It carefully timed these efforts to put indirect pressure on the Islamic Conference that was to meet in Kuwait at the end of January. A series of small bombing incidents occurred in Baghdad, artillery shells hit the Kuwaiti island of Failaka, and on January 20, three fires were set in oil installations in Kuwait. There were also indications that Iran had covertly attempted to mine Kuwait's harbors.[40]

It is unclear how much this Iranian pressure succeeded, but such intimidation was probably unnecessary. When the Islamic Foreign Ministers meeting did occur in Kuwait, it produced nothing more substantive regarding the Gulf than rhetoric and new peace initiatives. Iran did not attend, and Syria concentrated on the Arab-Israeli issue.

The main impact of the meeting was to bring Egypt back into the Islamic fold – a move that Saudi Arabia and Kuwait had already taken by quietly offering Egypt economic aid. It was clear that the southern Gulf states were seeking a potential source of military assistance in the event of further Iraqi defeats, although it was far from clear how much aid Egypt could give.

The Fighting During Late February and Early March: The End of Kerbala Five

During the rest of February and through most of March, Iran continued to pound at Basra while it built-up and deployed for major attacks elsewhere along the front. It continued to talk about final offensives, while it launched some additional limited attacks to the north and conducted a war of attrition.

Iraq continued to fight a relatively static defense on the ground and to use its air power to pound away at Iran's oil targets and cities. It kept up its air attacks on the thirteen major cities in western Iran until late February, and Iraqi aircraft continued to hit Tehran, something it had not done consistently since the "war of the cities" in 1985 – when it claimed to have bombed Tehran 30 times.

Although US and Israeli shipments of Hawk parts and missiles did seriously reduce Iraqi ability to attack Kharg Island and the otherwise vulnerable bridges and supply lines to the rear of Faw and the Iranian positions near Basra, it also became clear that most of Iran's ground radar stations were no longer functioning – if, indeed they had been functioning at the start of the year. While Iran scored some kills in selected areas with its Hawks, it seem to be scoring as many kills with the far less capable variants of the SA-2 it had received from the PRC, and with the short range laser-guided Robot-70 surface-to-air missiles it had bought illegally from Bofors in Sweden.[41]

Iraq sustained some losses to ground based defenses and fighters during its attacks on Iranian cities, but these were comparatively limited – particularly in the case of air-to-air combat. In fact, a defecting Iranian Air Force officer claimed that only one-third of Iran's remaining 65 F-4s and less than a third of its 1,000 helicopter gunships were really operational.[42] The most Iran could do in the air was to launch a few more

Scud missiles at Baghdad, and make futile calls for Iraq's population to evacuate the city.

On February 18, 1987, this series of counter-city attacks came to a temporary end. Iraq declared a halt on its anti-city attacks – supposedly because Rajavi had asked Sadam Hussein to halt attacks which were hurting Iran's "struggling masses" rather than its leadership – but more probably because the Khomeini regime agreed to call off its artillery attacks on Basra. In any case, Iran publically agreed to a two-week ceasefire in which Iraq suspended its air attacks on population centers and Iran limited its artillery attacks on Basra's population.

By this time, however, Iran claimed 3,000 killed and 9,000 wounded. Iraq claimed to have hit 35 Iranian towns and cities since January 9. Iraq, in turn, reported eleven missile attacks on Baghdad since January 9, plus the Iranian shelling of several towns. It indicated it had suffered 300 killed and more than 1,000 wounded. Although both sides were claiming violations of the ceasefire as early as February 22, it continued into April.[43]

On the ground, however, Iran continued to try to push forward at Basra. It moved many of its regular army units south from the Sumar front, and raised speculation that it was redeploying its armor and heavy artillery to strike at Basra.

While Iran did not use this armor in its next series of attacks against the Iraqi positions around the city, it did launch new infantry assaults. These new assaults included a two-pronged infantry assault on February 22-23 against the Iraqi positions east of Basra and along the road from Salamcheh to Basra.

This "Ya Zahra" attack scored limited gains, and caused some 2,000 casualties in Iraq's 98th, 705th, and 437th infantry brigades. It also, however, marked the official end of Kerbala Five. On February 27, the Iranians announced that the offensive was over and a new phase had begun. At this point in the fighting around Basra, Iran claimed to have caused 56,500 Iraqi casualties while Iraq claimed 230,000-280,000 Iranian casualties.[44] Although both claims were exaggerated, the fighting had been extremely bloody by any standard.

The end of the offensive also did not mean a pause in the fighting. The Iranian leadership began to talk of yet another "final offensive" by the Iranian New Year holiday at the end of March.

On March 1 Iraq attempted a limited counterattack on the Iranian positions around Fish Lake. Both the commander of the Iraqi Air Force, Air Marshal Hameed Shaban and the new commander of Iraq's 3rd Corps – Lt. General Diauldine Jamal, made claims to have destroyed large numbers of Iranian troops. In fact, Iraq took losses of 500 to 1,500 casualties, and 50 tanks and armored vehicles. The Iraqi troops were committed in head-on attacks against Iranian positions during daylight.

While Iraq did try to take advantage of its superiority in firepower, it failed to maneuver effectively or provide effective air and helicopter support. As at Faw, the Iraqi Army could defend, but took heavier losses than the Iranian forces when it tried to counterattack.[45]

The Launching of Kerbala Seven

In spite of the fact Iran tended to win most of its smaller battles with Iraq, it was still faced with the issue of what to do next. It was left with a number of near-term military options, all of which were certainly threatening to Iraq, but all of which also ran the risk of creating massive new Iranian casualties. These options included:

- Attempting to directly overrun the ring of massive and well-manned Iraqi defenses around Basra.
- Use the newly captured islands in the Shatt al-Arab as a springboard to attack across the Shatt in new areas.
- Attempt to thrust south of Basra and link up with the Iranian forces at Faw.
- Maintain a slow siege of Basra with artillery and missile fire in an effort to deprive the city of its strategic value and wear down the Iraqi troops with continuing casualties.
- Drive towards Baghdad from the Sumar basin southeast across heavily defended Iraqi positions, most of which were well entrenched in rough or mountainous terrain.
- Launch a limited or spoiling attack to the far north to try to take advantage of the Kurdish rebel groups hostile to Iraq, threaten Iraq's oil exports, and force Iraq to move troops north.

The option that Iran chose was to attack to the north. On March 4, 1987, Iran launched a new attack called Kerbala Seven. This offensive took place in the mountain area in the far north, called the Gerdmand Heights. These heights are in the region near Haj Omran region. They are west of Piranshahr in Iran, and east of the Iraqi town of Rawanduz in Iraqi Kurdistan.

This area had already been the scene of bitter fighting in 1983, and was important because it allowed Iran to take positions some 12 miles inside Iraq, to overlook the main valley road to Rawanduz, to strengthen its ties to the anti-Iraqi Kurdish rebel groups, and to increase its pressure on Kirkuk – some 60 miles to the south of Rawanduz.

The attack repeated a pattern where Pasadaran troops and troops from the regular 64th Urumiyeh Division skilfully infiltrated into fixed Iraqi positions which Iraq had the firepower to defend, but was too unprepared or inflexible to use it. Iranian infantry troops did this in spite of the fact they were attacking a snow-covered position some 8,300 feet above sea level which was held by the 96th Brigade of the Iraqi 5th Corps.

The Iranian forces attacked on foot, but used bulldozers and road graders to create a road directly behind the advancing troops that allowed rapid resupply and reinforcement in spite of the terrain. They seized the summit within less than 24 hours and held it, as well as the Iraqi town of Shuma Mustafa, in spite of repeated Iraqi counterattacks during 5-8 March.[46]

These new Iranian gains still left Iraq in a relatively good position to protect Kirkuk and the north, but they clearly were of deep concern to Sadam Hussein and the Ba'ath Party. On March 15, 1987, Hussein held a five-hour meeting with his commanders in Baghdad, including General Adnan Khairallah, the Minister of Defense; Ali Hassab Al MeJid, a senior member of the Ba'ath, and Information Minister, Latif Nasif Jassem. Although we cannot be certain what was talked about, Iraqi sources report they did discuss the risk of Iraq being slowly defeated by attrition. There is a growing Iraqi fear that a war of attrition might eventually lead to defeat.

It was also scarcely coincidental that Turkey soon issued another warning to Iran not to support any Kurdish attack on the Iraqi pipeline to Turkey. This warning paralled the warnings the Turkish Prime Minister and other officials had begun to issue in the summer of 1986, when Iran launched two Scud attacks against Kirkuk, and Iran's Hawks at Kharg made the risk of losses too high to justify major raids, and that Iran's improving use of other missiles was improving the defense of other oil targets.

Iraq did strike an Iranian shuttle tanker on March 8, but did not conduct any other major strikes until March 18, when it attacked three ships off the Iranian coast. It at least seemed possible that Iran's possession of Chinese anti-ship missiles and willingness to use the Sea Killer had created a climate where Iraqi attacks on Iranian shipping were far more vulnerable to retaliation than ever before.[50]

The only good news Iraq seemed to be getting was that the US was again making strong efforts to halt arms shipments to Iran and continued to declare it would escort cargo ships to Kuwait, and that the USSR declared it would reschedule Iraq's $15 billion debt to the Soviet Union – some $10 billion of which had gone to pay for arms. Further, the USSR made it clear that it would replace Iraq's air losses since the beginning of the year, which now totalled some 45-50 planes. These replacements were reported to include MiG-27 attack fighters and MiG-29s with full look-down shoot-down radars and air-to-air missiles.[51]

The Iranian New Year and the Prospects for Future Fighting

The Iranian New Year came on March 19, 1987. It did not bring the start of a final offensive, but neither did it bring any signs of peace. The net impact of Iran's offensives in 1987 was not so much to change the war, as to tilt it in favor of Iran while putting new strains on both nations.

Both nations also had problems within the senior military and political leadership. Iran and Iraq continued to exhibit serious economic difficulties, although basic services largely continued. Any boosts in morale were mixed with heavy losses, and the battles created a large new group of mourners. Equally significantly, the new battles involved major expenditures of materiel – up to one million artillery rounds per day were fired in the most intense exchanges – and caused serious losses of trained troops and leadership cadres. Iraq's costs for the war rose to well over $1 billion a month.

Both Iran and Iraq had also shown that they had serious military problems during the fighting. While Iran could claim significant gains in its strategic position, and Iraq could claim a largely successful defense of Basra. Iran again showed it could score limited gains, but lacked the firepower and support to sustain and expand them. It had much of its 750,000 man army still intact, but was increasingly short of heavy equipment and trained officers, NCOs, and ordinary troops.

Iran's political and economic problems continued in spite of a limited increase in oil prices. Nearly half the nation's industrial capacity was unutilised, the true price of a dollar was more than eleven times the official foreign exchange prices, and unemployment levels were higher than at the worst peak just before the fall of the Shah.[52]

While Khomeini seemed in good health, and made a long speech calling for unity and continued struggle against Iraq as part of Iran's New Year celebration, the internal political situation in Iran remained confused. Political executions and bombing incidents continued. Montazeri's position was uncertain, and Rafsanjani seemed to suffer from the public disclosure of just how deeply he had been involved in the covert arms deal with the US and Israel. There were increasing rumors that he had taken de facto command of the war to demonstrate his commitment to the revolution.[53]

Kerbala Eight and Kerbala Nine

Iran was again deploying forces for a possible major offensive in April, but it made few claims about a final offensive. It concentrated on relatively long-term actions like building up new supplies and logistic capabilities in the south, and beginning a major effort to drain the water barriers protecting Basra. It launched a "Kerbala Eight" offensive against the Iraqi defensive positions near Basra on April 3, 1987. While no significant gains were made, Kerbala Eight was sufficiently bloody to make it clear that Iran was still willing to pound away at Iraqi positions.

President Hojatoleslam Ali Khamenei and Speaker of Parliament Hajatoleslam Hashemi Rafsanjani stressed that the war would continue, that there would be no ties to the US, and that there were no "moderates" or "extremists" blocking Iran's commitment to the war.[54] At the same time, Iranian statements also stressed Khomeini's idea of war until victory in a "divine cause", rather than a single final offensive and made it clear that the war could last another year.[55]

Iran clearly had the potential to win further tactical victories, but its capabilities to create a major strategic breakthrough were far less certain. It still seemed to have major problems in fully utilizing its military strength, and continued to lose at least three times as many casualties as Iraq in the daily fighting around Basra. While Iran was on the attack, both nations were being ground down by the fighting to a point where it was difficult to be certain which would ultimately suffer the most.

Iraq's suffering was obvious. It had still not shown it could use air power with significant effect to halt a major attack by Iran's troops. It had far less flexibility in attacking Kharg Island. It had again demonstrated that it could not efficiently counterattack Iranian forces with armor, and that it continued to have problems with artillery – which often was wasted on mass barrages in marsh areas where much of the effect of Iraq's shells was lost because of the absorptive capability of the soft ground.

Iraq faced an increasing threat to Basra with each new Kerbala offensive and faced the prospect of being slowly depopulated by the constant threat of Iranian artillery fire. Iraq was clearly under even greater social and financial strain than in 1986. The fighting produced the same wave of funerals and mourning throughout Iraq as the fighting in Faw a year earlier, and costs were extraordinarily high.

By the end of April, the value of Iraq's carefully built-up capability to strike at Iran's oil facilities and shipping was increasingly uncertain even in the areas where Iran did have Hawk missiles. Iraq did continue to strike sporadically at Iranian oil fields. It hit Iran's Cyrus and Nowrouz fields in late March, as well as the Ardeshir oil field. Nevertheless, Iraq's leaders now had to consider the impact on the southern Gulf states if its attacks caused Iran to escalate its anti-ship strikes, or suddenly brought more US and/or Soviet warships into the Gulf.

Iran also used this time period to complete the deployment of at least two full batteries of Silkworm missiles near the Straits of Hormuz. By mid-April it had at least 12 launchers and 36-48 missiles on line. One battery was also relocated from the island of Onqeshim on the edge of the Straits to the Iranian naval base at Bandar Abbas, on the northwest shore of the Straits of Hormuz to provide surface-to-air missile protection. The other battery was located at Kuhestak to the east. While the missiles could just barely cover the 64 kilometer-wide straits with reasonable accuracy and their normal payload, they could reach up to 80 kilometers with less accuracy and a lower payload.[56]

Further, Iraq was running into more serious debt problems. A leading

Western export-import bank indicated that Iraq's foreign debt now approached some $50 billion, half of which was owed to Arab states – largely Kuwait and Saudi Arabia. Iraq's debt to the Western OECD (Organisation of Economic Cooperation and Development) was reported to have risen by over 53% in the preceding year, and from $7.69 billion to a total of $11.8 billion – largely to banks in France, the FRG and Japan.[57]

While two-thirds of this total debt was owed to banks in the form of government insured or guaranteed loans in 1985, Iraq owed far more to institutions with less ability to roll over debt payments. This made Iraq's October, 1986, failure to meet a $71 million payment of the principal on a $500 million commercial bank loan steadily more threatening as Iran's offensives of early 1987 forced it into heavier and heavier new expenditures on munitions and military equipment.[58]

Notes

[1] *Economist*, January 17, 1987, p. 36.
[2] *Washington Post*, December 4, 1986, P. A-49; *Washington Times*, December 2, 1986, p. 8A.
[3] *Jane's Defence Weekly*, December 13, 1986, p. 1372.
[4] *Christian Science Monitor*, December 12, 1986, p. 1.
[5] *New York Times*, December 11, 1986, p. A-23.
[6] Speech by Iraqi Minister of Defense Adnan Khairallh, December 27, 1986. The Mujahideen opposition movement claimed Iran had lost 16,000 killed.
[7] *Washington Post*, December 26, 27, and 28, 1986; *Economist*, January 3, 1987, pp. 26-27.
[8] *New York Times*, December 18, 1986, p. D-2.
[9] *Washington Post*, December 30, 1986, p. A-16.
[10] *Economist*, December 20, 1986, p. 46; *The Middle East*, November, 1986, pp. 6-7; *New York Times*, December 19, 1986, *Washington Post*, December 19, 1986.
[11] *Washington Post*, February 9, 1987, pp. A-13 and A-16. *Economist*, January 17, 1987, pp. 36-37; *Newsweek*, February 2, 1987, pp. 30-31.
[12] *Washington Post*, February 9, 1987, pp. A-13 and A-16.
[13] The geography involved is very complex, and current maps do not accurately show the changes in water barriers that have occured since the war. The extent of wet terrain is also seasonal and is visible only from satellite photography. In general, the Iranians picked a relatively dry period since the major floods do not hit the area until March. The north-south line that forms the Iran-Iraq border in the south is parallel to a line about one kilometer east of 48.00° longitude until it hits the Nahr el Khaiin River at a point called Boundary Pillar 1. It then runs along the Nahr el Khaiin for about eight kilometers until the river flows into the Shatt at a point called Boundary Pillar 2 (30.26.90N, 46.06.62E). The border then generally follows the east bank of the Shatt-al-Arab until it reaches the sea at the end of the Faw Peninsula, although it is to the west of a large island in the Shatt variously called Jazireh ye Salbukh or Muhalla Island.
[14] *Washington Post*, January 10, 1987, p. A-16.
[15] This was the 19th Iranian missile attack on Baghdad in two years.
[16] *New York Times*, January 12, 1987, p. A-1.
[17] Ibid, and *Washington Post*, January 15, 1987, p. A-1.

18 *New York Times*, January 12, 1987, p. A-1 and January 13, p. A-12; *Washington Post*, January 13, 1987, p. A-14.

19 *Wall Street Journal*, January 14, 1987, p. 27; *Washington Post*, January 14, 1987. p. A-19; *New York Times*, January 14, 1987, p. A-6; *Washington Times*, January 21, 1987, p. 6-A.

20 *Newsweek*, February 2, 1987, p. 31.

21 *Washington Post*, January 16, 1987, p. A-19; *Christian Science Monitor*, January 20, 1987, p. 1.

22 *Washington Times*, January 21, 1987, p. 6A.

23 *Washington Post*, January 20, 1987, p. A-1, January 28, 1987, p. A-15; *Christian Science Monitor*, January 20, 1987, p. I-1; *New York Times*, January 21, 1987, p. A-6; *Sunday Times*, January 25, 1987.

24 *Washington Post*, February 9, 1987, p. A-16.

25 January 27, 1987, p. A-1.

26 The killed on both sides now approached 1 million. To put this into some kind of perspective, this compares with 2.9 million in Korea, 2.4 million in Vietnam, and 2.2 million in Cambodia. *Washington Post*, January 16, 1987, p. A-1; and *New York Times*, January 16, 1987, p. A-9, January 20, 1987. p. A-8, and January 23, 1987, p. A-1; *Christian Science Monitor*, January 20, 1987, p. 1.

27 Ibid, and *Washington Post*, January 28, 1987, p. 16.

28 *Observer*, January 25, 1987.

29 *Wall Street Journal*, March 2, 1987, p. 2.

30 *Washington Post*, January 27, 1987, p. A-1. U.S. officials later said on a background basis that the Hawk parts had only added 3% to Iran's air defenses and the TOWs only knocked out a few dozen Iraqi tanks. *Washington Times*, January 29, 1987, p. 6A.

31 *New York Times*, January 20, 1987, p. A-1; *Philadelphia Inquirer*, January 21, 1987, p. 5A; *Observer*, January 25, 1987; *Washington Times*, February 5, 1987, p. 7A; *Baltimore Sun*, March 1, 1987, p. 24. Many of these attacks took place outside Iranian waters and off the shore of the UAE. Little effort seems to have been made to identify the targets. The *Wu Jiang*, for example, was a PRC registered freighter with no cargo of military value.

32 *Baltimore Sun*, March 29, 1987, p. 1A.

33 General Dynamics, *The World's Missile Systems - 1982*, Pomona, General Dynamics, 1982, pp. 233-234; Bill Gunston, *Modern Airborne Missiles*, New York, Arco, 1983, pp. 110-11.

34 *Washington Times*, February 5, 1987, p. 7A.

35 *Christian Science Monitor*, January 21, 1987, p. 1; *Washington Post*, January 28, p. A-1.

36 *Washington Post*, March 24, 1987, p. A-25.

37 *Washington Post*, March 24, 1987, p. A-25.

38 *Baltimore Sun*, March 29, 1987, p. 1A

39 President Reagan made the first statement on February 25, and this was followed up by statements by Secretary Weinberger beginning March 22. The US released details of the new Iranian missile build-up during the month of March. *New York Times* March 21, p. 4, March 24, 1987, p. A-1; *Washington Post*, March 23, 1987, p. A-19.

40 *Observer*, January 25, 1987.

41 The Chinese version of the SA-2 is an obsolete missile which first deployed in 1958, and is lethal only against fighters flying at medium to high altitudes which do not use their radar warning receivers effectively to allow them to maneuver and dodge the missile. It is a radar-guided system using the Fan Song radar and a computer aided command link. The missile has a maximum effective range of about 30 kilometers, a lant range of 50 kilometers, and a ceiling of around 5,500 meters. It is a large complex system requiring a well prepared ground sight. The missile alone weighs 2,300 kilograms.
The Robot 70, or RBS70, is a portable air defense system which is carried in three man-portable packs and which can be assembled in less than two minutes. One pack contains the stand, the second the sight and laser transmitter units, and the third the missile. The missile is 1.32 meters long and 106 centimeters in diameter. It weighs 13 kilograms and has a small high explosive fragmentation warhead with a proximity fuse. It has a maximum

range of five kilometers and a maximum altitude of 3,000 meters. It is normally a laser beam rider, but it has been installed in both Land Rovers and APCs using search radars. General Dynamics, *The World's Missile Systems – 1982*, Pomona, General Dynamics, 1982, pp. 85 and 197. The President of Bofors resigned on March 6, 1987 as a result of the sale after two years of investigation. *Washington Post*, March 7, 1987, p. A-24.

[42] These Claims were made by Colonel Behzad Moezi during Mujahideen-e-Khalq sponsored meetings with the press. He also claimed that (a) Iran had shot down 55 of its own planes because of the lack of functioning IFF and radar systems, including a Falcon Jet transport which he said was shot down by a US supplied Hawk missile in early February, (b) that only 30-40% of Iran's C-130 transports were flyable and that several had crashed because of poor maintenance, (c) that two-thirds of overall mix of 65 fighter that Iran had operational were not 100% functional, (d) that all RF-4Es were shot down or lost, (e) that only 1-2 of Iran's remaining P-3Cs out of a prewar total of 6 had serious computer and sensor problems, (f) that only 6-10 F-14s were still operational, (g) that only four tankers were still operational, (h) that over 180 pilots had defected and many with their aircraft, (i) that too few specialists remained to keep Iran's planes flying, and (j) that pilots were only briefed on their missions an hour or so before attacks to keep them from having time to plan defections. *Washington Times*, February 12, 1987, p. 6A, and *Aviation Week*, February 23, 1987, p.25

[43] *Washington Times*, February 20, 1987, p. 8A; *Washington Post*, February 24, 1987, p. A-1; *Washington Post*, February 19, 1987, p. A-23.

[44] *Washington Times*, February 28, 1987, p. 5.

[45] *Washington Times*, March 2, 1987, p. 7A.

[46] *Washington Post*, March 15, 1987, p. A-1.

[47] *New York Times*, March 16, 1987, p. A-3.

[48] *New York Times*, March 5, 1987, p. A-9.

[49] *Washington Times*, March 5 and 6, 1987, pp. 8A and 8A. *Washington Post*, March 8, 1987, p. A-30.

[50] *Christian Science Monitor*, March 19, 1987, p. 2.

[51] *Washington Times*, March 20, 1987, p. 11A.

[52] *Washington Post*, March 23, 1987, p. A-13.

[53] *New York Times*, March 22, 1987, p. 22; *Washington Post*, March 21, 1987, p. A-1.

[54] *New York Times*, February 17, 1987, p. A-1.

[55] *New York Times*, February 11, 1987, p. A-8. The quotations come from Khomeini's speech of February 10, his first in three months.

[56] *Jane's Defence Weekly*, March 28, 1987, p. 532.

[57] Current data on the breakdown of Iraq's debt are unavailable, but Iraq owed US banks only $200 million at the end of 1985. At the end of 1986, the US Export Import Bank had only guaranteed $7.5 million in US loans to Iraq, only $600,000 of which was in default.

[58] *Wall Street Journal*, February 12, 1987, p. 29.

Chapter Seven

The Prognosis: No Clear End in Sight

The grim truth is that recent events leave one unable to predict the course of the Iran-Iraq War, whether either side will win, or which side that will be. The shifts during 1984-1987 do not represent any firm trend in favor of Iran or Iraq.

An Iranian or Iraqi mistake could either reverse recent trends in the fighting on the ground or suddenly create a much worse situation. Similarly, the political, economic, and social factors that strain Iraq and Iran are so closely balanced that the net effect of the strains on each nation is completely unpredictable. While these strains may force either Iraq or Iran to exhaustion, they are equally likely to reduce both nations' ability to buy more weapons and munitions in rough proportion without shifting the balance or being severe enough to end the war.

What does seem likely is that the risk is rising that the war will broaden to include nearby states, and that the threat the war poses to Western strategic interests will continue to grow. Every month the war continues also means that its end is less likely to leave a legacy of peace and stability, and it is still all too possible that Iraq could suffer a major defeat. These issues become clearer, however, when the major possible outcomes of the war are examined in more detail.

A Continuing War of Attrition

There is no critical military, political, or economic reason why the war could not continue for several more years. Both sides already have sufficient military resources, and both are now locked into political positions that make it difficult to change their commitment to the war.

Iran is still receiving enough military resupply from states like Libya, Syria, Argentina, North Korea, Ethiopia, the PRC etc. to keep fighting, and is gradually expanding its military production base. Iraq can sustain its present manpower losses if it has to, and is getting enough economic aid from its Arab neighbors and the West to match Iran's equally weakened economy.

The fighting in early 1987 seems to be pushing the war towards some kind of final phase, but whether this phase will last two weeks, two months, or two years is totally unpredictable. The answer rests with intangibles like popular morale, the internal cohesion of the Iranian and Iraqi governments and their military forces, and the mistakes and successes of individual military commanders.

The war can easily go on until one side breaks for political reasons, or halt suddenly because an Iraqi commander makes a critical mistake at the front, or Iran makes mistakes in protecting its oil exports. The slow grinding attrition of the last two years can continue for some time to come.

Exhaustion and a Peace or Ceasefire

The sheer cost of the war is pushing both sides towards either conflict termination or further escalation. Iraq would clearly accept a peace based on the *status quo ante bellum* – even if it involved a tacit admission of defeat in the form of some kind of aid package to Iran from the Southern Gulf states.

For all its current denials, Iran may be forced in the same direction. Its present tactics of attrition are expensive in money and manpower, and while the Iranian government has consistently denied it could ever make a peace with Sadam Hussein, governments find it only slightly harder to find excuses to make peace than they do to find excuses to make war.

Political will may not be enough. Iran has the manpower to threaten Iraq, but lacks the conventional military means to threaten Iraq's current oil exports, and Iraq's exports will continue to increase. Iraq is now exporting averages of up to 1.7 MMBD, versus 2.5 MMBD before the start of the war. Iraq opened up its new link to the Saudi pipeline at Janbu on September 26, 1985.

As has been discussed in Chapter Two, these expansions have added an initial 600,000 BPD to Iraq's exports. Iraq will acquire another 500 MBD of export capacity through expansions to line through Turkey in the second quarter of 1987. While Kuwait and Saudi Arabia will then cease marketing their oil for Iraq, Iraq will still have a net gain in 1987 of an additional 250,000-300,000 BPD of export capacity.

Total Iraqi exports will rise from around 1.6 MMBD in 1986 to 2.6 MMBD in 1988. In the interim, Saudi Arabia and Kuwait would probably compensate Iraq for any temporary loss of its pipeline through Turkey.[1] This level of exports will not compensate Iraq for a prolonged drop in oil prices, but it will leave Iraq as well off in terms of export capability as Iran. It will also help persuade Iraq's creditors to continue to roll over current debts and extend at least some credits.[2]

Iran can probably count on future oil export revenues superior to those of Iraq. While Iran's population is far larger, its budget estimates indicate it can maintain both its war budget and essential civil expenditures with oil exports in excess of 1.5 MMBD. Nevertheless, total Iranian budget expenditures have ranged from $42-$48 billion during 1982/83 to 1984/85, while revenues have only reached $27-45 billion. Iran now has a major budget deficit and a serious shortage of hard currency. The war has imposed a major strain on Iran's economy and it has little flexibility if oil revenues drop even further. Iran has averaged as little as 1.6 MMBD per month in 1986, largely because of Iraqi air attacks, and this is pushing Iran near its limits.[3]

Accordingly, the central economic issue driving both sides towards a peace of exhaustion is probably oil prices. Both sides can continue the war, but both can only do so by steadily cutting the amount of "butter" in order to buy their "guns". While acute economic austerity seems to favor Iran – because of its broader popular base of support for the war – such calculations are difficult to make. Only time will tell how each country reacts, how these financial strains will interact with the military ones discussed earlier, and whether a rise in oil prices with strengthen Iran and Iraq's capability to keep fighting.

Iraqi Escalation to an All-Out Oil War

The recent shifts in both the oil market and in the course of the war give Iraq a strong incentive to conduct an even more intensive oil war. While Iran can probably continue the war indefinitely if it can export at levels of 1.5-2.5 MMBD, Iran cannot do so if its oil exports drop much below an average of 1.5 MMBD. Iran would then be forced to make massive additional cutbacks in its food imports and civil benefits. Such a further reduction in Iranian food imports might well threaten support for the Khomeini government and the war.

Iran also has uncertain ability to recover from any sustained loss of export capability from Kharg Island. Its only short-term hope is the extra capacity it has planned for by hiring Smith International to build two pipelines, 17 and 21 km long, to new loading points south of the Iranian coastal port of Ganaveh, just north of Kharg Island. Each pipeline will feed three single-point mooring buoys, and can load tankers of 80,000-100,000 tons dead weight. These buoys are similar to the 4-5 buoys Iraq bought earlier in the war so it would be ready to rapidly restore its export capability in the Gulf. Iraq stores these buoys in a friendly neighboring country. They have a maximum capacity of about 250 MBD each.

However, Ganaveh, the buoys, and the tankers loading from the buoy, will remain vulnerable to Iraq's Mirage F-1s and new "smart" air-to-surface weaponry. Unless Iran can improve its air defenses, Iraq could probably use its airpower to limit Iran to a maximum export capacity below 1 MMBD even if one considers Iran's other oil fields. While Iran can ship 220,000 BPD from the four offshore oil fields that feed its terminals at the island of Jazireh-ye Lavan, even this island is marginally within the range of Iraq's extended range Mirage F-1s.

It is highly likely that Iraq will also continue to use its new extended range Mirage F-1s and other attack aircraft to launch sporadic raids against Kharg, Sirri, Larak, and other Iranian oil targets regardless of the improvements in Iranian air defenses. The key issues are:

● Whether Iraq will take the risks and losses necessary to make continuing intensive efforts to halt most of Iran's oil exports, and
● Whether Iran will use its growing anti-ship warfare capabilities to retaliate against Kuwait or to try to force other southern Gulf states to halt their support to Iraq.

While Iraq may lack the air power to sustain suitable damage, no one can rule out the possibility that Iraq may succeed in crippling Iran's ability to finance the war.

Further, Syria is a wild card that could still turn against Iran at any time. There is no question that the rivalry between Syria and Iraq is a bitter one, and that Syria derives power and status from Iraq's current predicament. However, Iran is a long-term political threat to Syria and Syrian interests in Lebanon. Even though Iran renewed its agreement to provide Syria with one million tons of free oil a year on December 11, 1986, Syria is suffering from critical economic problems and may yet accept some settlement with Iraq if the Gulf states offer a large enough bribe in the form of aid.[4]

Iranian Escalation

Iran now has fewer than 40 F-4s it could use in a major air attack on the Southern Gulf, and the risk of U.S. intervention deprives Iran of much of the incentive to counter-escalate using its naval forces. It is unclear whether Iran has the conventional warfare capability to attack Iraq, the oil export facilities in other countries, or land targets in the southern Gulf states with great effectiveness.

Iran does, however, retain the option of violent counter-escalation directed at Gulf shipping, and can probably make effective selective strikes the southern Gulf states, Iraq, Turkey, and/or any other vital Western and Arab strategic target. Kuwait remains particularly vulnerable to indirect attacks on its shipping, terrorism, sabotage or even direct raids.

Iran seems to lack the assets to close the Gulf for more than the briefest period, and the US can easily counter with its Styx missiles – Iran now has only about 12 fire units and 36-48 missiles. The Straits are too deep and have too much current to make most mines effective. Nevertheless, Iran can use suicide small craft and light aircraft, its Sea Killer anti-ship missiles, and possibly its Harpoons to strike at tankers moving through the Gulf or Straits. It can easily raid most offshore oil facilities in the Gulf, particularly at night when local fighter coverage would be negligible. This could put powerful pressure on the southern Gulf states to try to halt their support for Iraq.

Much also would depend on Western resolve and especially on US willingness to make good on its claims that it will defend the right of passage through the Gulf. Iran's air force and navy may be in a state of acute decline, but Iran still has sufficient naval and air forces to create a Kuwaiti, Saudi or other GCC state demand for protection from U.S. forces and to force the U.S. Navy to protect shipping in the Gulf. Any delay in such a Western reaction might well lead the southern Gulf states to reduce their support for Iraq.

Iran has so far been more cautious in its deeds than in its words in reacting to these risks and uncertainties. It is exceedingly dangerous to assume, however, that Iran will not counter-escalate. Anyone who has read Khomeini, or the writing and speeches of those around him, must recognize his deep belief that a popular revolution can endure such escalation and damage far more easily than a Western state can endure even limited costs from such a conflict. Vietnam and Lebanon have scarcely been paradigms that act to control Iran at the point where it has to choose between peace and escalation.

One Sided Exhaustion: Iraqi Defeat and Iranian Counter-Revolution

The most extreme outcomes of the war would be (a) the defeat of Iraq or (b) the collapse of the Iranian effort and counter-revolution in Iran. Neither outcome now seems likely, but military and political analysts need to be cautious in making predictions that such events will not occur. The West may still be faced with the reality of at least short term Iranian dominance of Iran, or a political shift in Iran so drastic that it brought the USSR into Iran as its principal military and/or economic ally.

The past history of wars of attrition has not been one of exhaustion and peace. It has rather been that the internal tensions and costs in one side lead either to the equivalent of popular revolution or the catalytic collapse of one side's military forces for reasons unexplained by its military strength or previous combat history. One has only to point to World War I as a case in point. France came within the thin edge of such collapse in 1917, and Germany experienced it in 1918.

There are countless similar examples, all of which raise two major issues regarding the uncertainty inherent in predicting such outcomes. First, the internal cohesion of an army is not only never clear to outsiders, it is never clear to a nation's generals and political leaders. The process of defeat by attrition is difficult to detect. Second, coups and counter-revolutions succeed in repressive and one-party states precisely because they must be covert and unpredictable to succeed.

Both Iraq and Iran have special vulnerabilities in this area. Iraq's regime is no longer wealthy enough to offer massive civil compensation and benefits along with financing the war, and is not sufficiently popular to easily survive the effect of month after month of casualties with no clear end in sight. Iran's political rhetoric has also made it tempting to try to topple Sadam Hussein and his immediate supporters as a step towards a compromise peace – although it is far from clear where such a limited coup would stop or that Iran would actually accept any new secular government.

In contrast, Iran's regime is divided and its apparent unity is highly dependent on the life of one man: Khomeini. While its religious government does seem to be in firm control, such appearances can be highly misleading. There are few historical examples of a stable succession to a charismatic revolutionary leader, particularly under the outside pressure of war. Further, most outside analysis of Iranian politics commits the classic error of confusing a lack of knowledge of the new military commanders and elites in both countries with the absence of a potential leader of a coup or "man on horseback".

What is important for the U.S. and the West to recognize is that much of the risk of any Iranian victory will depend on how quickly and solidly it reassures the southern Gulf states, Turkey, and other Arab nations. Such a victory would pose a major threat to every other nation in the region, and even if Iran does not take further military action, states like Kuwait, Bahrain, and Saudi Arabia will be very vulnerable. Only a strong U.S. show of force and Western unity in seeking to contain Iran's political ambitions are likely to restore even moderate confidence and independence of action in the other Gulf oil exporting states.

Conflict Aftermaths

Finally, it is important to note that even a true peace settlement would leave grave uncertainties in the region. The minimum price of a stable peace would be some practical limit on the post-peace settlement arms race, Arab forgiveness of Iraq's war debts, de facto Iraqi and Iranian ability to export oil at something approaching their maximum practical capacity, Western and Arab efforts to rapidly rebuild civil trade with both Iraq and Iran, and the extension of major loans and credits. These conditions are possible, but not currently probable.

This, however, raises the issue of the probable evolution of Iraqi and Iranian forces, and the risks they will pose even with a "peace". It seems likely that any major pause in the Iran-Iraq War will lead both sides to cut their total active manning, although both will still have to maintain relatively high force levels. Such a "peace", ceasefire, or pause in the fighting will, however, probably allow Iran to make major arms purchases from Western Europe or the Soviet bloc. It may also be possible for Iran to rebuild or reactivate much of its U.S. supplied naval and air strength. At the same time, Iraq can be expected to continue to modernize its arms at a rapid rate and to buy the most advanced Soviet and Western European technology it can obtain.

A rough estimate of how present Iranian and Iraqi forces can be expected to evolve in the future is shown in Figure 11. Iran's choice of weapons types will be supplier dependent and is almost impossible to predict. Iraq is likely to rely on Soviet major weapons for most of its force structure, but to use Western aircraft for its first line combat aircraft and increasingly layer European C^3I/BM and EW gear over its Soviet supplied weaponry. The weapons types shown in both cases are illustrative of the expected level of technology and not predictions of buys of specific types.

There is no clear way to estimate the future trend in terms of numbers and type of combat unit. The estimates shown are largely speculative, and current unclassified Western reporting on Iran's divisions or brigades seems to ignore the fact that Iran is often calling far smaller formations "divisions", and some elite Iranian brigades are now larger than other units Iran calls divisions.

In theory, the Pasdaran, or revolutionary forces, were combined with the regular army in 1985. It seems possible, however, that Iranian forces will continue to have a highly irregular order of battle through 1995, with the new revolutionary forces gradually replacing those which existed under the Shah. It also seems likely that Iran will maintain the Hezbollah as trained reserves and its Basij Mustazafin as the equivalent of a mass mobilization system for popular warfare. This force has now given at least three million Iranians some form of paramilitary training.

It is unlikely that any Iranian units will have standardized TOEs (tables of organization and equipment) or U/Es (unit equipment). Some brigades may remain larger than divisions with sharply varying levels of armor, artillery, and communications equipment between units. Some squadrons may be two or three times as effective as others. Each unit will have to be characterized separately for intelligence purposes.

Figure 11. The Trends in Iranian and Iraqi Military Forces: 1987-1995

Force Category	1986/87 Iran	Iraq	1990-1995 Iran	Iraq
TOTAL ACTIVE MILITARY MANPOWER SUITABLE FOR COMBAT	750,000-1,050,000	750,000-850,000	1,000,000	600,000
LAND FORCES				
Regular Army Manpower				
Active	305,000	800,000	NA	450,000
Reserve	NA	(230,000)	NA	250,000
Revolutionary Guards/	350,000	-	500,000	-
Basij/People's Army	150,000	400,000	300,000	-
Hezbollahi (Home Guard)	−2,500,000	-	3,500,000	-
Arab Volunteers	-	6,000?	-	-
Division Equivalents				
Armored (Divisions/Brigades)	?	5	5/6	9/6
Mechanized	3-4? (a)	3	5	5
Infantry and Mountain	8-11 (a)	10+9 (b)	8	4
Special Forces/airborne	1/1	3/2	4/3	3/2
Pasdaran/People's Militia	9?/?	−/15	?	?
Major Combat Equipment				
Main Battle Tanks	900-1,250	4,600-6,000	4,000	5,000
Other Armored Fighting Vehicles	1,190-2,000	3,550-4,000	5,000	5,000
Major Artillery	600-1,300	4,000-5,500	4,000	6,000
AIR FORCES				
Air Force Manpower	35,000	40,000	50,000	50,000
Combat Aircraft	63-105 (c)	500 (d)	400	500
Combat Helicopters	45-75	120-170	220	250
Total Helicopters	150-370	360-410	400	500
Surface to Air Missile Batteries (e)	12	75	30	85
NAVY				
Navy Manpower	26,000	4,250	30,000	15,000
Destroyers	3(f)	0	3	1
Frigates	4(g)	2(h)	3	4
Corvettes	2	6 (i)	2	6
Coastal Submarines	0	0	6	3
Missile Patrol Craft	3-8(j)	8(k)	18	12
Major Other Patrol Craft	4-8	7-13	3	2
Mine warfare vessels	5-7	5	4	7
Hovercraft	10-12	0	0	0
Landingcraft and Ships	8	7	12	9
Maritime Patrol Aircraft	2 P-3F	0	6	6

(a) Estimates differ sharply. One detailed estimate of the regular army shows 7 mechanized divisions with 3 brigades each and a total of 9 armored and 18 mechanized battalions. Also 2 special forces divisions, 1 airborne brigade, plus eight Revolutionary Guard divisions and large numbers of other brigades and battalions.

(b) Includes 5 Infantry divisions and 4 mountain divisions. There are 2 independent special forces divisions, 9 reserve brigades, and 15 People's Volunteer Infantry Brigades.

(c) Includes 20-50 F-4D/E, 17-50 F-5E/F, 10-14 F-14A, and 3 RF-4E. Large numbers of additional combat aircraft are in storage due to lack of parts. Some Argentine A-4s and PRC or North Korean F-6 and F-7 may be in delivery. The number of attack helicopters still operational is unknown.

(d) Includes up to 7-12 Tu-22, 8-10 Tu-16; 4 FGA squadrons with 20 Mirage F-1EQ5 (with Exocet), 23 Mirage F-1EQ200, 4 FGA squadrons with 40-60 MiG-23BM/MiG-27, 3 with 75-95 Su-7 and Su-17/20, and 1 training unit with 12-15 Hunter FB-59/FR-10. There is 1 recce squadron with 5 MiG-25; and 5 interceptor squadrons with 25 MiG-25, 40 MiG-19, 150-200 MiG-21, and 30 Mirage F-1EQ. Figures for Mirage strength vary sharply according to assumptions about delivery rates and combat attrition. Typical estimates of combat helicopters are 40-50 Mi-24, 50-70 SA-342 Gazelle (some with HOT), 30 SA-316B with AS-12 and 44 MBB BO-105 with SS-11.

(e) The number of operational SAM units on each side is unknown. Many of Iran's 12 Hawk batteries are not operational. Iran also has extensive holds of SA-7s and some RBS-70. Iraq has shown very limited ability to use its Soviet made SAMs and some sites do not seem to be fully operational. Counts of Iraq's missile strength are controversial but Iraq seems to have roughly 20 SA-2 (120 launchers), 25 SA-3 (150 launchers), and 25 SA-6 batteries. It also has SA-7 and SA-9 units and some 60 Roland fire units.

(f) 3 equipped with Standard Arm SSMs. One Battle-class and two Sumner-class in reserve.

(g) Equipped with Sea Killer SSM

(h) 1 Lupo class with 8 Otomat-2 missiles and 1 × 8 Albatros/Aspide, plus 1 helicopter. 1 Yugoslav training frigate. 3 Lupo-class Italian made frigates on order

(i) 6 Wadi-class Italian made 650 ton corvettes. Each has 1 × 4 Albatros/Aspide. 2 have 2 Otomat-2 and 1 helicopter each; 4 have 6 Otomat 2 SSMs.

(j) Equipped with Harpoon surface to surface missiles.

(k) Equipped with Styx missiles.

Adapted from various editions of the IISS *The Military Balance,* JCSS, *The Middle East Military Balance,* and work by Drew Middleton for the *New York Times*

Similarly, one of the great uncertainties will be Iran's future reliance on mass mobilization and low technology "revolutionary" forces. Iran's religious leadership now talks a great deal about popular warfare. At the same time, Iran is scouring the world for advanced technology. A low technology and mass infantry force would be more defensive and less risky to the West, but it is doubtful that Iran's revolutionary rhetoric will translate into force plans if it can buy more advanced fighters, SAMs, and tanks.

The estimates in Figure 11 regarding the shifts in Iraqi and Iranian forces are comparatively moderate. They assume that some form of peace or ceasefire will allow the two states to reduce their total active forces, but sufficient tension will remain to force Iran to massively rearm and Iraq to steadily upgrade its level of force quality. Under these conditions, the forces driving each side's military development may be summarized as follows:

Both nations will retain a major mobilization base, but concentrate on building up their combat ready forces.

- Iran will place more emphasis on popular or infantry forces. Iraq will emphasize tank and attack helicopter forces. Artillery will increasingly include self-propelled types. Mechanized units will be equipped with modern MICVs (mechanized infantry combat vehicle) rather than older Soviet APCs and IFVs (infantry fighting vehicle) or M-113s. Modern 3rd and 4th generation anti-tank weapons will replace the present Soviet types still in service and many anti-tank guns. The extremely heavy load of infantry anti-tank rocket launchers will not be reduced, but will be replaced with the latest types available.

- Most armor on both sides will consist of Soviet made T-72 vintage and Western European Challenger/AMX-40/Leopard II tanks and associated MICVs. The artillery will be about 30% self-propelled in 1990, shifting steadily towards more self-propelled weapons. Both sides now favor Soviet-made artillery weapons. Attack helicopters will be of the Mi-24/Mi-28 vintage with large numbers of matching assault helicopters. Helicopters will be army, rather than air force weapons. Both nations will use helicopters more flexibly in maneuver warfare rather than armor and artillery.

- Regular land forces will have very large combat and service support units with heavy engineering, earth moving, and bridging forces. Both sides will have very large logistic stocks and transport units for Middle Eastern armies with large numbers of tank transporters and heavy movers. Their limitations in combat maneuver will be offset by rapid road mobility.

- Both sides will radically upgrade both their army air defense forces and their air defense forces for area and point defense. Iran will complete the full air defense and AC&W system it began under the Shah using European or Soviet technology. Iraq will heavily modernize its system. Both land forces and point targets will have large numbers of echeloned air defense weapons ranging from infantry held SAMs to SHORAD systems such as Crotale and the SA-8, and ranging up to Improved Hawk/SA-10 level surface-to-air missile launchers. These systems will be "netted" with the new warning and AC&W (air control and warning) systems. Both sides will emphasize modern EW/ECM systems of the kind available in Western Europe and from the Soviet bloc.

● The Iranians will rebuild their air force seeking fighters at the quality level of the MiG-29/F-16/Mirage 2000, although they will buy large numbers of lower quality Chinese fighters or Western dual-role trainers. Iraq will shift from a mix of Mirages and older Soviet fighters to similarly advanced types. Both sides will heavily shelter and actively defend their air bases, and acquire the most modern munitions and countermeasure gear available in Western Europe. Both sides will seek to emulate Western levels of training and reject Soviet training modes. Air-to-air missiles, air-to-surface/ship missiles, and air attack ordnance will be equivalent to that in the French, British, and Italian air forces.

● The Iranians will rebuild their navy by refitting existing major ships, buying new missile equipped frigates and MPA aircraft equipped with air-to-ship missiles, and by buying the most advanced and sophisticated air-to-ship missiles available. Iraq will follow suit.

● Both sides will gradually introduce modern European military communications gear, secure communications, and the best IFF (identification of friend or foe) gear commercially available from West Europe, plus some Soviet and PRC radars, fire control systems, and communications gear for individual weapons. Iran and Iraq have become increasingly aware of Western PHOTINT (photo intelligence) and SIGINT (signal intelligence) capabilities, and will buy the best secure gear commercially available in Western Europe for key command links although technical capability to establish an overall net will be poor, and communications discipline is likely to be lax with senior officials and commanders making extensive use of commercial or open telephone lines.

● Both sides will acquire modern Western maritime patrol and recce aircraft and some form of low cost AEW/AWACS aircraft. Both sides will buy modern commercial ESSM (electronic support measures) gear from Europe. Iran and Iraq will expand their intelligence efforts at both the unit and headquarters levels to improve intelligence processing and provide targeting support to air unit and artillery commanders. Extensive use will be made of armed helicopters in the recce role and of night vision aids and sensors. Both Iran and Iraq will continue, however, to rely heavily on infiltration, hostile political groups in the opposing country, and agents in place.

- The command and intelligence systems will remain heavily politicized, and be unable to accurately report bad news or problems in military proficiency. The key links in the system will be seen as threats to the regime and duplicate systems will exist with each echelon reporting on the political loyalty of the levels immediately above and below it.

- Overall military proficiency will be erratic with some units far more capable than others, relatively mediocre force-wide and large unit maneuver capability, and inadequate C^3I/BM integration and use. Politicisation will remain a serious problem.

Strategic Futility and Political Hatred

Even this conservative estimate of each side's future military capabilities, however, indicates the potential cost of another round of fighting. Both sides would be virtually certain to strike at the other's – and possibly neighboring – oil facilities, and they would be able to do so more effectively. The West and the other Gulf states have so far been lucky and may continue to be for the duration of this conflict. Another round of fighting would almost certainly mean far more ships sunk and damaged far more quickly, massive escalation against each side's oil facilities, and very probably escalation against each other's supporters and allies.

Unfortunately, both sides will also have to accept the fact that further quarrels over their borders, and the Shatt al-Arab boundary, are inherently absurd in order to avoid another round of fighting. More broadly, Iraq will have to accept that it has no conceivable military options – such as forcing Kuwait to lease or cede the marsh islands of Warba and/or Bubiyan near the Iraqi port of Umm Qasr – that can make up for the inherent vulnerability of its access to the Gulf to modern air power and missiles, and a bathymetry that means any expansion of its navy will still leave it so vulnerable to mining that it cannot survive.

It is hard to conceive of a more stupid and pointless struggle or debate than a continuing Iraqi-Iranian conflict over the 1937 boundary and 1975 Algiers protocol, or Iraq's effort to find a secure outlet to the Gulf. The issues are now strategically meaningless to the point of military absurdity. It is equally hard to conceive, however, that either Iraq or Iran will easily accept this reality.

Notes

[1] William L. Randol and Ellen Macready, *Petroleum Monitor*, New York, First Boston, November, 1986, pp. 16-17.

[2] The projections made here are highly uncertain. They are the author's estimates based on data published by the Economist Intelligence Unit and the U.S. Department of Commerce.

[3] Ibid, and William L. Randol and Ellen Macready, *Petroleum Monitor*, New York, First Boston, November, 1986, pp. 16-17.

[4] *Los Angeles Times*, December 12, 1986, p. I-23.

Chapter Eight

The Impact on Western Policy

Given this background, the West must be prepared for both "best" and "worst case" outcomes of the war. It must face the fact that it may have to aid the GCC states, and states like Turkey and Jordan, to suddenly cope with a radically more threatening environment. It is also clear that the need for Western power projection forces like those of the U.S. Central Command (USCENTCOM) continues to be as great as it was in the late 1970s. The West may yet be faced with a situation in the northern Gulf that is as threatening and unstable as the Arab-Israeli conflict.

As for the course of the war, there is little that the West can do to influence its present direction that it has not already tried. The West must continue to try to reduce the flow of arms to Iran and to help ensure Iraq's ability to obtain arms and financial support. The West should also back every regional peace initiative, and keep its political and economic lines of communication open to Iran so that it has no reason to feel it has no alternatives to isolation if it makes peace.

Speeding the Right Kind of End to the War

The war is far too dangerous to Western interests to be regarded as a means of paralyzing Iranian and Iraqi regional ambitions. The recent fighting has shown that the war becomes steadily more dangerous with time, and the West must make every effort to end the war as soon as possible.

The best outcome of the war is easy to define: it is to preserve the present national structure Iran and Iraq, without one side dominating the other. Both nations can act as major buffers between the Gulf and the USSR, but only if they remain strong, independent states.

The Right Kind of "Tilt" Towards Iraq

The West has no intrinsic reason to choose either side in the war. However, Iraq is now threatened by the risk of a successful Iranian invasion. Western policy must be shaped to limit the risk of any Iranian victory and a successful invasion. At the same time, the present division in the roles of the U.S. and Europe should be preserved.

The West will not benefit from U.S. efforts to directly supporting Iraq with weapons shipments or other major assistance. This is a role that France and other European nations can perform. U.S. support of Iraq should be indirect, and linked to efforts to open lines of communication to Iran and to strengthen the southern Gulf states. In practice, this means using every political means to limit arms shipments to Iran, providing indirect economic aid to ensure that Iraq can continue to finance the war, providing quiet intelligence support, and providing political support for every serious peace initiative.

The U.S. will, however, need to revitalize and sustain "Operation Staunch", the U.S. effort to halt the flow of arms to Iran that began in late 1983. It will need to continue to provide Iraq with agricultural credits, and be ready to support emergency aid by the EXIM (Export-Import) bank and collective action by the IMF (International Monetary Fund) and World Bank. The U.S. should continue to share intelligence with Iraq of the kind it has provided since mid-1984 and to make every effort to reduce the risk of a successful Iranian offensive or surprise attack.[1]

In contrast, Europe needs to halt its arms shipments to Iran as much as possible and to concentrate on building up economic ties. It needs to be ready to extend and renegotiate loans, and help ensure Iraq can keep fighting. France plays a particularly critical role. Its arms supplies to Iraq are vital not only to preventing an Iranian victory, but to reducing Iraqi dependence on the USSR.

The Right Kind of Opening to Iran

Iran is only beginning its current revolution. The West cannot hope to create stable and friendly relations with Iran for many years to come. The most it can do is to establish broad contacts with every reasonable Iranian faction and to try to use economic ties to restore some basis for correct relations and eventual friendship.

The Reagan Administration's disastrous flirtation with covert arms shipments to Iran has demonstrated that efforts to maintain and expand communications with Iran must be limited to political and economic contacts, and that these should be structured to act as incentives towards peace, not as bribes to Iran's government.

Further, it is important to note that the U.S. must avoid opportunism and gamesmanship in its dealing with both Iran and Iraq. Falsified or altered intelligence, attempts to achieve short term gains through high risk covert programs, efforts to shape the Iranian revolution, and attempts to manipulate the war are both dangerous and largely absurd. The net result is almost inevitably to have secret programs become public and embarrass the U.S.

U.S. policy only acquires strength when it is applied consistently and with clear purpose. The U.S. is also virtually dependent upon the belief of foreign nations that – for all their problems with the United States – the U.S. still acts with more ethics and morality than the Soviet Union and it can be trusted. The U.S. must do everything possible to rebuild this reputation and confine covert action to professionals who can set realistic goals in broad policy context where covert action has only a limited place.

At the same time, the West cannot afford to ignore the various opposition movements in Iran. It is possible that Iran's current ruling elite may remain in power for the next decade, but it is not likely. This means the West must try to maintain low level ties with every major faction, and to build a relationship based on economic self-interest, not common political and social goals.

The Hostage Issue: Policy Not Bribes

No Western effort to buy the support of either Iraq or Iran will secure American and European citizens in the Middle East, protect Israel, or ease the problems of terrorism and hostage-taking. The most such an effort can do is to solve a short-term problem at the cost of making long term problems worse.

It is stable, well-balanced Western policy initiatives based on strength and consistency of purpose that will do most to win the enduring support of Iranian and Iraqi regimes. The U.S. must not give in to blackmail a second time, and it must make every effort to keep its friends and allies from doing so.

U.S. Economic Ties and Western European Arms

The West cannot hope to make Iran or Iraq into military allies. Neither state is likely to act as any kind of proxy for Western security interests in the Gulf. The most the West can hope for is that Iranian and Iraqi economic ties to the West can be rebuilt and strengthened to the point where these ties dominate political attitudes and actions.

The U.S. also will not benefit from major arms sales to either state. This is an area where Europeans can accomplish far more by ensuring that neither state has to depend on the USSR for arms after the war, and that a superpower rivalry does not develop as part of an Iranian-Iraqi arms race.

Supporting the Gulf Cooperation Council States

No outcome of the war offers a secure hope of long-term stability in the Gulf unless the Gulf Cooperation Council states can be built up into a significant and unified political and military deterrent. The West needs to revitalize its efforts to strengthen the GCC states, and its military ties to Saudi Arabia – the only southern Gulf state large and strong enough to underpin a regional military effort.

Strengthening USCENTCOM

Rightly or wrongly, Europe has largely opted out of the role of global power projection. Britain and France can deploy token forces, but the U.S. is the only nation with the credible out of area strength to demonstrate that the West will protect its main source of imported energy.

This means the U.S. must continue to strengthen USCENTCOM and its power projection capabilities in the region. It must have the military option of ensuring the flow of oil through the Gulf, and be able to provide "over-the-horizon" reinforcements to any southern Gulf state threatened by one of its larger northern neighbors. The U.S. must not only consider the risks inherent in an Iranian victory, but the threat of Iranian and Iraqi efforts to limit southern Gulf oil production after the war, the threat from Soviet-backed radical states in the Red Sea, and the long term threat of a Soviet victory over Afghanistan's freedom fighters. No other nation can play this role.

Dealing With the USSR

The West must accept the fact it is in a strategic rivalry with the USSR for power and influence in the Gulf. This is a rivalry where the USSR is strongly limited by its ethnic problems with Asian Muslims and presence in Afghanistan. At the same time, the USSR sometimes seems to be outplaying the West.

The USSR is a major arms supplier to Iraq, and is still rebuilding some of its ties to Iran. The USSR and Iran signed an agreement in Tehran in early December, 1986, that provided for limited cooperation and stressed "good neighborly relations". Soviet technicians will return to Iran to help it construct dams, and work on power stations, and will ship industrial equipment.

This shows the USSR is still trying to play the Iran card, but it is important to note that the new agreement did not set a date for resuming the Iranian gas shipments to the USSR, which the USSR suspended in 1980 because of Iran's price rises. Although the USSR maintains an embassy in Tehran, and First Deputy Foreign Minister Georgy Korienko visited Tehran in February, 1986, his Iranian counterpart Ali Akbar

Velyati has not made a return visit. It is unclear how long it will be before either side can forget the expulsion of 18 Soviet diplomats in 1983. The USSR has refused to do anything to halt the flow of Soviet arms to Iraq, or make concessions on the Soviet presence in Afghanistan. Iran has refused to ease Iranian pressure on Iran's Communists.[2]

Similarly, Iraq shows little gratitude to the USSR for its arms shipments. It has had to pay for them, has often complained about the terms and quality. Iraq is all too aware that the USSR regarded Iran as the major prize early in the Iranian revolution, and only turned back to Iraq when Iran rejected it. Iraq is far more interested in Western arms and in civil trade with the West, and its current leadership is all too conscious than only a decade ago the Iraqi Communist Party led a coup against the Ba'ath.

The West, therefore, has no incentive to over-react or to try to buy either Iranian or Iraqi support. It can afford to wait and to act in its own interests. It can limit its tilt towards Iraq to the policies outlined earlier, and it has no incentive to take chances in its contacts with Iran's leadership out of fear of Soviet gains. A consistent and balanced Western policy towards both nations – protecting Iraq from defeat while maintaining the offer of better relations and economic ties with Iran – is all that is necessary. Any Soviet adventurism is as unlikely to be successful as was the U.S. effort to support Iranian moderation through covert arms sales.

The Problem of Energy Policy

Finally, the West must return to a far more realistic policy towards energy dependence. The present "oil glut" will not last beyond the early 1990s, and could end sooner. At that point, one central strategic reality will remain: well over 50% of all the world's proven oil reserves will be in the Gulf. The West must act to secure this flow of oil, but it must also revitalize its efforts to create safe sources of nuclear power and energy from coal, to develop advanced means of oil recovery, to create a commercial synfuels industry, and to exploit alternative sources of energy like solar and geothermal power.

The present "oil glut" has done more than reduce the flow of Western money to OPEC, it has virtually killed every major Western effort at reducing the West's long term dependence on oil imports. No Western security policy can be successful which does not recognize this fact.

Near Term Policy Needs

The highest priority challenges for Western policy are to overcome the heritage of American and other covert arms sales to Iran, and to show that the West will now enforce tight controls on arms sales to Iran.

Western governments must also take steps to convince Iraq's Western and Arab creditors, and the GCC states, that even if Iraq suffers further reversals, it will be necessary to continue to finance Iraq and vital not to provide arms to Iran. Iraq is inherently far more vulnerable to any loss of confidence than Iran. Iraq depends on outside aid for its military, political, and economic survival, and its ability to fight is as dependent on outside perceptions as it is on not making further mistakes.

This financing issue may soon require action by both the richer GCC states and Western governments. It is difficult to see how private firms and banks can be persuaded to continue to expand their risks and exposure by betting that Iraq's current regime will survive. Governments, however, must accept the cost of the strategic realities listed at the start of this analysis.

While it is not clear what would happen if Iran won a major victory, or that changes in Iraq's top leadership would have a critical impact on the Gulf and the availability of oil, no policy maker can afford to take that chance. This means that the U.S., Western Europe, Saudi Arabia, and Kuwait must be prepared to ensure Iraq's finances while continuing to make every possible effort to push both sides towards peace.

Notes

[1] *Washington Post*, December 16, 1986, p. A-12.
[2] *Chicago Tribune*, December 7, 1986, p. I-9; *Washington Times*, December 15, 1986, p. 8A; and *Christian Science Monitor*, December 17, 1986, p. 12.

Bibliography

Abir, Mordechai, *Oil, Power, and Politics: Conflict in Arabia, the Red Sea and the Gulf*, London, Frank Cass, 1974

Abdulghani, Jasim M., *Iraq and Iran: The Years of Crisis*, Baltimore, Johns Hopkins University Press, 1984

Albrecht, Gerhard, *Weyer's Warships of the World 1984/85*, 57th ed., Annapolis, Md., Nautical & Aviation Publishing Co.,

Atkins, James E., et al., *Oil and Security in the Arabian Gulf*, New York, St. Martin's Press, 1981

Allen, Robert C. "Regional Security in the Persian Gulf", *Military Review*, LXIII, 12 (December 1983) pp. 17-29

Amirsadeghi, Hossein, ed., *The Security of the Persian Gulf*, New York, St. Martin's Press, 1981

Amuzegar, Jahangir, "Oil Weath: A Very Mixed Blessing," *Foreign Affairs*, 60 (Spring 1982)

Anthony, John Duke, "The Gulf Cooperation Council," *Journal of South Asian and Middle Eastern Studies*, 5 (Summer 1982)

ARAMCO *Yearbook* and *Facts and Figures*

ARCO Series of Illustrated Guides, New York: Salamander Books, ARCO
Weapons of the Modern Soviet Ground Forces
The Modern U.S. Air Force
Military Helicopters
The Israeli Air Force
The Modern Soviet Navy
The Modern U.S. Navy

Armed Forces Journal International, various editions

Army, Department of, *1985 Weapon Systems*, Washington D.C., Government Printing Office
Iran, A Country Study, DA Pam 550, Washington, D.C., 1985
Iraq, A Country Study, DA Pam 5501, Washington, D.C., 1985
Soviet Army Operations, IAG-13-U-78, April 1978

Army Armor Center, Threat Branch, *Organization and Equipment of the Soviet Army*, Fort Knox, Kentucky, January 1981

Auer, Peter, Ed., *Energy and the Developing Nations*, New York, Pergamon, 1981

Aviation Week and Space Technology, various editions

Axelgard, Frederick W., "The Tanker War in the Gulf: Background and Repercussions," *Middle East Insight*, III, 6 (November-December 1984), pp. 26-3

 Iraq in Transition: A Political, Economic and Strategic Perspective, Washington, CSIS, 1986

Ayoob, Mohammad, ed., *The Middle East in World Politics*, London, Croom Helm, 1981

El Azhary, M.S., *The Iran-Iraq War: Historical, Economic and Political Analysis*, New York, St. Martin's Press, 1984

Aziz, Tareq, *Iraq-Iran Conflict*, London, Third World Center, 1981

Bakhash, Shaul, "The Politics of Oil and Revolution in Iran," Staff paper Washington, D.C., Brookings Institution, 1982

Banks, Ferdinand, *The Political Economy of Oil*, Lexington, Mass., Lexington Books, 1980

Banuazizi, Ali and Myron Weiner, *The State, Religion and Ethnic Politics*, Syracuse, Syracuse University, 1986

Bass, Gail and Bonnie Jean Cordes, *Actions Against Non-Nuclear Energy Facilities: September 1981-September 1982*, Santa Monica, Calif., Rand Corporation, April 1983

Batatu, Hanna, "Iraq's Underground Shi'a Movements: Characteristics, Causes and Prospects," *Middle East Journal*, XXXV, 4 (Autumn 1981), pp. 578-594

 The Egyptian, Syrian and Iraqi Revolutions, Washington, Center for Contemporary Arab Studies, Georgetown University, 1984

Beeman, William O., Language, *Status and Power in Iran*, Indianapolis, Indiana University Press, 1986

Be'eri, Eliezer, *Army Officers in Arab Politics and Society*, New York, Praeger Publishers, 1970

Bernstam, Mikhail S., "Soviet Oil Woes", *Wall Street Journal*, January 10, 1986

Bertram, Christoph, ed., *Third World Conflict and International Security*, London, Macmillan, 1982

Betts, Richard K., *Surprise Attack*, Washington, D.C., Brookings Institution, 1982

Bishara, Ghassan, "The Political Repercussions of the Israeli Raid on the Iraqi Nuclear Reactor," *Journal of Palestine Studies*, Spring 1982, pp. 58-76

Blake, G. H. and Lawless, R. E., *The Changing Middle Eastern City*, New York, Barnes and Noble, 1980

Blechman, Barry M., Stephan S. Kaplan, *Force Without War*, Washington D.C, Brookings Institution, 1978

Borowiec, Andrew, "Turks Seek Aid to Upgrade Army", *Washington Times*, May 16, 1986, p. 7

Bradley, C. Paul, *Recent United States Policy in the Persian Gulf*, Hamden, Conn., Shoe String Press, 1982

Brassey's Defense Yearbook, (later RUSI and Brassey's Defence Yearbook), London, various years

Brodman, John R. and Hamilton, Richard E., *A Comparison of Energy Projections to 1985*, International Energy Agency Monograph Series, Paris, OECD, January 1979

Brossard, E. B., *Petroleum, Politics and Power*, Boston, Allyn and Bacon, 1974

Brown, Professor Neville, "An Out of Area Strategy?", *Navy International*, October, 1982, pp. 1371-1373

Brown, William, *Can OPEC Survive the Glut?*, Croton-on-Hudson, N.Y., Hudson Institute, 1981

Brzoska, Michael and Thomas Ohlson, *Arms Production in the Third World*, London, SIPRI, 1986

Carlsen, Robin Woodsworth, *The Imam and His Islamic Revolution*, New York, Snow Man Press, 1982

Carver, Michael, *War Since 1945*, London, Weidenfeld and Nicholson, 1980

Chaliand, Gerad, *Guerrilla Strategies*, Berkeley, University of California Press, 1982

Chicago Tribune, various editions

Choucri, Nazli, *International Politics of Energy Interdependence*, Lexington, Mass., Lexington Books, 1976

Christian Science Monitor, various editions

Chubin, Shahram, *Security in the Persian Gulf: The Role of Outside Powers*, London, International Institute for Strategic Studies, 1981

Chubin, Shahram, ed., *Security in the Persian Gulf: Domestic Political Factors*, London, International Institute for Strategic Studies, 1980

Chubin, Shahram and Charles Tripp, "Iran and Iraq: War, Society and Politics: 1980-1986," *PSIS Occasional Papers*, Number 1/86, Geneva, November, 1986

Cittadino, John and McLeskey, Frank, "C³I for the RDJTF." *Signal*, September 1981

Clark, Wilson and Page, Jake, *Energy, Vulnerability and War*, New York, W. W. Norton, 1981

Clarke, John I, and Bowen-Jones, Howard, *Change and Development in the Middle East*, New York, Methuen, 1981

Collins, John M. and Mark, Clyde R., *Petroleum Imports from the Persian Gulf: Use of U.S. Armed Force to Ensure Supplies*, Issue Brief IB 79046, Washington, D.C., Library of Congress, Congressional Research Service, 1979

Combat Fleets of the World 1986/87, Their Ships, Aircraft, and Armament, A. D. Baker III ed., Annapolis Md., Naval Institute Press, 1986

Conant, Melvin A., and Fern Racine Gold, *Access to Oil: The U.S. Relationship with Saudi Arabia and Iran*, Washington, D.C., Government Printing Office, 1977

The Oil Factor In U.S. Foreign Policy, 1980-1990, Lexington, Mass., Lexington Books, 1982

Congressional Budget Office, *Cost of Modernizing and Expanding the Navy's Carrier-Based Air Forces*, Washington, D.C., Congressional Budget Office, May 1982

Rapid Deployment Forces: Policy and Budgetary Implications, Washington, D.C., Government Printing Office, 1981

Congressional Presentation for Security Assistance Programs, Vol 1 and 2, Fiscal Year 1987

Congressional Research Service, Library of Congress, *Soviet Policy and the United States Response in the Third World*, Washington, D.C., Government Printing Office, 1981

Conine, Ernest, "Soviets Sit on Oil's Power Keg", *Los Angeles Times*, February 17, 1986

CONOCO, *World Energy Outlook Through 2000*, April, 1985

Conway's All The World's Fighting Ships 1947-1982, London, Conway Maritime Press, 1983

Cordesman, Anthony H., "The Crisis in the Gulf: A Military Analysis", *American-Arab Affairs*, 9 (Summer 1984), pp. 8-15

"Arms Sales to Iran: Rumour and Reality," *Middle East Executive Reports*, February 1986, pp. 15-19

Jordan and the Middle East Balance, Washington D.C., Middle East Institute, 1978

"Lessons of the Iran-Iraq War." *Armed Forces Journal*, April-June 1982, pp. 32-47, 68-85

"Oman: The Guardian of the Eastern Gulf," *Armed Forces Journal International*, June 1983

The Gulf and the Search for Strategic Stability, Boulder, Westview, 1984

"The 'Oil Glut' and the Strategic Importance of the Gulf States", *Armed Forces Journal International*, October 1983

"U.S. Middle East Aid: Some Questions", *Defense and Foreign Affairs*, June 1986, pp. 15-18

Western Strategic Interests in Saudi Arabia, London, Croom Helm, 1986

Cottrell, Alvin J. and Robert J. Hanks, "The Strait of Hormuz: Strategic Chokepoint", In *Sea Power and Strategy in the Indian Ocean*, Beverly Hills, Calif., Sage Publications, 1981

Cottrell, Alvin J. and Michael L. Moodie, *The United States and the Persian Gulf: Past Mistakes, Present Needs*, New York, National Strategy Information Center for Scholars, 1981

Croan, Melvin, "A New Afrika Korps," *Washington Quarterly*, no. 3 (Winter 1980), 21-37

Cummings, J. H. Askari, H. and Skinner, M., "Military Expenditures and Manpower Requirements in the Arabian Peninsula". *Arab Studies Quarterly 2* (1980)

Danziger, Dr Raphael, "The Persian Gulf Tanker War", *Proceedings of the Naval Institute*, May, 1985, 160-176

Darius, Robert G., John W. Amos II and Ralph H. Magnus, *Gulf Security into the 1980s: Perceptual and Strategic Dimensions*, Stanford, Hoover Institution Press, 1984

Davis, Jacquelyn K. and Pfaltzgraff, Robert L., *Power Projection and the Long Range Combat Aircraft*, Cambridge, Mass., Institute for Foreign Policy Analysis, June 1981

Dawisha, Adeed I., "Iraq: The West's Opportunity", *Foreign Policy*, no. 41 (Winter 1980-81) 134-154

"Iraq and the Arab World: The Gulf War and After", *The World Today*, March 1981

de Briganti, Giovanni, "Forces d'Action Rapide", *Armed Forces Journal*, October, 1984, pp. 46-47

Deese, David A., and Joseph Nye, eds., *Energy and Security*, Cambridge, Mass., Ballinger, 1981

Defense and Foreign Affairs, various editions

Defense News, various editions

Defense Update, "Helicopter Special", Number 60, March 1985

Dunn, Keith A., "Constraints on the U.S.S.R. in Southwest Asia: A Military Analysis", *Orbis*, 25, no. 3 (Fall 1981) 607-629

Dunn, Michael C., "Gulf Security: The States Look After Themselves", *Defense & Foreign Affairs*, June 1982

Dupuy, Trevor, N., *Elusive Victory: The Arab-Israeli Wars, 1947-1974*, New York, Harper & Row, 1978

Economist, various editions

Economist Publications, London and New York

"Growing Pains, The Gulf Cooperation Countries, A Survey", February 8, 1986

"Oil Turns Manic Depressive", February 15, 1986, pp. 61-62

Economist Intelligence Unit, *The Gulf War: A Survey of Political Issues and Economic Consequences*, London, Economist Publications, 1984

EIU Regional Review: The Middle East and North Africa, 1985, Economist Publications, London 1985

EIU Regional Review: The Middle East and North Africa, 1986, London, Economic Publications, 1986

Epstein, Joshua M., "Soviet Vulnerabilities in Iran and the RDF Deterrent", *International Security*, Vol. 6, no.2 (Fall 1981), 126-180

Eshel, David, *The U.S. Rapid Deployment Forces*, New York, ARCO Publishing Inc., 1985

Farad, Abd al-Majid, ed., *Oil and Security in the Arabian Gulf*, London, Croom Helm, 1981

Feldman, Shai, "A Nuclear Middle East," *Survival*, 23, no. 3 (May-June 1981), pp. 107-116

Fesharaki, Feridun, and David T. Isaak, *OPEC, the Gulf and the World Petroleum Market*, Boulder, Colo., Westview, 1983

Feuchtwanger, E. J. and Nailor, Peter, *The Soviet Union and The Third World*, London, Macmillan, 1981

Fiecke, D. B. Kroqully and D. Reich, "The Tornado Weapons System and Its Contemporaries", *International Defense Review*, No. 2/1977

Financial Times, London and Frankfurt

Fischer, Michael M. J., *Iran: From Religious Dispute to Revolution*, Cambridge, Mass., Harvard University Press, 1980

Flavin, Christopher, *World Oil: Coping With the Dangers of Success*, Worldwatch Paper 66, Washington D.C., Worldwatch Institute, 1985

Forbis, William H., *The Fall of the Peacock Throne*, New York, McGraw-Hill, 1981

Fukuyama, Frances, *The Soviety Union and Iraq Since 1968*, Santa Monica, Calif., RAND, N-1524, AF., 1980

Gail, Bridget, "The West's Jugular Vein: Arab Oil", *Armed Forces Journal International*, 1978, p. 18

Ghareeb, Edmund, *The Kurdish Question in Iraq*, Syracuse, Syracuse University Press, 1981

Grayson, Leslie E., *National Oil Companies*, New York, John Wiley, 1981

Green, Richard, Editor, *Middle East Review, 1986*, London, Middle East Review Company, 1986

Griffith, William E., *The Middle East 1982: Politics, Revolutionary Islam and American Policy*, Cambridge, Mass., M.I.T. Press, 1982

"The Revival of Islamic Fundamentalism: The Case of Iran", *International Security*, 5, no. 4, Spring 1981, pp. 49-73

Grimmett, Richard F., *Trends in Conventional Arms Transfers to the Third World By Major Supplier, 1978-1985*, Washington, CRS Report 86-99F, May 9, 1986

Grummon, Stephen R., *The Iran-Iraq War*, Washington Paper 92, Center for Strategic and International Studies. New York: Praeger Publishers, 1982

Gulf Cooperation Council. *Cooperation Council for the Arab States of the Gulf, Information Handbook*, Riyadh, Bahr Al-Olum Press, 1982

Gunston, Bill, *Modern Airborne Missiles*, ARCO, N.Y., 1983

Modern Soviet Air Force, ARCO, New York, 1982

Martin Streetly, "Su-24 Fencer C; Major Equipment Change", *Jane's Defence Weekly*, June 22, 1985, pp. 1226-1227 and various editions

Haffa, Robert P., Jr., *The Half War, Planning U.S. Deployment Forces to Meet a Limited Contingency, 1960-1983*, Boulder, Colo., Westview Press, 1984

MERIP *Reports*, various editions

Halloran, Richard, "Poised for the Persian Gulf," *The New York Times Magazine*, April 1, 1984, pp. 38-40, 61

Hameed, Mazher A., *Arabia Imperilled: The Security Imperatives of the Arab Gulf States*, Washington D.C., Middle East Assessments Group, 1986

Hanks, Robert, *The U.S. Military Presence in the Middle East: Problems and Prospects*, Cambridge, Mass., Institute for Foreign Policy Analysis, 1982

Hardt, John P., "Soviet Energy: Production and Exports", Issue Brief no. 12B75059, Library of Congress, Congressional Research Service, Washington, D.C., 1979

Hargraves, D., and Fromson, S., *World Index of Strategic Minerals*, New York, Facts on File, 1983

Hedley, Don, *World Energy: The Facts and the Future*, London: Euromonitor, 1981

Heikal, Mohammed, *Iran: The Untold Story*, New York, Pantheon, 1982 (also published as *The Return of the Ayatollah*), London, Andre Deutsch, 1981)

Heller, Mark, Dov Tamari and Zeeve Eytan, *The Middle East Military Balance*, Jaffe Center for Strategic Studies, Tel Aviv University, 1985 and 1986

Helms, Christian Moss, *Iraq: The Eastern Flank of the Arab World*, Washington, Brookings Institution, 1984

Hetherton, Norris, S., "Industrialization and Revolution in Iran: Force Progress or Unmet Expectation", *Middle East Journal*, 36, no. 3 Summer 1982, pp. 362-373

Hickman, William F. *Ravaged and Reborn: The Iranian Army*, 1982 Staff paper, Washington, D.C., Brookings Institution, 1982

Hiro, Filip, *Iran Under the Ayatollahs*, Boston, Routledge & Kegan Paul, 1985

Horwich, George and Edward Mitchell, eds., *Policies for Coping with Oil Supply Distributions*, Washington, D.C., American Enterprise Institute, 1982

Hottinger, Arnold, "Arab Communism at Low Ebb", *Problems of Communism*, July-August 1981, pp. 17-32

"Does Saudi Arabia Face Revolution?", *New York Review of Books*, June 28, 1979

Howarth, H. M. F., "The Impact of the Iran-Iraq War on Military Requirements in the Gulf States", *International Defense Review*, 16, no. 10, 1983

Hunter, Shireen, ed., *Political and Economic Trends in the Middle East*, The Center for Strategic and International Studies, Boulder, Colo., Westview Press, 1985

Hurewitz, J. C., *Middle East Politics: The Military Dimension*, New York, Praeger Publishers, 1969

Ibrahim, Saad Eddin, *The New Arab Social Order: A Study of the Social Impact of Oil Wealth*, Boulder, Colo., Westview Press, 1982

International Defense Review, Switzerland, Geneva, various editions

International Defense Review, Special Series, various editions

International Energy Statistical Review, Washington D.C., National Foreign Energy Assessment Center, CIA, various editions

International Institute for Strategic Studies, *The Middle East and the International System*, Parts I and II, Adelphi Papers No. 114 and 115, London, 1975

  The Military Balance, London, various years

International Journal of Middle East Studies, New York

International Monetary Fund, *Direction of Trade Statistics*, various editions

  Direction of Trade Yearbook, Washington D.C., various years

Isby, David C., *Weapons and Tactics of the Soviet Army*, New York, Jane's, 1981

Ismael, Tareq Y., *The Iran-Iraq Conflict*, Toronto, Canadian Institute of International Affairs, 1981

  Iraq and Iran: Roots of Conflict, Syracuse, N.Y., Syracuse University Press, 1982

Iungerich, Ralph, "U.S. Rapid Deployment Force – USCENTCOM – What Is It? Can It Do the Job?", *Armed Forces Journal International*, CXXII, 3 October 1984

Jane's, *All the World's Aircraft*, London, various years

  Armour and Artillery, London, various years

  Aviation Annual, London, various years

  Combat Support Equipment, London, various years

  Defense Review, London, various years

  Fighting Ships, London, various years

  Infantry Weapons, London, various years

  Military Annual, London, various years

  Military Communications, London, various years

  Naval Annual, London, various years

  Weapon Systems, London, various years

Jenkins, Brian Michael, et al., "Nuclear Terrorism and Its Consequences", *Society* 17, no. 5, July-August 1980, pp. 5-25

Johnson, Major Maxwell Orme, U.S.M.C., *The Military as an Instrument of U.S. Policy in Southwest Asia: The Rapid Deployment Joint Task Force, 1979-1982*, Boulder, Westview, 1983

  "U.S. Strategic Operations in the Persian gulf," *Proceedings of the Naval Institute*, February 1981

Jones, Rodney W., *Nuclear Proliferation: Islam, the Bomb and South Asia*, Washington Paper no. 82, Center for Strategic and International

Studies. Beverly Hills, Calif., Sage Publications, 1981

ed., *Small Nuclear Forces and U.S. Security Policy*, Lexington Mass., Lexington Books, 1984

Jordan, Amos, "Saudi Arabia: The Next Iran," *Parameters: The Journal of the Army War College*, 9 (March)

Jordan, John, *Modern Naval Aviation and Aircraft Carriers*, New York, ARCO, 1983

Joyner, Christopher C., and Shah, Shahqat Ali, "The Reagan Policy of 'Strategic Consensus' in the Middle East", *Strategic Review*, Fall 1981, pp. 15-24

Judge, John F., "Harpoon Missile Targets Ships and Cost", *Defense Electronics*, April, 1985, pp. 92-98

Kaplan, Stephen S., *Diplomacy of Power*, Washington D.C. Brookings Institution, 1981

Karsh, Efraim, *The Cautious Bear*, Boulder, Colo., Westview Press, 1985

Soviet Arms Transfers To The Middle East In The 1970s, Tel Aviv, Tel Aviv University, 1983

Kazemi, Farhad, *Poverty and Revolution in Iran*, New York University Press, 1980

Keddie, Nikki R. and Eric Hooglund, *The Iranian Revolution and the Islamic Republic*, Syracuse, Syracuse University, 1986

Keegan, John, *World Armies*, New York, Facts on File, 1979

World Armies, 2nd ed., London, Macmillan, 1983

Kerr, Malcolm and El Sayed Yassin, eds., *Rich and Poor States in the Middle East*, Boulder, Colo., Westview, 1982

Khaddur, Majid, *Socialist Iraq: A Study in Iraqi Politics Since 1968*, Washington, Middle East Institute, 1978

Klare, Michael T., *American Arms Supermarket*, Austin, Texas, University of Texas Press, 1984

Kolodziej, Edward A. and Robert E. Harkavy, *Security Policies of Developing Countries*, Lexington, Lexington Books, 1982

Korb, Edward L., ed., *The World's Missile Systems*, 7th ed., Pamona, Calif., General Dynamics, Pamona Division, 1982

Krapels, Edward, N., ed., "International Oil Supplies and Stockpiling", Proceedings of a conference held in Hamburg, 17 and 18 September 1981, London, Economist Intelligence Unit, 1982

Kurian, George, *Atlas Of The Third World*, New York, Facts on File, 1983

Kuwait, *Annual Statistical Abstract*, Kuwait City, Ministry of Planning, Central Statistical office, various editions

Laffin, John L., *The Dagger of Islam*, London, Sphere, 1979

War Annual 1, London, Brassey's, 1986

Leites, Nathan, *Soviet Style in War*, New York, Crane, Russak & Co., 1982

Leltenberg, Milton and Sheffer, Gabriel, eds., *Great Power Intervention in the Middle East*, New York, Pergamon Press, 1979

Lenczowski, George, "The Soviet Union and the Persian Gulf: An Encircling Strategy", *International Journal*, 37, no. 2, 1982

Library of Congress "The Persian Gulf: Are We Committed?" Washington, D.C., 1981

Liebov, Robert J. "Energy, Economics and Security in Alliance Perspective," *International Security*, Spring 1980, pp. 139-163

Imbert, John W., *Iran: At War with History*, Boulder, Westview, 1986

Litwak, Robert, ed., *Security in the Persian Gulf: Sources of Inter-State Conflict*, London, International Institute for Strategic Studies, 1981

Los Angeles Times, various editions

MacDonald, Charles G., "The U.S. and Gulf Conflict Scenarios", *Middle East Insight*, 3, no. 1, May-July 1983, pp. 23-27

Maddy-Weitzmann, Bruce, "Islam and Arabism: The Iraq-Iran War", *Washington Quarterly*, Autumn 1982

Mansur, Abdul Karim (pseud.), "The Military Balance in the Persian Gulf: Who Will Guard the Gulf States from Their Guardians?", *Armed Forces Journal International*, November 1980

Marr, Phoebe, *The Modern History of Iraq*, Boulder, Westview, 1984

Martin, Lenore G., *The Unstable Gulf: Threats from Within*, Lexington, Mass., D.C. Heath, 1984

McLaurin, R.D., "U.S. Strategy in the Middle East and the Arab Reaction," *Journal of East and West Studies*, XI, 2, Fall-Winter 1982

McNaugher, Thomas L., "Arms and Allies on the Arabian Peninsula, *Orbis*, Volume 28, No. 3, Fall 1984, pp. 486-526

   Arms and Oil: U.S. Military Security Policy Toward the Persian Gulf, Washington, D.C. Brookings, 1985

   Shireen Hunter, ed., *Gulf Cooperation Council: Problems and Prospects*, CSIS Significant Issues Series, VI, 15 (1984), pp. 6-9

   "Rapid Deployment and Basing in southwest Asia," In *Strategic Survey* (London, International Institute for Strategic Studies, April 1983), pp. 133-137

   "The Soviet Military Threat to the Gulf: The Operational Dimension", Working Paper, Washington, D.C., Brookings Institution, 1982

   "Pipelines and Power in the Gulf: Shifting Balances," Cambridge, CERA, 1986

Macksey, Kenneth, *Tank Facts and Feats*, New York, Two Continents Publishing Group, 1974

Masters, Charles D., "World Petroleum Resources – A Perspective", USGS Open File Report, pp. 85-248

Masters, Charles D., David H. Root, and William D. Dietzmann, "Distribution and Quantitative Assessment of World Crude-Oil Reserves and Resources", Washington, USGS, unpublished, 1983

Meir, Shemuel, *Strategic Implications of the New Oil Reality*, Westview Press, Boulder, 1986, p. 55

MERIP Reports, "The Arabian Peninsula Opposition Movements", February, 1985, pp. 13-19

Middle East, "Guarding Turkey's Eastern Flank", April, 1986, pp. 9-10

Middle East Economic Digest Special Report Series, *France and the Middle East*, May 1982

   Oman, November 1982

   Qatar, August 1981 and August 1982

   UAE: Tenth Anniversary, November 1981

   U.K. and the Gulf, December 1981

Middle East Insight, various editions

Middle East Journal, Washington, D.C., Middle East Institute, various editions

Middle East Review 1985, World of Information, Saffron Walden, England, 1985

   1986, World of Information, Saffron Walden, England, 1986

Miller, Marshall Lee, "The Soviet General Staff's Secret Plans for Invading Iran," *Armed Forces Journal*, January 1987, pp. 28-32

Mottahedeh, Roy Parviz, "Iran's Foreign Devils", *Foreign Policy*, no. 38 Spring 1980, pp. 19-34

Mullen, Thomas D., "The Security of Oil Supplies," *Survival*, November-December, 1986, London, IISS, pp. 509-523

Naff, Thomas, ed., *Gulf Security and the Iran-Iraq War*, National Defense University Press, 1985

National Foreign Assessment Center, *International Energy Statistical Review*, Washington, D.C., Photoduplication Service, Library of Congress, 1978-1986

Natkiel, Richard, *Atlas of The 20th Century*, New York, Facts on File, 1982

Navy, Department of, Office of the Chief of Naval Operations, *Understanding Soviet Naval Developments*, Washington D.C., Government Printing Office, April 1985

"Nearby Observer", "The Afghan-Soviet War: Stalemate or Solution?", *Middle East Journal*, Spring 1982, pp. 151-164

Neuman, Stephanie, *Defense Planning in Less-Industrialized States*, Lexington, Mass., Lexington Books, 1984

Neumann, Robert G. and Shireen T. Hunter, "The Crisis in the Gulf: Reasons for Concern but not Panic," *American-Arab Affairs*, 9 Summer 1984, pp. 16-21

New York Times, various editions

Novik, Nimrod, *Encounter With Reality: Reagan and the Middle East*, Boulder, Colo., Westview Press, 1985

Noyes, James H., *The Clouded Lens*, Stanford, Calif., Hoover Institution, 1982

O'Ballance, Edgar, "The Iran-Iraq War," *Marine Corps Gazette*, February 1982, pp. 44-49

Odell, Peter R. and Rosing, Kenneth E., *The Future of Oil: A Simulation Study*, London, Nichols, 1980

OECD/IEA, *Oil and Gas Statistics, 1985*, No. 4, Paris, 1986

The Oil and Gas Journal, "Worldwide Report", December 31, 1984

Olson, William J., "The Iran-Iraq War and the Future of the Persian Gulf", *Military Review*, LXIV, 2, March 1984, pp. 17-29

    ed., *U.S. Strategic Interests in the Gulf*, Boulder, Westview, 1986

Organization of Petroleum Exporting Countries, *Annual Report*, Vienna, various years

Pahlavi, Mohammed Reza, *The Shah's Story*, London, Michael Joseph, 1980

Perlmutter, Amos, Handel, Michael and Bar-Joseph, Uri, *Two Minutes Over Baghdad*, London, Corgi, 1982

Perry, Charles, *The West, Japan and Cape Route Imports: The Oil and Non Fuel Mineral Trades*, Cambridge, Mass., Institute for Foreign Policy Analysis, 1982

Petroleum Intelligence Weekly, New York

Pierre, Andrew J., *The Global Politics of Arms Sales*, Princeton, N.J., Princeton University Press, 1982

Pipes, Daniel, "Increasing Security in the Persian Gulf", *Orbis*, 26, Spring 1982

Plascov, Avi, *Security in the Persian Gulf: Modernization, Political Development and Stability*, Aldershot, Gower, 1982

Platt's Oil Price Handbook, New York

Quandt, William B., "The Crisis in the Gulf: Policy Options and Regional Implications", *American-Arab Affairs*, 9, Summer 1984, pp. 1-7

Ra'anan, Uri, *The USSR Arms The Third World*, Cambridge, Mass., M.I.T. Press, 1969

Ramazani, R. K., *Revolutionary Iran, Challenge and Response in the Middle East*, Baltimore, Johns Hopkins Press, 1986

Randol, William L., "Petroleum Monitor", First Boston Corporation

Ransom, David M., Lt. Colonel Lawrence J. MacDonald and W. Nathaniel Howell, "Atlantic Cooperation for Persian Gulf Security", *Essays on Strategy*, Washington, D.C., National Defense University, 1986

Record, Jeffrey, *The Rapid Deployment Force*, Cambridge, Mass., Institute for Foreign Policy Analysis, 1981

Roberts, Hugh, *An Urban Profile of the Middle East*, London, Croom Helm, 1979

Ross, Dennis, "Considering Soviet Threats to the Persian Gulf", *International Security 6*, no. 2, Fall 1981

    Soviet Views Toward the Gulf War," *Orbis*, XVIII, 3, Fall 1984, pp. 437-446

Rouleau, Eric, "Khomeini's Iran", *Foreign Affairs*, Fall 1980, pp. 1-20

"The War and the Struggle for the State", *MERIP Reports*, no. 98, July-August 1981, pp. 3-8

Royal United Services Institute/Brassey's, *International Weapons Development*, 4th ed., London, Brassey's, 1981

Rubin, Barry, *Paved with Good Intentions*, New York, Oxford University Press, 1980

Rubinstein, Alven Z., *The Great Game: Rivalry in the Persian Gulf and South Asia*, New York, Praeger, 1983

  Soviet Policy Towards Turkey, Iran and Afghanistan: The Dynamics of Influence, New York, Praeger Publishers, 1982

Russi, Piere, *Iraq, the Land of the New River*, Paris, Les Editions, J.A., 1980

Rustow, Dankwart, *Oil and Turmoil: America Faces OPEC and the Middle East*, New York, Norton, 1982

Saikal, Amin, *The Rise and Fall of the Shah*, Princeton, N.J., Princeton University Press, 1980

Salameh, Ghassane, "Checkmate in the Gulf War", *MERIP Reports*, XIV, 6/7, July-September 1984, pp. 15-21

al-Salem, Faisal, "The United States and the Gulf: What Do the Arabs Want?", *Journal of South Asian and Middle Eastern Studies*, 6, Fall 1982

Sciolino, Paulo, "Iran's Durable Revolution," *Foreign Affairs*, Spring 1983, pp. 893-920

Schmid, Alex P., *Soviet Military Interventions Since 1945*, New Brunswick, N.J., Transaction, Inc., 1985

Schmitt, Richard B., "U.S. Dependence on Oil, Gas Imports May Grow", *Wall Street Journal*, April 23, 1985

Schrage, Daniel P., "Air Warfare: Helicopters and the Battlefield", *Journal of Defense and Diplomacy*, Vol. 3, No. 5, pp. 17-20

Schultz, James B., "New Strategies and Soviet Threats Spark EW Responses", *Defense Electronics*, February, 1985, pp. 17-21

Sella, Amon, *Soviet Political and Military Conduct in the Middle East*, London, Macmillan, 1981

Senger, F. M. von, and Etterlin, *Tanks of the World 1983*, Annapolis, Md., Nautical & Aviation Publishing Co., 1983

Shwardran, Benjamin, *The Middle East: Oil and the Great Powers*, Boulder, Westview, 1985

Sick, Gary G., *All Fall Down: America's Tragic Encounter with Iran*, New York, Random House, 1985

  Alvin A. Rubenstein, ed., *The Great Game: Rivalry in the Persian Gulf and South Asia*, New York, Praeger, 1983

SIPRI, *World Armaments and Disarmaments: SIPRI Yearbook 1985*, London, Taylor & Francis, 1985

Snyder, Jed C., Samuel F. Wells, Jr., eds., *Limiting Nuclear Proliferation*, Cambridge, Mass., Ballinger Publishing Co., 1985

Staudenmaier, William O., "Military Policy and Strategy in the Gulf War," *Parameters: The Journal of the Army War College*, 12 (June 1982)

Stempel, John D. *Inside the Iranian Revolution*, Bloomington, Indiana University Press, 1981

Stewert, Richard A. "Soviet Military Intervention in Iran, 1920-46," *Parameters, Journal of the U.S. Army War College 11*, no. 4 (1981), 24-34

Stobach, Robert and Yergin, Daniel, eds., *Energy Future*, New York, Random House, 1979

Stockholm International Peace Research Institute, *Tactical Nuclear Weapons: European Perspectives*, New York, Crane, Russak & Co., 1978
World Armaments and Disarmament: SIPRI Yearbook, various years (computer print out for 1982), London, Taylor & Francis, Ltd

Stookey, Robert W., *The Arabian Peninsula: Zone of Ferment*, Stanford, Hoover Institution, 1984

Sullivan, William H., "Iran: The Road Not Taken," *Foreign Policy*, no. 40 (Fall 1980), 175-187
Mission to Iran, London, W. W. Norton, 1981

Sweetman, Bill, "New Soviet Combat Aircraft", *International Defense Review*, 1/1984, pp. 35-38

Szuprowicz, Bohdan O., *How to Avoid Strategic Materials Shortages*, New York, John Wiley, 1981

Tahir-Kheli, Sharin and Shaheen Ayubi, *The Iran-Iraq War: New Weapons, Old Conflicts*, New York, Praeger Publishers, 1983

Taylor, Alan, *The Arab Balance of Power*, Syracuse, N.Y., Syracuse University Press, 1982

Thompson, W. Scott, "The Persian Gulf and the Correlation of Forces," *International Security*, Summer 1982, pp. 157-180

Tillman, Seth, *The United States in the Middle East*, Bloomington, Indiana University Press, 1982

Tripp, Charles, "Iraq – Ambitions Checked," *Survival*, November-December, 1986, London, IISS, pp. 495-508

Truver, Dr Scott C., "Mines of August: An International Whodunit", *Proceedings of the U.S. Naval Institute*, May 1985, Volume III5/987, pp. 94-118

Turner, Louis and Bedore, James M., *Middle East Industrialization: A Study of Saudi and Iranian Downstream Investments*, London, Saxon House, 1979

Twitchell, Hamilton A., "The Iran-Iraq Oil War," *Geopolitics of Energy*, vol. 5, no. 10, October 1983

U.S. Arms Control and Disarmament Agency, *World Military Expenditures and Arms Transfers*, various editions, Washington, D.C., 1980

U.S. Central Intelligence Agency, *Economics and Energy Indicators*, DOI, GIEEI, Washington, D.C., Government Printing Office, various years
Handbook of Economic Statistics, various editions

International Energy Situation: Outlook to 1985, 041-015-00084-5, Washington, D.C., Government Printing Office, 1977

International Energy Statistical Review, NFAC, GI-IESR, Washington, D.C., Government Printing Office, various years

USSR Energy Atlas, Washington, CIA, 1985

World Factbook, Washington, D.C., Government Printing Office, various years

U.S. Congress, House of Representatives, Committee on Foreign Affairs, *Proposed Arms Sales for Countries in the Middle East*, 96th Cong., 1st Sess., 1979

   U.S. Interest in, and Policies Toward, the Persian Gulf, 1980, No. 68-1840, Washington, D.C., Congressional Printing Office, 1980

   U.S. Security Interests in the Persian Gulf, No. 73-354-0, Washington, D.C., Government Printing Office, 1981

U.S. Congress, House of Representatives, Committee on Foreign Affairs and Joint Economic Committee, *U.S. Policy Toward the Persian Gulf*, 97th Cong., 1st sess., 1975

U.S. Congress, Senate, Committee on Energy and Natural Resources, *Geopolitics of Oil*, No. 96-119, Washington, D.C., Government Printing Office, 1980

U.S. Congress, Senate, Committee on Foreign Relations, *Fiscal Year 1980 International Security Assistance Authorization: State Department Briefing on the Situation in Yemen*, 96th Cong., 1st Sess., 1979

Persian Gulf Situation, 97th Cong., 1st Session, 1981

U.S. Arms Sales Policy, 94th Cong., 2nd Sess., 1976

War in the Gulf, 98th Cong., 2nd Session, Staff Report, 1984

U.S. Defence Security Assistance Agency, *Foreign Military Sales, Foreign Military Construction Sales and Military Assistance Facts*, Washington, D.C., Government Printing Office, various years

U.S. Department of Defense, *Soviet Military Power*, Washington, D.C., Government Printing Office, various years

   Foreign Military Sales, Foreign Military Construction Sales and Military Assistance Facts, September 1984

U.S. Department of Energy, *Secretary of Energy Annual Report to the Congress*, DOE-S-0010(84), September, 1984

   Energy Projections to the Year 2000, DOE/PE-0029/2, October, 1983

   Annual Reports to Congress, Washington, D.C., Government Printing Office, various editions

   Petroleum Supply Monthly, various editions

   World Energy Outlook Through 2000, April, 1985

U.S. Energy Information Administration, *International Energy Annual* Washington, D.C., DOE/EIA-02 (84)

   Impacts of World Oil Market Shocks on the U.S. Economy, DOE/EIA-0411, July, 1983

Monthly Energy Review, Washington, D.C., Government Printing Office, various editions

International Energy Annual, Washington, D.C., Government Printing Office, various editions

U.S. Department of Energy, International Affairs, *International Energy Indicators*, DOE/IA-0010, Washington, D.C., Government Printing Office, various years

U.S. Library of Congress, Congressional Research Service, Foreign Affairs and National Defense Division, *Western Vulnerability to a Disruption of Persian Gulf Oil Supplies: U.S. Interests and Options*, 1983

U.S. News and World Report, various editions

Van Hollen, Christopher, "Don't Engulf the Gulf," *Foreign Affairs*, Summer 1981, pp. 1064-1078

Volmann, Daniel, "Commanding the Center," *MERIP Reports*, XIV, 6/7 (July-September 1984), pp. 49-50

von Pikva, Otto, *Armies of the Middle East*, New York, Mayflower Books, 1979

Wall Street Journal, various editions

War Data, Special editions of the "Born in Battle" series, Jerusalem, Eshel-Dramit

Washington Post, various editions

Washington Times, various editions

Weinbaum, Marvin G., *Food Development, and Politics in the Middle East*, Boulder, Colo., Westview Press, 1982

Weissman, Steve and Herbert Krosney, *The Islamic Bomb*, New York, Times Books, 1981

Wenger, Martha, "The Central Command: Getting to the War on Time," *MERIP Reports*, XIV, 9 (Fall 1984), pp. 456-464

White, B. T., *Wheeled Armoured Fighting Vehicles In Service*, Poole, Dorset, Blandford Press, 1983

Wiley, Marshall W., "American Security Concerns in the Gulf," *Orbis*, XXVIII, 3 (Fall 1984), pp. 456-464

Wohlstetter, Albert, "Meeting the Threat in the Persian Gulf," *Survey*, XXV, 2 (Spring 1980), pp. 128-188

Wolfe, Ronald G., ed., *The United States, Arabia and the Gulf*, Washington D.C., Georgetown University Center for Contemporary Arab Studies, 1980

World of Information, *Middle East Review*, London, various years

World Industry Information Service, *Energy Decade: A Statistical and Graphic Chronicle*, San Diego, Calif., 1982

Yodfat, Aryeh Y., *The Soviet Union and the Arabian Peninsula: Soviet Policy towards the Persian Gulf and Arabia*, New York, St. Martin's, 1983

Index